ATHOLL AND GOWRIE

Atholl and Gowrie
North Perthshire

A Historical Guide

Lindsay J. Macgregor

Richard D. Oram

Birlinn

Published by
Birlinn Limited
Unit 8
Canongate Venture
5 New Street
Edinburgh EH8 8BH

ISBN 1 84158 029 5

British Library Cataloguing in Publication Data
A Catalogue record for this book is available from the British Library

Typesetting and origination by Brinnoven, Livingston
Printed and bound by Creative Print and Design Wales, Ebbw Vale

CONTENTS

ACKNOWLEDGEMENTS

Many thanks to friends who have contributed in different ways to this volume. Special thanks to Alison Mackay and the mechanic at Cambusmichael. I should also like to acknowledge the work of the Royal Commission on the Ancient and Historical Monuments of Scotland and their publications, *South-East Perth* and *North-East Perth*, which provide much of the groundwork for this volume.

L.J.M.

This is my old stamping ground and a vast debt is owed to all my friends, past and present, and to my late grand-parents – a Meigle man raised in Balbeggie and Pitlochry and a Perth woman – who stimulated and encouraged my early interest in the archaeology and history of Atholl and Gowrie.

R.D.O.

LIST OF PLATES

LIST OF MAPS

LIST OF ILLUSTRATIONS

ESSENTIAL VIEWING

PREFACE

Atholl and Gowrie lie at the very heart of Scotland. From the wild, mountainous highland landscape of Atholl to the more gentle rolling hills of Gowrie, these two regions of contrasts and contradictions have provided the backdrop for the shaping of so much of Scotland's history, literature and legend. But Macbeth's Dunsinane, Birnam Wood and the Stone of Scone are not even half the story. For there is a great unwritten, long-forgotten history of people and places in Atholl and Gowrie, stretching back over 8000 years.

Atholl and Gowrie may for centuries have been subsumed into the pre-1974 county of Perth, remembered largely as district names with no political significance in the modern world, but their origins are as medieval earldoms, and yet earlier, as Pictish sub-kingdoms which had themselves emerged from more ancient Iron Age tribal lands. Atholl is a rugged land, stretching from Rannoch Moor in the west to Glen Isla in the east and to the River Almond in the south. It is mountainous, including Schiehallion at 1083 m and Beinn a' Ghlo at 1121 m, with vast tracts of open moorland across Breadalbane in the west to Glen Shee in the east. In the past, forest cover was much greater: remnants of the ancient Caledonian pine forests can be found at the Black Wood of Rannoch. Mountain, moor and forest are punctuated by river valleys, such as Glen Shee, Strathardle, Glen Lyon and Strath Tay, which have always attracted settlers.

To the south and east of Atholl lies Gowrie, the Sidlaws separating the low-lying Carse of Gowrie from the fertile river valleys of Strathmore and Strath Tay to the north and west. The broad plain of the Carse of Gowrie along the north bank of River Tay is very productive, known today as the 'Garden of Scotland', the result of drainage, first by the Cistercians of Coupar Angus in the twelfth century, and later by agricultural improvers of the eighteenth and nineteenth centuries. Names containing the element 'inch' – for example Megginch, Inchture, and Inchcoonans – identify former islands or pockets of high ground: banks of sand and gravel which stood above the wet, clay flood-plains around.

The survival of archaeological sites in Atholl and Gowrie is dependent on a number of factors. Much of Gowrie's prehistoric past has been long ploughed out and in populous river valleys like Strath Tay, modern settlements no doubt overlie millennia of settlements beneath. By contrast, in areas of boggy moorland, no longer attractive for settlement, the foundations of Bronze and Iron Age homesteads have been largely preserved. Increasingly, aerial photography is indicating that settlement in the upland zones was largely similar in both Atholl and Gowrie.

Despite the effects of agricultural improvements and modern settlement, both regions are still extremely rich in archaeological sites and it has proved impossible to present them all in one slim volume. Instead, sites have been selected to represent the diversity of settlement and lifestyle in Atholl and Gowrie through the ages, from *c.* 3500 BC to *c.* 1900 AD. So industrial and agricultural workers' cottages are included as well as palaces, mansions and castles. However, sites which are very difficult of access, being located for example in the midst of dense forestry plantations, have been excluded.

The majority of the sites in the gazetteer are in eastern Atholl and in Gowrie, a reflection not only of the predominant settlement pattern on the ground, but also of the current state of archaeological investigation.

While most of the key sites are well signposted and easily accessed by visitors – including disabled visitors – you will need appropriate Ordnance Survey maps to visit many of the remoter sites as well as compass, stout footwear and plenty of patience and imagination. The best detail is provided in the Ordnance Survey 1:25000 Pathfinder Series but the 1:50000 Landranger maps are quite adequate and the majority of sites in the gazetteer are marked on them. Sheets 42, 43, 50, 51, 52, 53 and 58 cover the whole area. A compass is useful, not only to locate the more remote moorland sites but also to follow the site descriptions in the gazetteer. Patience will help when searching for low walls in deep heather and will be, hopefully, well rewarded. Finally, a vivid imagination will greatly enliven a visit to all the sites in this book, aided by excellent museum displays in Dundee, Perth, Blair Atholl and Alyth, and a growing number of Heritage Centres and working industrial sites.

The vast majority of sites in the gazetteer are on private land and permission to visit them should therefore be sought from the nearest farm, house or estate office to ensure right of access. Sites marked with an asterisk (*) are in the guardianship of the State, the National Trust for Scotland or are opened on a regular basis by private owners. Several – particularly castles, palaces, museums and working industrial sites – have restricted seasons and opening times and charge an entrance fee. Sites and monuments within the gazetteer which are felt to be outstanding in their class and, therefore, *Essential Viewing*, have been highlighted in italics.

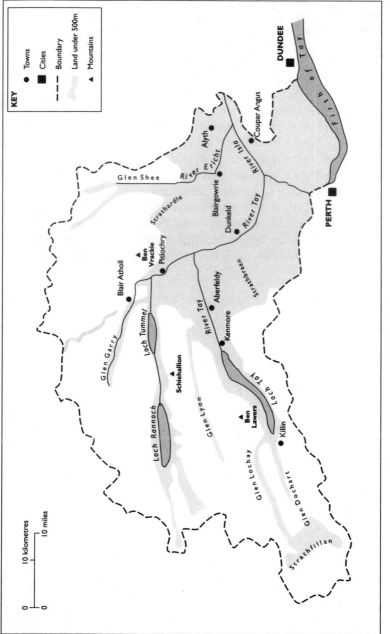

Atholl and Gowrie

PART I

PALAEOLITHIC PERIOD

Before *c*. 7000 BC

The Palaeolithic period or 'Old Stone Age' is characterised by a series of Ice Ages, when a deep ice sheet advanced and retreated across the northern hemisphere until *c*. 10,000 years ago, making Scotland a very inhospitable region for human settlement during much of this era. Between the phases of ice cover, hunters of the tundra ranged across the low-lying plains which connected Britain with the continent, tracking prey which included reindeer, mammoth, woolly rhinoceros, bear, bison and horse. Successful hunting and food-gathering required the development of basic tools like stone choppers, hand axes and wooden spears, and food-sharing necessitated effective communication and social organisation. Distinct populations with those skills evolved from early hominids, including *homo erectus* and *homo sapiens neanderthalensis*, before the appearance of our own very distant ancestors, *homo sapiens sapiens*, about 30,000 years ago.

Around that time more specialised hunting groups emerged, camping along estuaries and lake-sides in the caves of south-west England and Wales. Some of these groups exploited hunting-grounds in colder and wetter regions to the north, perhaps even ranging into Scotland when the climate allowed. Major advances, including the ability to manufacture fire, to make clothes from furs and skins, and to construct artificial shelters, no doubt also made hunting more feasible in these less favourable northern areas. The palaeolithic tool-kit also expanded greatly during this period with the development of scrapers for preparing skins, thin blades of flint and other fine-grained stone for spear and harpoon points, and a range of tools and weapons manufactured from ivory, antler and bone. We have no way of knowing, however, just how tasks like hunting, food-gathering and tool-making were allocated – whether according to gender, status or age.

Even when conditions allowed, settlement in Scotland was probably neither large-scale nor permanent, and any evidence has been scoured away by subsequent glaciers. Scotland was still buried under ice 18,000 years ago, but 3000 years later temperatures began to rise, the glaciers retreated, and vegetation, animals and probably hunters returned to the Arctic-like grasslands. Then, around 11,000 years ago, the climate in Scotland deteriorated again for another 1000 years and glaciers once more eradicated any possibility of human settlement. This time the mammoth, woolly rhinoceros and reindeer did not survive – though elk, deer, auroch or wild cattle, horses, wolves, lynx, bear and boar all returned, followed by small groups of hunters and gatherers who moved in from England, Ireland and across the North Sea plains which the sea now fills. Although the way of life of those settlers may have been little different in many of its aspects from their predecessors', they had developed a new stone-using technology, manufacturing tools and weapons of quite different forms from those of the Palaeolithic cultures. To distinguish them from the earlier peoples they are labelled 'Mesolithic', or 'Middle Stone Age'. And with them, the archaeological record in Scotland begins.

MESOLITHIC PERIOD

c. 7000 BC to *c.* 4000 BC

During the Mesolithic period, rising sea levels resulting from the great ice-melt and the heat-expansion of the ocean waters isolated Britain from mainland Europe and Ireland, and generally decreased the amount of land available for exploitation, requiring more efficient hunting techniques and advances into new hunting areas. By 8000 BC Scotland, with its forests of birch, hazel, alder, oak, elm and pine and open tracts of heath and grasslands, was eminently suitable for just such advances. The earliest Scottish Mesolithic site so far excavated, at Loch Scresort, Rum, dates to *c.* 7000 BC and by at least 6000 BC there were further west coast encampments around Oban and on Arran, Islay, Jura and Ulva. Excavation of sites from Inverness to Galloway suggests that there were probably populations along most of the major Scottish rivers and around the coast, hunting migrant game, fishing and gathering leaves and berries. They did not settle permanently in one place but followed the herds seasonally, setting up temporary base-camps to which they returned each year.

Groups of hunter-gatherers had reached the River Tay by at least 6000 BC. At Morton in north-east Fife, small groups of eight to twelve people built temporary seasonal camps of lightweight timber-framed huts with hearths and sleeping places from which they fully exploited the post-glacial environment of the surrounding region. A mid 7th-millennium dug out canoe found beneath the clays at Friarton on the Tay below Perth was of a type which would probably have been familiar to the people who camped and fished at Morton. Activities at the camp included shell collection, food preparation and cooking, and flint, skin and wood-working. Their middens or refuse heaps indicate that they enjoyed a varied diet, including a wide variety of shellfish, all of which can still be found in the vicinity: deer, wild cattle, pigs, hedgehog and vole; and seabirds, cod, salmon and sturgeon. Tools included a variety of new narrow blades, scrapers and chisels unknown to the Palaeolithic peoples and scatters of these have been recovered from along the Lunan Burn, south of Blairgowrie. It is highly probable that these Mesolithic hunter-gatherers also camped along the old shoreline of the Carse of Gowrie, on the north bank of the Tay, but any evidence of their activities is still buried beneath the estuarine deposits.

There is some evidence that the Mesolithic hunter-gatherers were attempting to control and manipulate their environment. For example, the percentage of hazel and alder pollen rises at this time, suggesting that trees were coppiced for fuel and building materials and swathes of land seem to have been deliberately burned to encourage the growth of grasses for grazing by deer. Basically, however, the subsistence economy of the Mesolithic peoples was dependent on the availability of a food supply over which they had very limited control. All of that was to change in the course of the greatest revolution in human social development, the emergence of settled communities founded on agricultural exploitation of the land.

NEOLITHIC PERIOD

c. 4000 BC to *c.* 2500 BC

The arrival of newcomers whose society and economy was founded on the growing of crops and the keeping of flocks and herds heralded the dawn of a new age. Improved tool-making technology and the emergence of settled communities with a recognisable architecture marked a decisive change from the Mesolithic past. This was the Neolithic or New Stone Age. In this period much greater control over food production emerged, creating static communities with the potential to produce food surpluses and thereby to support specialist craftspeople. Settled farming was established in the Near East and adopted by adjacent communities, reaching the plains of central Europe by *c.* 6000 BC. The earliest agricultural communities arrived in Britain from the continent, probably in skin boats, around 4000 BC, moving north into Scotland across the usual routes from England and Ireland and across the North Sea. These small groups of immigrants introduced sheep and goats and primitive forms of wheat and barley, none of which are native to Scotland, and developed skills in cultivation, pottery manufacture and tool-making. Though the nomadic Mesolithic lifestyle no doubt co-existed with settled farming for several centuries, in the long term it was incompatible with the developing need for territorial boundaries, land-clearance, cultivation and stock-rearing.

As yet, there is no firm evidence in Atholl and Gowrie of the actual settlements of these Neolithic farming communities and we have to look further afield to gain some idea of the types of homes which may have been in use. Orkney long provided the most concrete evidence for the houses of the first farmers, with well-preserved stone-built sites such as Knap of Howar or Skara Brae displaying considerable sophistication in their design. There, it is still possible to visit single or two-room houses focused on a central hearth and furnished with waterproofed storage pits, stone box-beds and dressers for the display of pottery. An alternative and distinctive building tradition was established in Angus and the Mearns. There, at Balbridie on the River Dee in Kincardineshire, the site of a massive, timber-built aisled hall, dating to *c.* 3500 BC, was excavated in the 1970s. The structure, which was traced only through the slots and pits which held its long-rotted timbers, was revealed to have been roughly 24.5 m long by 13 m wide, with straight side walls and slightly bowed gables. To support the wide roof-span the roof members would have been supported on a double row of timber uprights. As no other structures were detected in the vicinity, this timber longhouse has been interpreted as the communal dwelling-place of an early farming community comprising up to twenty-five families. Although no similar evidence has been recognised as yet in Atholl and Gowrie, it is not unlikely that here too, timber would have been the dominant building material, leaving little archaeological record. Recent exavations at Grandtully in Perthshire have revealed Neolithic pits and pottery suggestive of domestic activity, though no dwellings have been identified .

If there is no evidence of permanent Neolithic settlement in Atholl and Gowrie, there is nonetheless evidence of early industrial activity in the area. Across Strathmore, the Carse of Gowrie and the Sidlaws, a large number of Neolithic tools have been discovered, in particular stone axes. Axes were a vital part of the Neolithic tool-kit for felling trees and clearing scrub and – like the large decorated maceheads peculiar to eastern Scotland – were probably also objects of prestige with social and possibly religious significance. The major centres of axe production were at Great Langdale in the English Lake District, Tievebulliagh in County Antrim, and a number of sites in Cornwall, and axes from these sites were traded and exchanged over long distances. Only two axe production centres have as yet been identified in Scotland, one of them at Creag na Caillich on the southern flank of the Ptarmachan ridge overlooking Loch Tay near Killin. Axes from this 'factory', formed from a distinctive fine-grained grey-green stone, were also widely traded and have been discovered as far south as Buckinghamshire.

Other innovations in the Neolithic period include the

practice of communal burial which marks the development of a sophisticated belief system. Although the actual practice of excarnation – the exposing of the bodies until the flesh was completely removed or rotted off, and then the placing of the disarticulated bones in tombs – was common to Neolithic farmers across much of Britain and Ireland, the actual construction of the tombs into which the remains were deposited varied regionally. In the west and north of Scotland in particular, successive generations were buried collectively in stone-built chambers within cairns of stone, but such *chambered cairns* are largely absent from Atholl and Gowrie. There is only one poorly-preserved chambered cairn at *Derculich* in Strath Tay, but outwith the region to the south-west in Strathearn there is a cluster of well-preserved examples in the district from Crieff to St Fillans. The presence of this group suggests that other forms of communal burial may have been preferred in eastern and northern Perthshire.

Long barrows or elongated earthen mounds up to 130 m long were favoured in other areas of Britain, especially in Yorkshire, and in Atholl and Gowrie there are two known examples at *Bridge of Lyon* and *Herald Hill* near Caputh. The latter measures 60 m in length and is 9 m wide at its west end, widening characteristically at the east end to 18 m. The excavation of a similar monument at Dalladies in Kincardineshire revealed that it had been reared over a timber 'mortuary enclosure', presumably where the bodies were excarnated, and which had been levelled before the construction of a small timber structure, covered by the broader eastern end of the barrow, in which the bone was deposited. Close parallels have been identified between tomb forms and house types, with the Dalladies barrow interpreted as the burial place of builders of Balbridie-style houses. At *Pitnacree* in Strath Tay, a similar procedure was followed but the covering mound was not an earthen long barrow but a round cairn of earth and stones. Excavation within the cairn revealed a rectangular stone mortuary enclosure containing four cremations dated to *c.* 2800 BC. Free-standing mortuary enclosures have also been identified as crop-marks in south-east Perthshire as ditched or fenced enclosures. At Inchtuthil, excavation of a site revealed by cropmarks indicated that the mortuary enclosure had been deliberately burned and back-filled in the late 4th or early 3rd-millenium BC.

A third burial form found particularly in eastern Atholl, where it may represent an outlier of a tradition which expanded southwards from Badenoch and the north-east of Scotland, is the *ring cairn* (which looks like a stone doughnut!). An outer ring of large stones or slabs set on edge to retain the cairn material (smaller stones and pebbles), encloses a smaller inner court also defined by a ring of large stones. Burials were deposited over a period of many years within this court. Often the stones of the outer (and in some cases the inner) kerb have been deliberately graded in size, with the largest in the south-west arc, a distinctive feature of the related *Clava Cairn* class of monuments, found in the region around Inverness and central Strathspey. At *Muir of Merklands* in Strathardle, *Lair* in Glenshee and *Middleton Muir*, there are good examples of ring cairns where both the inner and outer kerbs are still visible. Local variants of the ring cairn may also have developed. For although there is no evidence of an internal court at the cairn at *Ninewells*, its external platform, large kerb graded to the south-west and shallow depth of cairn material are all associated with the ring-cairn tradition.

Another monument allied to burial sites and mortuary enclosures is the *cursus* or ceremonial avenue, a long rectangular earthwork defined by pairs of banks within ditches or by rows of pits, identifiable from aerial photography. These avenues have often been found in close association with long barrows and may have functioned as ceremonial ways along which the dead were carried. The earthwork known as *Cleaven Dyke* near Meikleour, which extends for about 2.6 km, has been tentatively identified as a cursus, and another has been identified from aerial photography at Blairhall in association with a cemetery of small barrows.

Henge monuments or ceremonial complexes, typically with one or two opposed entrances and a broad enclosing ditch flanked by an external bank, have not yet been identified with any certainty in Atholl or Gowrie. However, cropmarks at

Mains of Gourdie are suggestive of an enclosure in the henge tradition and elsewhere in the region aerial photography has identified a variety of pit alignments and enclosures which have parallels in Neolithic ceremonial complexes.

Ceremonial circles also provided a focus for community ritual activity in the Neolithic period. Excavations at the Perthshire site of *Croft Moraig* near Kenmore in Strath Tay, one of the most informative circles in Britain, provided valuable evidence of a timber prototype circle which preceded the surviving stone-built circles. Fourteen post holes held upright timbers in a penannular or horse-shoe shape until, later in the Neolithic period, the timbers were replaced by a stone setting which was itself enlarged and added to in the Bronze Age. Given the evidence from Balbridie in Kincardineshire as well as from Pitnacree and Croft Moraig in Perthshire, there is a strong likelihood that timber was a vital building material in Atholl and Gowrie in the Neolithic period for domestic, ceremonial and funerary structures, but it left behind little trace.

The monumental scale of these communal tombs, henges, circles and avenues suggests a high level of organisation and corporate activity, probably requiring the convening of a large number of people from widely dispersed areas. So, although largely self-sufficient agricultural and pastoral communities may have lived for much of the time in fairly isolated extended family groups, they may well have come together in larger social groups for the construction of ritual and burial sites and to attend associated group ceremonies.

THE BRONZE AGE

*c.*2500 BC to *c.* 700 BC

During the middle centuries of the 3rd millenium BC, waves of immigrants from northern Europe, particularly the Rhineland and Low Countries, brought major technological, economic, social and cultural changes to Britain. Analysis of bone material indicates that these incomers were taller and more heavily built than the indigenous Neolithic people but it has not been ascertained whether immigration was by large-scale invasion or small-scale integration with the exisiting population. It is clear, however, that population levels, which had been rising steadily throughout the Neolithic period, continued to grow after 2500 BC, maintaining pressure on the land. Farmers and stock-rearers as well as warriors, the incomers sought land for cultivation and pasture and continued the inexorable clearance of woodland for agriculture which had begun 2000 years before at the dawn of the Neolithic period. Indeed, the peak of forestry clearance was reached in the period *c.* 2000 BC to *c.* 1800 BC.

Despite the preponderance of weapons in early Bronze Age burials in southern England, the survival of several aspects of Neolithic culture into the Bronze Age suggests that the influx was not one of conquest and obliteration but of mutual adaptation and adoption, resulting in an integrated and innovative, native and immigrant Bronze Age culture.

Whatever the scale of the immigration, the implications of the advent of metallurgy were far-reaching. Gold had been worked in the Near East since 4500 BC and copper axes and tools were being manufactured in the Balkans from around the same time. But in Neolithic Britain prospecting, smelting, casting and metalworking skills seem to have been quite unknown. The earliest surviving metal objects in Britain are copper knives, axes and daggers produced from central European and Irish ores. Around 1800 BC, however, copper began to be superceded by bronze, a superior, stronger metal alloy of copper and tin. Though small deposits of copper and gold were available around Loch Tay and towards the head of Strathfillan in this region – and elsewhere in Scotland – Ireland remained one of the principal sources of copper ores for British metalworkers, and Cornwall held the monopoly on tin supply. This limited geographical distribution of resources probably led to attempts to establish control over both raw materials and the vigorous trade which had developed with the European mainland. Furthermore, the introduction of metalworking skills greatly expanded both the range of goods available and the market for those goods, from improved axes and weapons to sophisticated ornaments including penannular rings, ear-rings and collars.

The resulting economic and political changes within Bronze Age society were accompanied by changes in belief systems. The collective burials of the Neolithic period were at this time replaced by individual crouched burials in slab-lined stone coffins or *cists*, like that exposed at *Muir of Merklands*. These were often covered over with round earthen barrows or stone cairns. The cairns and barrows are by no means uniform but vary greatly in size, location and construction. Many of the smaller ones were removed during land improvements in the 19th century but a number of the larger burial mounds survive, both along fertile river valleys, like *Monzie* and *Dunfallandy*, and on hilltops, commanding views along the glens below, like *Strathgroy* and *Pole Hill*. They vary in diameter from 6 m to 38 m and at least three of them, at *Pole Hill*, *Shien Hill* and *Culfargie*, were clearly built in two or three separate stages. At *Cairn Gleamnach* the kerb which retained the since-robbed cairn material is still almost entirely intact, while at *Grey Cairn* the distinctive cairn material of large boulders has survived at least two 19th-century excavations.

Pottery vessels and other grave goods found with human remains at excavated grave sites are also characteristic of the Bronze Age – so characteristic that the immigrants who introduced metalworking to Britain have been named the 'Beaker People' after the drinking cups or beakers which are often found in association with their burials. These vessels were a long-lived cultural tradition, originating in the later

14

Neolithic period and developing in style and form over a thousand years down to *c.* 1600 to *c.* 1500 BC. The beakers are typically decorated with impressions or incisions made with blunt-toothed combs, strands of twisted cord, seeds or small bones. Analysis of a beaker from a cist burial in Fife showed that it had contained a mead made from lime-blossom honey, flavoured with meadowsweet.

From around 1500 BC another change in funeral practices occurs with a marked increase in cremations. Bodies were burned on pyres and the ashes deposited in large *cinerary urns* which were buried, often upside down, in shallow pits. A Bronze Age cemetery discovered near Grandtully within an area of Neolithic occupation contained seven such pits with cremations. At East Essendy in Gowrie, a jet necklace was found in association with two cremations and a *Food Vessel* – a smaller, squatter, bowl-like container named as such in the 19th century because of the Victorians' belief that they held food offerings, placed in the grave to sustain the dead on their journey to the afterlife. Jet was greatly favoured for jewellery in the Bronze Age and much of it probably originated near Whitby in Yorkshire. Token cremation deposits are also found in association with several Bronze Age ritual monuments in Atholl and Gowrie.

Like the burial mounds, there is no standard form for Bronze Age ritual monuments. Stone circles vary in shape from simple circles to ellipses and ovals and in diameter from 5 m to 10 m. Some, like *Meikle Findowie*, are located high on hillsides; others, like *Kinnell Park*, are on valley floors. Although most circles contain six to ten stones and, like the late Neolithic ring cairns, the largest stone tends to be located in the south-west quadrant, there are variations in the form of circles which must have developed in response to local rituals or beliefs. At *Shian Bank* and *Fortingall*, for example, there are pairs of circles; at *Meikle Findowie* the circle has an inner and outer ring; and at *Druid's Seat Wood* short and tall stones alternate.

Local innovation also accounts for the development in Bronze Age Atholl and Gowrie of diminutive *four-poster* settings. Up to only 4 m in diameter, the four-posters consist of four small upright stones, and, like the larger stone circles, one stone is often decorated with cupmarks. The largest stone is usually in the south-west arc. Cremation deposits have been discovered at several sites.

Single standing stones and two and three-stone alignments were also focal points for ritual activity. Single stones vary in height from around 1 m, to the unusually large *Macbeth's Stone* which stands 3.6 m high. Most of the aligned stones are over 1.5 m high and they are rarely more than 3 m apart. One of the most impressive three-stone alignments is at *East Cult* where a massive cupmarked boulder lies beside two colossal upright stones on a ridge overlooking the River Tay. Elsewhere in Scotland, for example at Kingussie and Ballintomb in Badenoch, Keig in Aberdeenshire, and the Clochmabenstane in Dumfriesshire, the Neolithic and Bronze Age monuments appear to have preserved a significance into the Middle Ages as places of assembly, especially as the meeting places of fairs and of local law courts. Such a role seems to be recorded at *Courthill* near Rattray, where there are a number of standing stones.

While this later medieval role as places of secular assembly may represent continuity of purpose from the distant past, the exact prehistoric function of the circles, four-posters and standing stones remains a mystery. Like the Neolithic ring cairns, some importance seems to be placed on grading the stones in size, often with the largest in the southern arc. This suggests some sort of astronomical significance – though without the level of exactitude claimed for the larger British stone circles and henges. Rather, along with the surrounding hills, rivers and woodlands, they may have provided a spectacular backdrop for particular seasonal rituals. The cupmark decorations, token cremation deposits and quartz pebbles associated with many sites may have 'charged' them with a special spiritual or fertility-enhancing power.

Cupmark decorations have their origins in the Neolithic period and represent an important aspect of cultural continuity into the Bronze Age. They appear on rock outcrops like Braes of Balloch and Balmacnaughton in Atholl, on boulders like those at *Newbigging* and *Rait*, and on standing stones including *MacBeth's Stone* and *Colen*. They were made by grinding the surface of the rock with a small stone to produce hollow cups and rings. Some stones, like that at Rait, have cupmarks only, around 70 mm in diameter and 40 mm deep, but on others some of the cups are surrounded by one or more concentric rings. One of the most impressive examples of cup-and-ring marks is *Duncroisk* in Glen Lochay where there are over 150 cups along a 20 m outcrop. Other less common forms of decoration include channels and dumbells. Like the ritual sites, the function and meaning of the cup-and-ring marks found throughout Scotland, and which have parallels in Ireland and Spain – remain unknown.

While there are as yet no firmly-identified Neolithic settlement sites in Atholl and Gowrie, suddenly from the late Bronze Age there is a proliferation of sites which have survived because they are in upland areas where they have been preserved from agricultural destruction on the peat-covered moorlands. There was no doubt dense settlement in the lower lying lands too, as aerial photography is beginning to identify in Gowrie, but it is in areas of settlement expansion onto land which is now more marginal, that the remains of *hut circles* can still be seen on the ground as penannular banks of stone and earth. Most usually, small communities of several hut circles are found rather than single isolated huts but there is evidence from many sites that they were not all inhabited at the same time but were instead variously occupied and abandoned between the late Bronze Age and the Iron Age. The hut circles are generally about 5 m–12 m in internal diameter with walls spread up to 3 m thick. Very few have been excavated but evidence from *Dalrulzion* and *Tulloch Field* indicates that inner rings of posts supported the roofs. Most hut circles are single-walled but other forms developed, including double-walled huts and paired or tangential huts and courtyards enclosed by an outer wall. Around the hut circles there are usually heaps of stones, cleared to allow cultivation, the remains of low field walls and even trackways linking groups of huts and outlying fields.

Another feature of later Bronze Age settlement is the *burnt mound*, a heap of heat-cracked stones. These are mostly found along streams or on marshy areas, occasionally with a large stone trough nearby. They have been identified as communal cooking places used by groups of people without pottery suitable for use over an open fire. Water in the trough could be kept on the boil to cook meat for two hours or more by dropping into it stones which had been heated in an adjacent fire. Stones could only be used a few times before the repeated stress of heating and cooling caused them to fracture. The shattered remains were then discarded to either side of the preparation area, forming over time the burnt mounds.

Many of the changes identified in Bronze Age society may have stemmed from the progressive climatic deterioration which occurred from about 2000 BC onwards. While the population continued to expand and further land was taken into cultivation, agriculture was reaching its natural limits and pushed beyond those into areas that even in the better Bronze Age climate would have been highly marginal. This was a society living on a knife-edge and as climatic conditions worsened through the 2nd millennium, with a general cooling coupled with increased rainfall and strengthening winds from the Atlantic, crop-failure and food shortages may have been an ever-present threat.

In such circumstances we may see evolution of the more hierarchical society evident in the Bronze Age and the development of the warrior-aristocracy whose splendid weapon sets were designed for use as well as for show. Competion over good land and resources may have spilled over into conflict, and it is clear from the archaeological record throughout Scotland that by the last two centuries of the 2nd millennium BC Scottish Bronze Age society was in crisis. The crisis tipped over into catastrophe around 1100 BC, evidently precipitated by the violent eruption of the Icelandic volcano, Hekla, in 1159 BC. This threw vast amounts of ash into the atmosphere and consequently produced several cold and wet years in succession. Coupled with the progressive cooling over much of the preceding millennium, this sharp drop in annual temperatures and increased rainfall saw the abandonment of high altitude cultivation and the acceleration of peat growth in the uplands. Population levels may have collapsed to as low as 50 per cent of earlier Bronze Age levels and whole areas of upland settlement, such as those still visible in northern and eastern Atholl, were simply abandoned or at best given over instead to cattle-raising rather than cultivation, the former farmsteads sealed beneath a thick blanket of peat.

THE IRON AGE

c. 700 BC to c. AD 500

Further technological, social, cultural and political changes around 700 BC in Britain have inevitably led to theories of large-scale hostile invasions, on this occasion by Celtic-speaking peoples from the Continent bringing with them newly-learnt skills in extracting and working iron. However, although use of iron certainly appears across Britain as an innovation around this time, it was probably adopted peacefully by communities which were already Celtic-speaking and which continued to enjoy trading and other links which had been established during the Bronze Age with fellow Celts on the European mainland. Indeed, much of the Iron Age population would have been descendants of the indigenous Neolithic and Bronze Age peoples. Some level of immigration continued into the Iron Age with the expansion of Germanic tribes and the Romans causing the *Delgae* of northern France and the Lower Rhine to cross into southern Britain. On the whole, however, Julius Caesar's report in the mid 1st-century BC that the tribes of Britain claimed descent from the earlier indigenous peoples is upheld by the archaeological record.

With the Iron Age we no longer have to rely solely on archaeology, for valuable, if somewhat biased, written accounts of Celtic customs and historical events by Roman historians have survived. They describe Celtic society as tribal and hierarchical, with farming communities and slaves led by a warrior-aristocracy and priestly elite. A map of the 2nd century AD produced at Alexandria by the geographer Ptolemy shows the territories of sixteen major tribes in Scotland, including the *Caledones* in the central Highlands from the basin of the Tay-Tummel complex across the mountains into Strathspey. The Caledones are remembered in the Perthshire place-names, Dunkeld ('fort of the Caledones') and Schiehallion ('fairy hill of the Caledones'). The Roman campaigns against these Iron Age tribes during the 1st to 3rd centuries AD (see p. 27) seem to have stimulated alliances and treaties between the tribes, with the emergence in the late 2nd century AD in Tayside and Fife of a major supra-tribal confederation, recorded variously as the *Maeatae* or *Verturiones*.

Already in the Bronze Age there is some evidence for occupation of hill-top sites, which later emerge as a principal feature of the Iron Age. The deterioration of the climate in the late Bronze Age, with falling annual temperatures and increasing rainfall, had badly affected harvests and restricted the availability of cultivable land. It is likely that the resulting competition for resources led to increased aggression and the need for well-defended strongholds. Most hill forts were therefore sited on naturally-defended high ground, taking advantage of cliffs, ravines and promontories or following the contours of hills and plateaux. Artificial defences include one or more lines of wall or bank with external ditches and sometimes a small bank or *counterscarp* beyond the ditch. Ramparts and walls at some of the hill forts like those on *Barry Hill* and *Dunsinane Hill* were timber-laced, timbers positioned horizontally in bands within them to add strength. When timber-laced walls were subjected to fire, either by accident or under siege, the heat of the burning wood caused the stones to vitrify or fuse, forming a distinctive mass (it has also been suggested that the vast amounts of timber needed to generate the necessary heat indicate considerable control over local resources, and that vitrification may therefore have been a mark of social distinction). Further lines of defence were added at later stages to several hill-forts like *Evelick* and *Inchtuthil*, suggesting that they were either in use over a long period or were re-occupied and refurbished after periods of abandonment. Other elements in defence include *chevaux de frise* or jagged stones set upright and close together in the ground to make approach by enemy forces extremely slow and difficult. An example of this technique can be seen at *Law Hill*.

The hill forts were probably the permanent residences of the upper echelons of very hierarchical tribal societies, rather than the occasional retreat of the whole community during times of hostility. While some of the larger British hill forts enclose over 50 ha, the smaller are less than 0.5 ha and probably could not have accommodated all of the local population, even during sieges. Not only did the hill-top strongholds provide places of safety for tribal leaders, they also outwardly symbolised the authority and power of those leaders who could muster and organise the considerable labour force required to construct the forts. Leaders like Calgacus, who was recorded by the 1st century AD Roman historian Tacitus as a leader of a cohesive military resistance to the Romans in the 80s AD, probably had significant power bases, many of which probably survived the Roman period largely intact.

At only a few Perthsire sites, like *Evelick* and *Dunsinane Hill*, is there any surviving trace of internal buildings. These are usually *round houses*, sometimes with a *ring ditch* around the inner perimeter in which the timber roof supports were positioned.

Elsewhere in Scotland, the Iron Age saw the development of a range of other defensive, high status fortified sites, notably the *duns* and *brochs* of the West and North. Atholl and Gowrie have no known examples of duns or fortified circular farmsteads, though there are three in neighbouring Angus. On *Little Dunsinane Hill* there is a broch, a dry-stone circular tower with tapering profile, probably 5 m–6 m in height originally and 12 m in diameter with walls up to 5 m thick. Most of the 500 or so brochs which date from the 2nd century BC to the 2nd century AD, are located in the Northern and Western Isles, the northern mainland districts and along the west coast, with only fifteen so far identified outwith those regions. These outlying brochs like *Little Dunsinane Hill* were possibly commissioned by local leaders as outward signs of their power and sophistication, or alternatively may have been built by colonists from the broch-building areas who moved south and east following the Roman withdrawal, *c.* AD 100.

Peculiar to the Scottish Iron Age and concentrated in Angus and Perthshire are *souterrains* (earth houses) or underground storage areas of the 1st and 2nd centuries AD. These are generally 8 m to 30 m long and found both singly and in clusters on freely-draining soils near good arable land. Accordingly, none have been located in Glen Shee, Strathardle or the uplands of western Atholl but in Gowrie they are increasingly identified from aerial photography. They probably provided storage for grain, allowing control of agricultural surpluses, and are usually found in association with high-status timber-built round houses. One of the largest yet investigated by archaeologists lay at *Newmill* near Bankfoot on the A9 north of Perth, excavated in advance of destruction of the site during the realignment of the road. There, the passage was 20 m long and opened into a bulbous 4 m wide end, the whole of the passage being revetted by a well-constructed dry-stone wall. The round house with which it was associated was 17.6 m in diameter. When souterrains were abandoned, their roofs were often deliberately removed – as appears to be the case at Newmill – and the interior filled in.

Aerial photography has also produced a mass of new evidence of unenclosed and enclosed rings, discs and crescents, many of which may represent the dwellings and associated buildings of the Iron Age – the lowland remains of the unenclosed settlements so much more visible on the higher land in Atholl. The hut circles of the Bronze Age remain the dominant form of dwelling in the upland areas during the early Iron Age, many of them now featuring internal ring ditches.

Another distinctive feature of the Iron Age – although excavations at *Loch Olabhat* in North Uist and at *Oakbank* on Loch Tay have established the Neolithic and Bronze Age ancestry of the tradition – are the easily-defended *crannogs* or artificial islands on which timber houses were built. Layers of timber and brushwood were consolidated by stones and vertical wooden piles and can be identified today as tree-covered, stony islands, though many are now submerged. Crannogs were evidently a useful response to the need for security and a means of exploiting loch and lochside resources, for in Loch Tay alone seventeen have been identified. They remained a feature of settlement in Atholl and Gowrie into the 17th century. A typical Iron Age crannog, modelled on findings from the excavated example at Oakbank near Fearnan, has been reconstructed at Croft-na-Caber near Kenmore on Loch Tay.

Specialist occupations probably developed to serve the demands of an increasingly hierarchical society. A priestly class, the Druids, emerge in the Iron Age, worshipping not at the old stone circles but at natural locations like rivers, lochs, wells and woods. Another specialist group probably produced the horse gear, weaponry and jewellery of the period, much of it crafted in iron – more readily available in Scotland than copper and gold. Glass-working also developed in the Iron Age and in the 1st century BC wheel-thrown pottery appears. Other crafts were probably more widely practised: tools associated with weaving are amongst the most commonly found Iron Age artefacts. Native Iron Age society with its tribal and religious leaders, specialist craftspeople and farmers, seems to have emerged intact and relatively unscathed from the undoubted turbulence and insecurity endured during periods of Roman occupation during the first four centuries AD.

ROMAN PERIOD

c. AD 78 to *c.* AD 215

In Scotland, the three major recorded Roman invasions between AD 79 and the 3rd century AD were relatively short-lived and wholly military in character. As a result, the Romans made much less visible cultural impact on native communities than in England where their influence was pervasive and long-lasting.

The first Roman invasion of Britain was led by Julius Caesar in 55 BC but his claim that he completely subjugated the whole island was nothing more than crafty public relations work to impress the citizens back home. It was almost a century later in AD 43 that the Emperor Claudius staged what was to be the beginning of a protracted process of invasion, conquest and domination of the British Isles. Following civil war in Rome, AD 68–69, the *Flavian* dynasty came to power in the person of the veteran general Vespasian, who had earlier commanded a legion during the conquest of south-west England. Under the Flavians the military offensive in Britain was resumed, their long-serving governor Gnaeus Julus Agricola spearheading the drive northwards. Agricola had arrived in Britain around AD 77, campaigned in northern Wales and northern England and in *c.* AD 78 arrived in what is now southern Scotland with 20,000 legionary soldiers plus auxiliaries. In his third campaigning season in AD 79 he reached the Tay estuary and spent the two following years consolidating his conquests behind a frontier line defended by a line of forts strung across the isthmus between the Forth and the Clyde. His biographer, Tacitus, claims that Agricola contemplated the invasion of Ireland from south-western Scotland, but continuing pressure on his northern frontier from the as yet unsubdued tribes beyond the Forth forced him to abandon his plans and prepare for a campaign against them instead. So in AD 82, Agricola turned his attention to the centres of native Celtic population on the east coast plains, from the Tay up through Strathmore and round

the north-eastern end of the Grampian Mountains into Aberdeenshire and the Moray Firth coastlands. His campaigns
climaxed in a pitched battle in *c.* 83 AD against a confederacy of Caledonian tribes led by Calgacus at a hill which
Tacitus named *Mons Graupius*, possibly Bennachie in central
Aberdeenshire or Knock Hill at the Pass of Grange in Banffshire. Though the tribesmen were defeated by the superior
Roman forces, the battle did not give Agricola his sought-
after final victory. Although there is some evidence that Agricola's forces may have pushed on towards the area of Inverness and may even have returned to their southern bases via
the hill routes followed by the modern A9, the Roman grip
over the country north of the Grampians was never secured
and was probably abandoned the following season. Instead,
Agricola and his successors concentrated their resources on
securing the country up to the mountains.

Conquests in eastern Scotland were secured by a network
of forts, watch-towers and roads along the river valleys to
the south of the Highland Line, centred on the legionary
fortress of *Inchtuthil* on the River Tay just below Dunkeld,
where the river breaks out of its narrow Highland gorge
and debouches into the broad lowland plain. Inchtuthil was
built to house a legion – identified as the Legio XX Valeria
Victrix – of around 5500 troops, plus support staff and
commanding officers. It had not been completed, however,
when the temporary labour camp, officers' accommodation
with bath-house and the fortress itself were abandoned
around AD 87 as part of a planned withdrawal forced on
the Roman commanders in Britain by the removal of one
of the four legions based in the island to bolster the Rhine-
Danube frontier. Legio XX moved south and was based for
the remainder of its time in Britain at Chester.

For a brief period, Inchtuthil had been the centre of a
massive engineering project which involved shipment of materials up the navigable reaches of the Tay, quarrying of stone
for the facing of the rampart from several sites in the vicinity,
including the outcrops at Gourdie, and the firing of lime for
mortar, possibly at the adjacent site known as *Steedstalls*.

Inchtuthil was intended as the command centre for an

extensive network of smaller garrison posts which would control the country between the Forth and the mountains and act as a springboard for future campaigns. The crop-mark site of *Cargill*, which accommodated a 'century' of between fifty and eighty men, is an example of a smaller fortlet. It was situated to control the roadway up Strathmore from the crossing of the Tay above Perth, which led to larger forts – which would have housed a *cohort* of about 480 men – at Cardean, Inverquharity and Stracathro in Angus.

At the bottom end of the scale were signal towers. *Black Hill*, commanding an imposing prospect and visible from both Inchtuthil and Cargill, was the site of a timber watch tower from which the native populations could be observed and movements along the valleys followed, with fire or smoke signals being used to relay information to other look-out posts. Like Inchtuthil upon which they depended, all these outposts north of the Tay were abandoned when heavy defeats in the course of the emperor Domitian's campaigns on the Danube forced the recall of several fighting units from northern Britain. Before they went, however, the Romans carefully dismantled their fortifications, salvaging materials which could be recycled, and burning or burying any others to prevent native tribes from re-using materials.

During the 2nd century AD, the Romans attempted to strengthen their northern frontier in Britain by building garrisoned walls, first Hadrian's Wall across the Tyne-Solway isthmus in AD 122–5 and later the Antonine Wall across the Forth-Clyde line, built *c.* AD 142–3 for the emperor Antoninus Pius by his governor in Britain, Lollius Urbicus. The forts of southern Scotland were rebuilt and re-garrisoned, as was the line of forts along the road from the Forth to the Tay, culminating at *Bertha* where the River Almond flows into the Tay just to the north of Perth. Though the tribes of eastern Scotland paid tribute to the Romans in grain and other produce – presumably stored before collection by the Roman *procuratores* or tax-gatherers in the large souterrains which dot this region – little significant advance appears to have been made into northern Scotland, and after a tempo-rary withdrawal in *c.* AD 154, by AD 170 the forts along the

Antonine Wall had been abandoned and the northern frontier reverted south to Hadrian's Wall and a handful of outpost forts in southern Scotland.

The third and final major recorded incursion into Scotland was made early in the 3rd century AD when the emperor Septimius Severus came in person to Britain with his sons Caracalla and Geta. For some time, the *Maeatae* – a confederacy of tribes between the Forth and the Mounth (the mountainous barrier extending eastwards from the Grampians) and their northern neighbours the *Dicalydones* – had been raiding deep into the Roman-held south and it was Severus's intention to bring them back into the Roman peace and secure the northern frontier of the settled province. With his imperial capital based at York, campaigns between AD 208 and 211 penetrated deep into the north. Rather than depend on extended and vulnerable supply lines up the old military roads from Hadrian's Wall, supply bases were established at harbours on the Forth at Cramond to the west of Edinburgh and on the Tay at Carpow near Abernethy, where bulk stores could be brought in by sea.

The army's progress itself can be followed in the huge temporary *marching camps* which it built to accommodate itself, extending through southern Scotland and across the Forth into Strathearn, Strathmore and on as far as Muiryfold in Banffshire. Several marching camps have been identified as fairly standard-sized encampments of 25 ha, 44 ha, 52 ha and a truly massive 66 ha. Lines of encampments of similar size have been interpreted as the products of particular campaigns. Thus 25 ha marching camps at *Scone*, *Longforgan* and *Lintrose* mark the routes of march of troops employed in a campaign directed against the native centres in Strathmore and north Fife. *Grassy Walls* near Scone at 52 ha was probably built to accommodate a much larger force which campaigned through the same area, but penetrated further to the north-east. Despite truces and treaties agreed with the Maeatae and Dicalydones, the tribes chose to capitalise on Roman weakness and break the agreements at the first opportunity, prompting Severus in AD 210 to solve the problem through genocide. Caracalla was sent north with the full imperial army and instructions to annihilate the Maeatae, but the death of his ailing father at York saw a rapid end to the bloody policy and the patching up of a hasty truce in AD 211; Caracalla was eager to secure a negotiated settlement before returning to Rome to consolidate his grip on the empire.

Although there were still some permanent Roman forts in the frontier zone north of Hadrian's Wall at the end of the 3rd century, Caracalla's peace treaty appears to have held for the remainder of the century. However, the early 4th century saw a rapid deterioration in the security of the northern frontier, provoking Roman military responses. In AD 306, Emperor Constantius Chlorus died at York following a campaign into Scotland, while in AD 314 further campaigns were conducted in the name of his son, Constantine. Further raids occurred on the Roman province in AD 342–3, forcing the emperor Constantine to come to Britain in person, while in AD 360–3 his cousin, Emperor Julian, sent an army to repel invaders. In the late 360s the great Roman general, Theodosius, campaigned extensively in Britain and attempted to set the defences of the province into good order, but further problems in the early 380s and 390s showed that no long-term solution had been found. While many of the attacks on Britain were the work of *Scots* from Ireland and *Saxons* from northern Germany, pressure from the north was coming in the shape of a new grouping which was emerging from the older confederacies – the *Picti*.

PICTISH AND EARLY
MEDIEVAL PERIODS

c. AD 500 to *c.* AD 1050

The tribal amalgamations which had originated in the struggle to resist Roman conquest in the Iron Age, later fostered by the stability which Roman might imposed on the bickering tribes beyond their political frontier, culminated in the emergence of the confederations known to the Romans as the *Maeatae* or *Verturiones* and the *Dicalydones*. The Romans referred to these peoples collectively as *Picti* or 'painted ones'. The Picts of the Tay basin were the descendents of the Maeatae or Verturiones – whose name was preserved in the later Pictish kingdom of *Fortriu*, centred on Strathearn – while those living to the north of the Grampian and Cairngorm mountains were descended from the Dicalydones. For most of the period until the takeover of Pictland and the forming of a national kingship by the Gaelic-speaking Scots from Argyll in the mid 9th-century, it is probably wrong to think of a unified Pictish kingdom. Rather, a patchwork of Pictish kingdoms on occasion recognised the authority of an overking or kings. It is as elements in this patchwork that Atholl or *Adtheodle* and Gowrie (*Gouerin*) emerge as distinct provinces in the Pictish period. An early centre of Pictish power may be recognised at Dunkeld, possibly at the hill fort of *King's Seat* which commanded the important routes north and west along the Tay out of the lowlands. A second likely site in Atholl is *Logierait* at the confluence of the Tay and Tummel, whose name preserves the Gaelic element *rath*, signifying a fortified centre, and where the 12th- and 13th-century earls of Atholl, and presumably their remoter ancestors, had their chief seat. Other Iron Age hill forts like *Dunsinane* may also have continued in occupation into the Pictish period and beyond.

In the 8th century, Atholl, ('New Ireland'), emerged as the power centre of a lineage of rulers evidently opposed to the spreading authority of the powerful kings of Fortriu to the south. These kings may not, given the name of their kingdom,

have been purely Pictish, and their kingdom may have originated in a migration of Gaelic-speaking settlers eastwards
out of Argyll. However, the kings of Fortriu were to impose
lordship over all of southern Pictland and achieve domination over the kingdom of the Scots of *Dalriada* (Argyll).
The intensity of the conflict was revealed in AD 738 when
Talorcan, son of Drostan, king of Atholl, was drowned by
Oengus mac Fergus, king of Fortriu, who then installed his
brother as king.

Not only were there internal factions struggling for power
within the Pictish kingdoms, but rival peoples to the south
and west were also keen to exert their influence over the
Picts. From AD 653, the southern Picts were under the domination of the *Anglians* of Northumbria, a Germanic people of
Continental origin, related to the Saxons who were progressively taking over the southern part of the old Roman province in England, who had established a powerful kingdom
which occupied most of the region between the Humber and
the Forth. This domination lasted until AD 685, when the
Picts defeated and killed the Northumbrian king, Ecgfrith, in
battle at Nechtansmere or Dunnichen near Forfar. A degree
of Northumbrian overlordship was re-established in the early
8th century, but as Anglian power declined from the middle
of the century Scottish influence grew. Intermarriage with
the ruling elites of Dalriada brought Gaelic cultural domination and the steady spread of Gaelic language into Pictland,
which spoke another Celtic language akin to modern Welsh,
and by the end of the 8th century a line of kings who ruled
in both Pictland and Dalriada. This paved the way for the
traditional union of the Picts and the Scots under Cinaed
mac Ailpin (Kenneth MacAlpin) in the years after AD 849,
but whether this was achieved largely by peaceful means or
conquest is still a matter of academic debate.

Opinion differs as to the nature of Cinaed's takeover in
the 840s. Views that it was a largely peaceful phenomenon,
representing the natural culmination of centuries of progressive gaelicisation of Pictish society must be tempered by an
awareness that such a union is without parallel in European
history. The vision of Picts and Scots going off hand-in-hand

into the dawn of a new era is one which can no longer be sustained and more value should perhaps be placed in traditions of bloodshed and the elimination of the Pictish leadership. There are also indications of a rival line of rulers, all bearing strongly Pictish names – Talorgen, Uurad, Bridei, Drust and Kineth – surviving down to AD 843. They appear to have been based mainly in Angus and eastern Gowrie – Uurad appears to be recorded in an inscription on the so-called 'Drosten Stone' from St Vigeans near Arbroath, which seems to have been an important monastic centre – and it is possible that the spiritual centre at Meigle was closely associated with them. Their abrupt disappearance in AD 843, after a succession of five kings in four years, strongly suggests that they were eliminated in the course of a protracted rearguard defence of the rump of a Pictish kingdom.

A major influence was played by Christianity in this ebb and flow of power in southern Pictland. Missions directed by St Ninian and his successors from bases in Galloway in south-west Scotland are credited with the early conversion of the southern Picts, reinforced in the later 6th century by missions stemming from the monastery founded by St Columba on Iona. Atholl formed a strategic routeway for these early missions. Drostan, a saint associated with Angus and the North-East, appears to have pushed his influence northwards through Atholl into Badenoch, where a number of early churches were dedicated to him, while dedications to saints of the Ionan tradition at churches in Glen Lyon and Strathtay mark the passage of missions from the West and the continuing affiliations of the peoples whom they converted. Domination by the church based on Iona brought powerful Gaelic influences into Atholl and Gowrie, as the missionaries and monks of the early church were drawn largely from the Gaelic-speaking Scots of Dalriada.

Pictish symbols and symbol stones
Relative stability in 7th- to 9th-century Pictland allowed for the development of a sophisticated Pictish art which has survived in the wealth of carved stones found in both northern and southern Pictland. These are classified as

'Class I' stones bearing characteristic symbols incised into the surface or roughly dressed slabs (as on the fragments found at *Collace* or *Longforgan* in Gowrie, or at *Struan* in Atholl); 'Class II' stones bearing symbols and Christian images, especially the cross, carved mainly in relief (such as some in the collection at *Meigle Museum*, or those at *Dunfallandy* and *Logierait*); and 'Class III' stones which have Christian imagery and figures, but no symbols (for example in the collection at *Meigle Museum* or in the old churchyard at *Benvie*). The symbols on the earliest stones of the 7th to 8th centuries are mostly high-status objects related to warfare, hunting and craftwork. They include mirrors, combs, tongs, beasts and less easily classified abstract shapes, like the V- and Z-shaped rods and the crescent and double disc, probably motifs adopted from metalworking.

Class I stones were marked using a hammer and punch to mark individual dots which were then linked together to form continuous lines. Because of the simplicity of the technique and the lack of any obvious Christian iconography, they are thought to pre-date the introduction of Christianity. Their function and meaning, however, despite recent extravagant claims, are unknown. The symbols are found across northern and southern Pictland, indicating a shared understanding, and many are found in association with burial sites. The *Inchyra Stone*, for example, now in Perth Museum, covered an extended inhumation. The symbols may therefore be a form of hieroglyphics, providing information on names, tribal affiliations, lineage or occupation or they may have conveyed particular strengths or powers. The stones themselves may record deaths, marriages or political alliances, or form territorial markers. The paucity of Class I stones in Atholl and Gowrie probably reflects a relatively early conversion to Christianity in those areas. By contrast, great concentrations of this class of stone are found in the territories of the northern Picts, in Aberdeenshire, Easter Ross and around Inverness, perhaps indicating their later conversion – Christianity appears to have made little headway in this area before the 7th century – and also their political dominance at that time over the southern Picts.

The symbols evidently remained relevant with the introduction of Christianity for they appear along with Christian symbolism and figurative sculpture on the Class II cross-slabs carved in relief. The distribution of these Class II stones complements that of the Class I slabs, with a greater concentration in the south. This probably reflects the late spread of Christianity amongst the northern Picts, the greater and earlier cultural and artistic influences of the Scots and the Northumbrians in the south and a decisive shift in the locus of power within Pictland to the more prosperous south in the course of the 7th century. Although the symbols are unique to the Picts, the iconography and style of many aspects of the Class II sculptured stones indicate a familiarity with contemporary art and craftwork from other regions of Europe, including the Byzantine Empire in the eastern Mediterranean.

The Class II stones in particular illustrate the Pictish interest in monsters, an interest which was shared with contemporary peoples throughout 8th- and 9th-century Europe. The monsters are allegorical, like the symbols, conveying messages and meanings to a largely illiterate people. Christian themes and Biblical stories are illustrated using symbols and metaphors which would have been familiar and well understood. Popular scenes include Daniel in the Lion's Den (found at *Meigle*) and Jonah and the Whale as well as symbolic representations of Christ as a stag (overcoming a serpent). The image of a lion breathing life into its cub on the *Dunfallandy Stone* was probably a well-understood image, symbolising the Resurrection. Contact with Mediterranean art is suggested by the vocabulary of gryphons and centaurs borrowed from that region, while the decorative spirals and linear animals used to fill in spaces indicate an awareness of Irish and Anglo-Saxon art. The *hog-back* stone from the *Meigle* collection suggests that contact with Anglo-Scandinavian sculptors in Yorkshire continued into the 10th century.

Many of the Class II sculptured stones and Class III cross-slabs without symbols are found in association with medieval parish churches like *Alyth*, *Logierait* and St Madoes (from where the stone has now been moved to *Perth Museum*) and there may already have been churches or consecrated sites at these places by the 8th century. Given the large number of carved stones found in and around *Meigle* church, there must have been a significant sculpture workshop there in the 8th to 10th centuries, probably attached to an important monastic and administrative power centre. Long cist burials have been found in the graveyard and amongst the carved stones are two architectural fragments which hint at an early stone building. Documentary evidence also confirms that Meigle was an important Pictish centre – a scribe called Thana is recorded as working there in AD 840.

The Class II stones reveal a society interested in hunting, horse-riding and war, as well as with salvation through Christianity. They were probably carved for an aristocratic elite who advertised their authority, power and influence in part through the stones. The *Rossie Priory* stone for example depicts a hunting scene, including two hunting dogs, and bearded horsemen feature on several of the Meigle stones, one wearing a broad scabbard. Little is known of other sectors of society, however. Women, for example, do not appear on any of the carved stones in Atholl and Gowrie, but those who are depicted in carvings elsewhere in Pictish territory are clearly of high status.

The Kingdom of the Scots

It was in the years after AD 843, when the last member of a line of evidently Pictish kings based in eastern Gowrie and Angus was eliminated, that the lasting union of the Scots and the Picts was achieved under Cinaed mac Ailpin (Kenneth MacAlpin). He established his power centre at the former Pictish royal seat of Forteviot in Strathearn but shrewdly maintained the importance of the other chief centres of Pictland. Dunkeld, with its carved Pictish stones, was already established as a major ecclesiastical centre before Cinaed mac Ailpin built a church there in *c.* AD 849 and brought to it some of the relics of St Columba from Iona, which was under increasing attack from Viking raiders. He clearly intended this to be the spiritual heart of his new kingdom, for on his death in AD 865 Tuathal mac Artgus, head of the Dunkeld community, was described as 'chief bishop of Fortriu and abbot of Dunkeld'. Certainly, the new monastery was intended to replace Iona in the consciousness of the Scots. This would have been reinforced in the same year as the 'foundation' of Dunkeld, when the abbot of Iona, Indrechtach, took the remainder of the relics to Ireland and abandoned the island monastery to Viking raiders. Ironically, Dunkeld itself was plundered by Vikings in the late 9th and early 10th centuries. Religious life there survived the onslaught, maintained by powerful men such as Abbot Crinan, father of King Donnchad (Duncan I), who appears to have entered the church after a long and successful career in lay society, possibly as ruler of Atholl. Nevertheless, by AD 943 St Andrews in Fife had won ecclesiastical supremacy over the Scottish church from Dunkeld.

Cinaed mac Ailpin may also have established Scone as a place of inauguration, bringing to it the Stone of Destiny, and the Moot Hill there may already have been an important Pictish assembly and judgment site. Other important power centres include Rathinveramon, possibly at the site of the old Roman fort at Bertha, where Cinaed's brother and successor, Domnall mac Ailpin (Donald I) died, and Clunie, which is recorded in AD 843–58 and 903 and was probably a centre of political and administrative importance over the district between Atholl and Gowrie properly known as Stormont. That this was the heartland of Cinaed's kingdom is suggested strongly by the attack on it by Danes at some stage in his reign, when they were recorded as wasting the country to Clunie and Dunkeld. In AD 864 and 866, the Danes again ravaged the political heartland of the new Scottish realm, bringing into Scotland the terror and devastation which the same force had been wreaking throughout the Anglo-Saxon kingdoms in England.

The warfare between the Scots and the Vikings continued for much of the remainder of the 9th century. Just like the estuaries of the Humber and Thames in England, so the firths of the Forth and Tay acted like motorways along which these sea-borne raiders could penetrate. It was in battle

against a Viking force which had entered the Tay estuary in
AD 877 that Cinaed's son, Causantin I, was slain. His reign
(862–77) had seen successive waves of attack from Danish
Vikings based in York and Dublin, who overwintered in his
kingdom on more than one occasion. Despite his ultimate
defeat and death, he did score some successes against them,
particularly in AD 864 when he defeated a major Danish expe-
dition and killed their leader, Olafr Godredsson. Chronicle
accounts of Causantin's death vary, but most agree that the
defeat saw the invaders establish themselves within the heartland of the kingdom for at least a year. One account records
that the defeated Scots fled into the fastnesses of Atholl.

At the beginning of the reign of Causantin II (900–43),
a major Norse raid struck deep into Strathearn and Atholl,
Dunkeld again falling prey to raiders. The following year
Causantin crushed the invaders in battle in Strathearn
thereby ending for the time being the Viking threat. After
the traumas of the previous sixty years, the kingdom of the
Scots was at last established on secure foundations and his
long reign was to confirm the emergence of their kings as the
most powerful rulers in northern Britain.

The Church and the Gaelicisation of Pictland
Although the accession of Cinaed mac Ailpin no doubt inten-
sified the movement of Scottish settlers eastwards into Pictish
territories, contact between the two peoples had been established much earlier. Amongst the earliest Scots to make the
journey east were missionaries who introduced *ogam*, a form
of script which originated in Ireland and which can be seen
on the Inchyra Stone in Perth Museum. Early church sites
are represented by names beginning in *kil*, like Kilspindie,
while larger territories or portions of Church-owned land
under the jurisdiction of an abbot were referred to as *abthania*,
remembered in the district still known as the Appin of Dull.
Similar districts are also recorded at Rossie, Kirkmichael and
Megginch, where they do not necessarily indicate the former
presence of a monastery but betray the origin of these lands
as portions of church property. The small handbells now in
the churches of Fortingall and Innerwick in Glen Lyon are

probably also associated with the early Christian missions of ultimately Irish origin which were active in Pictland.

The arrival of these missionaries, and later of settlers, had a profound impact on Pictish society, particularly in relation to language. The Picts spoke a different form of Celtic language from that of the Gaelic-speaking Scots and place name elements in Perthshire illustrate the encroaching settlement of the Scots into Pictish territory. *Pit* names like Pitlochry ('stony share') are definitively Pictish, with a distribution in eastern Scotland from the Firth of Forth northwards. The second element in these names, however, is usually Gaelic, dating them to a period of bilingual naming in the 9th or 10th centuries. *Baile* or *bal* is a Gaelic term meaning farm or settlement and it is sometimes found in use interchangeably with *pit*, as with Pitlochry.

While no certain evidence of Pictish settlement survives in Atholl and Gowrie, many massive stone round-houses dated to the 8th to 13th century have endured in Atholl in particular, which may represent the settlement of Gaelic-speaking Scots coming eastwards. These circular settings are built of huge boulders with 3 m-wide walls and averaging 20 m in diameter. They have been classified as ring forts because of their obvious strength and size and their similarity in design and construction to the ring forts of Ireland. However, few of the Atholl ring forts are in easily defensible locations. Like the cluster in close proximity to one another at the upper end of Glen Lyon, many are situated by rivers on low-lying land by routes through the glens. The massive walls were probably necessary to bear the load of their vast thatched roofs, for concentric rings of post-holes which held timber roof-supports have been excavated at *Litigan*. A central hearth was also discovered there but excavations at the *Allean Forest* site suggested that at least part of the enclosure there may have been used to shelter animals. An early 9th-century silver Pictish brooch was recovered from the ring fort at Aldclune, near Blair Atholl.

Soon after AD 1000 another expansion of settlement occurred on to higher ground previously settled in the Bronze and Iron Ages. This phase of settlement is represented by long, sub-rectangular buildings known as *Pitcarmick*-type buildings from the type-site in Atholl. Characteristically, they are 10 m to 30 m long, 7 m to 8.5 m wide, with rounded ends and curved side walls. Broader at one end than the other, the floors of most of the known examples are partially sunken, usually at the narrower end – possibly indicating the byre area.

THE MIDDLE AGES

c. AD 1050 to c. AD 1600

The political union of the Picts and Scots in the mid 9th-century by no means ended the rivalry for the throne of Scotland. The old Pictish territories were still ruled by local dynasties under provincial rulers called *mormaers* ('great stewards'). Two of the foremost mormaers, in Moray and Atholl, were to continue their struggle for greater power into the early Middle Ages. With the political centre of power of the kingdom continuing to lie at Forteviot and Scone, it is not surprising that many of these struggles were played out in surrounding Atholl and Gowrie. Dunkeld was burned in 1027. The perpetrator is not known, but the close association between its abbot, Crinan, who may previously have been mormaer of Atholl, and the powerful King Maelcoluim mac Cinaeda (Malcolm II) may shed some light on the question. King Donnchad mac Crinan (Duncan I), son of the abbot of Dunkeld and grandson of King Maelcoluim mac Cinaeda, was killed by his kinsman Macbethad mac Findlaich (Macbeth), mormaer of Moray, in 1040. Donnchad's father staged a rebellion in 1045 in a bid to secure the throne for his grandson, Maelcoluim mac Donnchada (Malcolm III Canmore), but was defeated and killed by Macbethad. Nine years later, with English backing, Maelcoluim pressed the claims of the Atholl family to the kingship of the Scots. A large Anglo-Scandinavian army commanded by Earl Siward of Northumbria joined forces with Maelcoluim's Scottish supporters and defeated Macbethad in battle, possibly at Dunsinane near Scone. Maelcoluim's victory, however, was far from complete and Macbethad continued to rule over much of Scotland. In 1057, at Lumphanan in Aberdeenshire, Macbethad was killed in battle with Maelcoluim's army. Since Macbethad's step-son, Lulach mac Gillecomgain, is named by the chroniclers as king of Scots in succession to him it would seem that victory in battle had continued to elude Maelcoluim despite the death of his opponent. Only in 1058 did Maelcoluim succeed in killing Lulach too, and it is from that date that his contemporaries deem his reign to have begun. Atholl remained an important powerbase for Maelcoluim and his family – his younger brother, Maelmuire, was installed as mormaer.

The Earldom of Atholl and Medieval Lordships

From the later 11th century onwards, a series of marriage alliances between Scottish kings and English ladies led to the gradual introduction of foreign – Anglo-Norman – traditions into the royal household. Kings such as Edgar (1097–1107), Alexander I (1107–24) and David I (1124–53) – sons of Maelcoluim mac Donnchada by his second wife, the Anglo-Saxon princess Margaret – used these new traditions in part to bind together their kingdom more tightly and to begin a gradual centralising of power in the hands of the monarch.

The reign of David I in particular has been portrayed as a time of profound change, marked by the introduction of colonists from the Anglo-Norman kingdom of England and from north-west France. David's up-bringing at the court of his brother-in-law, Henry I of England, had opened him to the benefits of royal power offered by the bureaucratic administration and control of justice at national and provincial level enjoyed by the English Crown, and on his accession to the Scottish throne in 1124 he began to introduce personnel to Scotland who could help construct a similar system there. Their arrival is widely regarded as signalling the appearance of 'feudalism' and the beginning of a rapid decline in the significance of Celtic institutions, but current research is tending to suggest that this is an overly cataclysmic view of the long-term consequences of colonisation. Indeed, within the great provincial lordships – or 'earldoms' as the old mormaerdoms were now re-labelled – life continued with little obvious sign of change or royal interference until well into the 13th century.

The 12th century marks the beginning of a clearer division between the culture and society of largely lowland Gowrie and highland Atholl, a separation which was to last into the late 19th century. One of the chief mechanisms for this process was colonisation. Anglo-Norman families were encouraged to settle in Scotland by the king, David I, and his grandsons and successors Malcolm IV (1153–65) and William the Lion (1165–1214) in particular exploited their personal royal or *demesne* lands, granting out blocks of property as knight's feus or fiefs. Gowrie, which had been one of the chief centres of royal power and the location of significant royal estates in the reign of Alexander I, saw the grant of many royal lands to fresh colonists and loyal retainers from the anglicised country south of the Forth in Lothian, in return for military service in the royal army or an equivalent money rent. Roger de Mortemer, for example, held Fowlis Easter from William the Lion in return for the service of one knight, and Kinnaird was held for the same fee by another Anglo-Norman settler, Ralph Rufus.

Some feus, like Errol, which was held by William de Hay in the 12th century, formed the basis for the development of medieval settlement patterns. In these, the lordship of the knight shared the same boundaries as the parish and, in some cases, the dependent village territory. The charters by which the king granted these colonists their feus record an evidently profound change in the pattern of lordship and the relationship between Crown and nobility, but it is easy to overstate the degree of change. Even within Gowrie, native land holders were not entirely displaced or eclipsed.

But it is in the earldoms that there is least sign of change, for the king could not force the earls to introduce colonists onto their lands. As a consequence, the earldoms, including Atholl, have been seen as bastions of Celtic conservatism in the face of a 'feudalising' Crown. Provided the earls were doing a satisfactory job in governing their earldom, there was no need for the Crown to interfere in their administration and while kings from David I onwards could encourage the Celtic earls to adopt and embrace elements of Anglo-Norman culture, they could not force the pace of adaptation. Even within Fife, where the earl had surrendered his earldom to the king and received it back as a feu, Celtic traditions continued largely unchanged.

Despite the numbers of Anglo-Norman and continental colonists introduced to the kingdom after 1100, the Crown continued to depend on the earls for government of the provinces. As kinsmen of the king, the earls of Atholl were expected to play a key part in the extension of Crown authority. Maelmuire's son, Matad or Maddad, is the first to emerge in such a supporting role, featuring prominently in David I's schemes for the government of the rebellious province of Moray and the wider control of northern Scotland. His significance was underscored soon after 1130 by his marriage to Margaret, daughter of Earl Hakon of Orkney and Caithness. In 1138 their five-year-old son, Harald Maddadsson, was accepted as co-ruler of those northern earldoms in return for military support from Atholl and Scotland in securing the other half for another claimant, Rognvald. This Atholl-Caithness axis played a central part in establishing strong royal control over the central Highlands and Ross for the remainder of David's lifetime, but after 1153 Earl Harald proved to be an untrustworthy agent and until his death in 1206 was a source of frequent threat to Scottish authority in the far north.

Gaelic Earls and colonial Lords

This wider role for the earls of Atholl brought rewards and also introduced them to the culture and society of the Anglo-Norman colonists who dominated the royal court. As a sign of favour, the earls received new lands from the Crown, the grants being made on exactly the same terms of service as the new settlers. Thus, while the earls may have kept the spread of colonists into their own territories at bay, they themselves were being drawn into the emerging 'feudal' society of the kingdom. Marriage was a powerful medium for strengthening such bonds. Matad's son by an earlier marriage, Earl Maelcoluim, married Hextilda, grand-daughter of King Domnall Ban (Donald III) and widow of Richard Comyn, the head of the Comyn kindred. Hextilda was not only of royal blood – albeit of a line which had been violently excluded from the succession by the sons of Maelcoluim mac Donnchada – but was the heiress through her father, Uhtred of Tynedale, to extensive lands in the Anglo-Scottish borders.

The interests of the earls of Atholl were extending far

beyond their home territories. Earl Maelcoluim's son by a previous marriage, Earl Henry, continued this policy by marrying a second Comyn lady, Margaret. His half-sister, daughter of Maelcoluim and Hextilda, married another powerful nobleman, Thomas Durward, lord of extensive lands in Gowrie and Angus and grandson of Gilchrist earl of Mar. Their son, Alan Durward, was briefly to be earl of Atholl in the 1230s, to emerge as one of the most powerful men in the kingdom during the reigns of Alexander II (1214–49) and Alexander III (1249–86). All these marriages, however, produced daughters and not sons, and in the early 1200s Atholl was to pass through the hands of a succession of heiresses.

While women could lawfully inherit land and titles, they were not expected at this period in history to manage and rule it for themselves. Instead, the king would find them a suitable husband who would become lord in right of their wife and rule in their place. It was particularly important to the king that the heiress to some great lordship such as the earldom of Atholl should marry the 'right' man: someone who was of proven loyalty to the crown. Thus, in *c.* 1210, Earl Henry's eldest daughter, Isabel, was married to Thomas of Galloway, younger brother of one of the most influential men in Britain, Alan, lord of Galloway and constable of Scotland. There is little evidence that Thomas was regularly active within his earldom, his interests lying instead in Anglo-Scottish affairs and in the carving out of a personal domain in Ulster, where his brother was a major landholder. Thomas, indeed, often provided the English king, John, with mercenaries and galleys for his Irish campaigns, possibly drawing the former from the military resources of his wife's earldom. He was, moreover, a man who moved at ease between the new 'feudalised' society of the royal court and the Anglo-Norman nobility and the older world of Celtic tradition, appearing both as a feudal knight and Celtic warlord. His love of the trappings of knighthood, however, cost him his life when he was accidentally killed in 1231 in a tournament.

Countess Isabel died a few years after her husband, leaving as her heir their young son, Patrick. As a minor, he was placed in the care of his Comyn kinsmen who were thus able to enjoy control of Atholl, much to the disgust of their rival, Alan Durward. Durward used his influence with King Alexander II to secure the earldom for himself, but lost possession in 1237. Five years later, the young Patrick of Atholl, who had not yet been invested with his earldom by the king, died in mysterious circumstances at Haddington. The Comyns at once cried foul play and accused one of Alan Durward's leading supporters, who happened to be Patrick's uncle by marriage, Walter Bisset, lord of Aboyne, and his nephew John Bisset – of murdering the young man. Walter, it was claimed, coveted Patrick's Galloway inheritance, to which his wife was an heiress. The murder of Patrick of Atholl, however, benefitted neither the Comyns nor Durward, who may have expected to be restored to the earldom, but which instead passed to the husband of Countess Isabel's younger sister, the peculiarly-named Forwht. Her husband, David de Hastings, lord of Dun in Angus, was a comparative lightweight and had no clear association with either faction in the Comyn-Durward rivalry. No children resulted from the marriage and when Earl David died in about 1247 it seems that the native line ended with him, for there is no sign that Durward revived his claim to the earldom.

When a new succession of earls emerged in the 1260s, it was in the person of David de Strathbogie, kinsman of the earl of Fife and a man with no known connection to the old line of earls of Atholl. It may have been the instability and uncertainty in Atholl caused by these repeated changes in lordship and the power vacuum which developed after the death of David de Hastings which encouraged the Comyns to attempt to expand their power southwards out of Badenoch into Atholl. In 1269 this provoked a confrontation between John Comyn of Badenoch and Earl David de Strathbogie, who complained to the king that Comyn had built a castle at *Blair* 'which harmed the interests of this earl'.

During this period of most intense Anglo-Norman settlement in Scotland in the 12th and 13th centuries, the estates of the incomers tended to be focussed upon a new form of power centre imported by them – the castle. The earliest castles were of earth and timber, of which only the earth-works now remain. The most prominent feature of these sites is the flat-topped earthen mound, known as the *motte*, which would have been crowned originally by a timber palisade enclosing a timber tower. Some mottes had a lower courtyard, called the *bailey*, enclosed by an earthen bank and ditch and containing buildings such as stables and workshops. Excavations of such sites elsewhere in Britain have indicated that motte and bailey castles tend to be earlier in date (before *c.* 1175), while bailey-less mottes are later in origin. Indeed, excavations on bailey-less mottes in Scotland have shown that new ones were still being constructed in the early 14th century and older ones continued in occupation in some cases into the 15th century. Some estate centres like the *Hallyards* and *Bridge of Lyon* moated sites or the ringwork at *Cargill* were less elaborate. Cargill was granted to Richard de Montfiquet by William the Lion *c.* 1190 and the castle is recorded in a charter of *c.* 1195.

Royal castles which served as administrative centres and royal hunting seats also increased in number at this time. One of the earliest stone castles in south-east Perthshire was probably *Clunie* in Stormont on the western shore of the Loch of Clunie. A castle can be inferred here as early as *c.* 1140 when a charter of David I makes mention of the royal forest of Clunie. William the Lion also had a castle at Alyth adjacent to the royal forest in lower Glen Isla.

The Gaelic earls were slower to embrace the castle as a symbol of their power. They, after all, were the greatest noblemen in the land, second only to the king in status and representative of an office which had its roots in the provincial sub-royalty of the Picto-Scottish kingdom. Throughout the 12th and into the early 13th century, the earls of Atholl had their chief base at Logierait. This occupied an elevated site on the headland above the confluence of the Tay and the Tummel, but little can now be seen and much of the area is planted with forestry. In the middle of the 13th century an unknown earl, possibly David de Hastings or his de Strathbogie successors, started work on a new stone castle at *Moulin* further up the Tummel. This structure, a quadrangular enclosure with round towers at the angles, symbolised the change in the social order of the earldom and signalled its closer integration into the kingdom.

Atholl and the Wars of Independence

The de Strathbogie earls of Atholl represented a significant new departure in the history of the earldom. Although their power was based primarily on the land from which they drew their title, they were to use that power to make an impact on the national political scene. The second de Strathbogie earl, John, was an early supporter of Robert Bruce. He emerges in 1295 as one of the members of the twelve-man council which took over the running of the kingdom from King John Balliol and negotiated a treaty of mutual defence with France, but he does not appear to have enjoyed a close relationship with the Comyn family which effectively controlled the government of Scotland. From the outbreak of war with England in 1296 he took an active role in the field and was captured with many leading Scots in the crushing defeat at Dunbar, but was to take up arms again against Edward I after the Scottish victory at Stirling Bridge. As the tide turned decisively against the Scots in 1304, Earl John made his peace with Edward and was to be rewarded by appointment as the English king's warden between Forth and Spey. In 1306, however, he joined immediately in Robert Bruce's coup and was one of three earls present at his inauguration at Scone on 25th March. His defection to the 'rebel' cause sealed his fate. Having been charged by King Robert with the safety of the queen and other important ladies at Kildrummy Castle in Aberdeenshire, Atholl withdrew further north as an English army closed on the fortress. Apparently heading for the safety of Norwegian Orkney (King Robert's sister, Isabel, was the dowager queen of Norway), the earl and his charges were captured at Tain and handed over to Edward. For his treason, Earl John was hanged in London.

Earl John's son, David, did not share his father's enthusiasm for Scottish independence and the Bruce family. He was, after all, son-in-law of the man Bruce had murdered at the outset of his coup (John Comyn, Lord of Badenoch), and evidently enjoyed a closer relationship with that family than his father had done. Loyal service to the English Crown saw him restored to his father's forfeited lands and titles and through 1307 and 1308 he was at the forefront of Scottish action against the insurgents. Despite the great success of King Robert in crushing the power of the Comyn family and his main Scottish opponents such as Atholl, by mid-1308 Earl David continued to adhere to the English side. Down to 1312 the earl was an active field-commander in English service, but as Edward II's position in Scotland collapsed in that year David decided to salvage what he could from the wreck. He immediately proved his worth to his new master, and Atholl levies feature prominently in the capture of Perth, the last English-held burgh north of the Forth. The relationship, however, was almost immediately thrown into the balance when the king's brother, Edward Bruce, seduced the earl's sister, fathered her a child, then abandoned her for the daughter of the earl of Ross. Atholl gained his revenge in June 1314 for, on the eve of Bannockburn, he defected once again to the English and attacked the Scottish supply depot in Cambuskenneth Abbey, killed its commander and carried off provisions and prisoners. It was an unpardonable crime and led to his forfeiture in the aftermath of the battle. Effectively a refugee in England, he lived out his days as a pensioner of the English Crown and died in exile in 1326.

It was important for King Robert that the highly strategic earldom of Atholl should be placed in safe hands. In the redistribution of forfeited lands and titles which followed Bannockburn, Atholl was granted to John Campbell, son of Sir Neil Campbell, a long-standing Bruce loyalist and brother-in-law of the king. No line of Campbell earls was founded, for Earl John died without heirs in 1333, killed in the carnage of the battle of Halidon Hill fighting against Edward III of England and his protégé as king of Scots, Edward Balliol, son of the King John who had been deposed in 1296. Amongst Balliol's key supporters was David de Strathbogie, son of the forfeited Earl David, who was seeking restoration of his patrimony. Strathbogie was the stormy petrel of the civil wars which followed, his repeated changes of side in a bid to hang on to the lands which he had recovered signalling sharp shifts in the course of the struggle. In 1335, however, he made one side-change too many and on 30th November was defeated and killed at the battle of Culblean in Aberdeenshire. The earldom thereafter remained vacant until 1341 when King David II granted it to Sir William Douglas, a man whose chief interests lay in the Borders.

Stewards, wolves and serpents – the Stewart Earls

In 1342, in a very suspect property deal, Douglas exchanged Atholl with the king's nephew and heir presumptive, Robert the Steward, for the lordship of Liddesdale in the Borders. The transfer of Atholl to Stewart control marked a decisive stage in the development of Stewart power in the central Highlands. It was here that Earl Robert began to build up his close links with the chief Gaelic kindreds of the region which were to underpin his family's later dominance of the area. Central to his plans was the forging of ties with *Clann Donnchaidh* – the Robertsons – a kindred who claimed descent from the male line of the old Celtic earls of Atholl. They had cashed in on the destabilisation of power in the earldom and the surrounding region in the repeated upheavals of the previous forty years to establish their own local dominance in northern Perthshire and were to provide Robert with much-needed military muscle. Around this same time, he granted Glen Tilt to Euan MacRuaridh, brother of one of the most powerful West Highland and Hebridean lords, Ranald MacRuaridh of Garmoran, and it is probable that Euan was expected to provide him in return with more warriors.

By 1371 when Robert succeeded his uncle on the throne as King Robert II, Stewart power straddled Drumochter. Although the king himself had granted Atholl in 1367 to his eldest son, John, he encouraged his third son, Alexander, to expand his interests in the area. Alexander's chief centre of power lay to the north, in Badenoch, but he also acquired the lordship of the Appin of Dull, which then embraced most of western Atholl including upper Strath Tay, Fortingall and Glen Lyon. Following the family tradition for shady property transactions, he added to this significant block of properties through the acquisition from a Menzies heiress of the lands of *Garth*, much of Strath Tummel and Rannoch. His chief allies in this area were his father's old associates, *Clann Donnchaidh*, who effectively became Alexander's hired muscle in his bid for domination of the northern and central Highlands in the 1380s and 1390s. Alexander's ambitions, however, collided with those of his skillful and devious elder brother, Robert, who likewise was seeking to build up a powerbase within the Highlands and tap into the reserves of military manpower which they contained. As earl of Fife since 1372, Robert had acquired the superiority of lands in Strath Tay and Strathbraan, lands occupied by *Clann Donchaidh* for over forty years. This immediately pitched him into head-on confrontation with his brother's chief supporters, a collision which erupted with spectacular consequences in the 1390s. From 1389 onwards, Fife, who was in effective control of the government of the kingdom, had been able to dismantle his brother's north Perthshire lordship piecemeal and transfer most of it into the hands of his own son, Murdach. This was a clear challenge to Alexander's allies, the *Clann Donnchaidh*, and to the interests of his own bastard sons whom he had established on his Garth and Rannoch properties. In Autumn 1391 the new king, Robert III, who as Earl John had received Atholl as a wedding gift from his father, toured north Perthshire in an attempt to pour oil on troubled waters through an assertion of his own lordship, but the simmering hostility towards Fife and his allies spilled over in early 1392.

The flashpoint was an inheritance in Angus claimed by the chief of the Robertsons but held by Sir David Lindsay, one of Fife's henchmen. A raid into Angus by a force drawn from *Clann Donnchaidh* and the kindreds of northern Atholl was intercepted in Glen Brerachan on its return by a force of Angus knights, but in the bloody batle which followed it was the Highlanders who scored a dramatic victory. Despite the victory, however, it was Fife's influence in Atholl which was to prevail.

Lordship in Atholl was passed on in 1398 by Robert III to his son, David, duke of Rothesay. Rothesay's determination to exploit his rights there at the expense of his uncle (by then Duke of Albany), was one of the many factors which contributed to his downfall and murder in 1402. In a bid to consolidate his hold over the earldom, Rothesay turned to his second uncle, Alexander, who still controlled substantial properties in northern Perthshire, and appointed him his baillie in Atholl. Alexander's continued prominence in the earldom is underscored by his burial in *c.* 1405 in *Dunkeld Cathedral*, where his magnificent tomb with his effigy in full armour can still be seen. Rothesays's efforts, however, came to nothing and following his death Albany's authority was confirmed over Atholl.

In 1404, King Robert III granted the earldom of Atholl to his youngest surviving brother, Walter Stewart, who already held the earldom of Caithness. Walter, earl of Atholl, has earned a somewhat black reputation in Scottish history as the evil genius of the Stewart family – 'that old Serpent and Ancient of evil days' as one chronicler called him – plotting the downfall first of his elder brother's family, the Albany Stewarts, in 1424–5, and then being deeply implicated in the assassination in 1437 of his nephew, King James I. He had profited greatly from the destruction of the Albany Stewarts – against whom James I had turned following his release from eighteen years of captivity in England – with many of their former lands and titles in Perthshire and Fife being granted to him by his nephew.

By the late 1430s, however, despite his position as the last surviving royal uncle, Atholl was being excluded from influence in government and feared for the long-term prospects of his family at the hands of a king who was eyeing his great complex of estates greedily. It is probable that Walter hoped to exercise power in the kingdom as lieutenant for his infant great-nephew, James II, but whether he actually plotted the king's murder or simply knew of the conspiracy but chose to remain silent, is unknown.

The murder took place at in the royal residence attached to the Dominican friary at Perth, close to Earl Walter's power-base in the lordship of Methven and the earldom of Atholl. His Highland lordship in Atholl provided a bolt-hole for the king's murderers, with whom his only grandson and heir,

Sir Robert Stewart, was actively involved in conspiring but the widowed queen and her supporters hunted them down and brought them to swift and savage justice. Walter himself, accused of complicity in the murder, was condemned to death and executed with great barbarity – fitting punishment, it was felt, for so heinous a crime.

Following the death and forfeiture of Walter Stewart, Atholl remained crown property for the duration of the minority of James II. This break in active local lordship further undermined the authority of the earl and gave local families an opportunity to expand their freedoms and influence. This decline was arrested when James II granted Atholl in *c.* 1455 to his half-brother, John Stewart, who began to rebuild the position of the earls. Although Earl John's power-base extended beyond his earldom into Highland Moray and Banffshire, where he held the lordship of Balvenie, *Blair Atholl* served as his principal seat and his nephew, James III, clearly saw him as the chief royal agent in northern Perthshire. As such, he became a target for attack in 1475 in the disturbances in the Highlands which followed James III's seizure of the earldom of Ross from the MacDonald Lords of the Isles. According to tradition, it was from the church at *Blair* that Earl John and his countess, Margaret Douglas, were kidnapped by a raiding party led by Angus Og MacDonald. Although he had been closely associated with his nephew, the king, in the action against the MacDonalds, Earl John had his own ambitions and in 1482, with his brothers, James Earl of Buchan and Andrew Bishop of Moray, staged a successful coup to seize the king and place him under ward in Edinburgh Castle. Ever the political survivor, John made his peace with his nephew and, while continuing to intrigue in his own interests, remained loyal to James III in the final rebellion against him in 1488 and took the field in the king's army at Sauchieburn, where James was slain. Despite his association with the old king's regime, Earl John survived the violent upheaval which brought his great-nephew, James IV, to the throne and retained control of his lands and titles.

The direct line of Stewart earls descended from John held

Atholl until their extinction in 1595, whereupon the earldom passed to a junior branch of the family. In 1629, Atholl passed into the hands of the Murrays of Tullibardine, with which family it has remained to the present.

New families for old

It was not just the earldom which witnessed upheavals in tenure. The 14th century was a period of great social disturbance in Scotland. Crop failure and famine followed climatic deterioration at the end of the 13th century and outbreaks of plague caused further devastation, evidenced by burial sites of plague-victims like that at Fortingall. Added to these natural catastrophes were the effects of the prolonged series of wars now known as the Scottish Wars of Independence, which lasted intermittently from 1296 to 1357 and which in the periods 1300–04, 1307–12 and 1332–6 saw widespread destruction of crops, burning of property and slaughtering. This was also a civil war fought out with great bitterness by the supporters of the usurper, Robert Bruce and the exiled John Balliol. Local lords, like the Macnabs of Glendochart opposed Bruce and faced the forfeiture of their land, expulsion, imprisonment, execution or death in battle. Other families emerged to fill the vacuum. For example, the de Meyners or Menzies family, already well established in north-eastern Perthshire by the middle of the 13th century profited from their support for the new regime and received for their loyalty much of the land forfeited by the Macnabs. By the end of Robert I's reign, the Menzies family controlled estates from Aberfeldy in the east to Glenfalloch in the west. Conflicting claims to large parts of this spread of possessions embroiled the family in the protracted squabble between Robert and Alexander Stewart. In 1374, Alexander Menzies surrendered his rights in Glendochart to Robert, initiating a bitter struggle for control between the two brothers from which Robert emerged triumphant in the late 1380s. On the forfeiture of the Albany Stewarts in 1425, the lordship of Glendochart was taken into Crown possession but was administered on the king's behalf by his uncle, Walter, Earl of Atholl. The Menzies family was one of a few north Perthshire kindreds who did not readily fall into dependence on Walter (others included Clann Donnchaidh and the sons and grandsons of Alexander Stewart) – instead associating themselves closely with the royal household. Sir David Menzies of Weem was a prominent servant of James I's queen, Joan Beaufort, and was rewarded with the grant of the bailliary of the Appin of Dull, which formed part of the queen's dower lands. On Atholl's fall in 1437, Sir David recouped many of the earlier losses to his family, but Glendochart remained Crown property. By the 1460s, the influence of the Campbells of Glenorchy was spreading eastwards into Glendochart, an influence which was to become almost absolute in the 16th century when *Finlarig Castle* at the west end of Loch Tay became one of the principal seats of the Glenorchy Campbells and their descendants, the earls of Breadalbane.

The 14th and 15th centuries in Scotland generally saw successive changes of lordship in many estates in the aftermath of the civil and foreign wars which scarred the first half of the 14th century. It was as a consequence of the great reallocation of property post-1350 that the Stewarts began to secure their domination of the central Highlands. While the main branches of the family present in the region by 1370, the Albany and Badenoch Stewarts, had been eliminated in the legitimate, male lines by 1425 – collateral lines, descended from the bastard sons of Alexander Stewart, continued. The principal of these were the Stewarts of *Garth*, who controlled most of the patchwork of properties built up by Alexander in the Glen Lyon and Rannoch area. A related family were the Stewarts of *Grandtully*, who, like their more senior kinsmen, were new arrivals in the area in the 14th century and were to build up a substantial block of properties in the area between Aberfeldy and Logierait.

In sharp contrast to Atholl, where the earls dominated the social hierarchy and where power was vested in the hands of a few important families, Gowrie was a region where no one family exercised outstanding influence throughout the Middle Ages. This was largely a consequence of the Crown's break up of its own estates in the area and its parcelling of them out to colonial families or as endowments to the Church. This produced a patchwork of lesser lordships interspersed with blocks of territory controlled by ecclesiastical landlords. Grants, such as that made *c.* 1172–4 by William the Lion of Kinnaird to Ralph Ruffus, appear fairly typical. This was a compact lordship, its bounds marked by those of the parish of the same name, with Ralph's motte at *Barton Hill* as its administrative and economic centre. The site was excavated in the early 1970s, when the pits which had contained the four massive corner-posts of its timber tower were revealed. This tower, five square metres on plan, had stood within a rectangular enclosure on the summit of the motte, defined by a dry-stone wall-base which may have supported either a turf bank or timber palisade. Around the foot of the motte was a 2 m-deep ditch.

Few of the 12th-century lordly families of Gowrie survived into the later Middle Ages. One notable exception was the Meigle family, which took its name from its properties on the northern side of the Sidlaws. The family is first recorded in the reign of William the Lion, when Simon of Meigle granted the church and chapel of his lordship to the priory of St Andrews in Fife. His son, Michael, was a benefactor of Coupar Angus abbey in the early 1200s. The late 13th-century head of the family, also called Michael, was captured by the English in 1296 in the defeat at Dunbar and subsequently imprisoned at Nottingham. He was released only in 1299, when he was exchanged for an English knight held prisoner by the Scots. On his release he appears to have quickly rejoined the struggle for independence, although in 1305, after the Scots had submitted to Edward I, he was the subject of a specially commissioned inquiry which found that he had been forced against his will to join with William Wallace, and had in fact twice attempted to escape from Wallace's army. As a result of this finding, he was confirmed in his possessions by the victorious English king. His descendants held Meigle until 1404 when William Meigle resigned in favour of David Lindsay, Earl of Crawford.

The Crown still retained important estates within Gowrie, including the manors of Scone, Kinfauns and Rait – despite the founding of the priory and abbey there. It was in the aftermath of the Wars of Independence that many of these properties were granted away. The western half of Kinfauns, for example, was given by Robert I to one of his favourites, Hugh Ross, son and heir of the earl of Ross. Through the marriage of Hugh's grand-daughter, Euphemia, to Alexander Stewart, third son of King Robert II, it passed temporarily into Stewart hands in the 1380s. Eastern Kinfauns and the neighbouring lordship of Rait also ultimately became Stewart possessions, Robert II granting the properties to his bastard son, James Stewart of Cardeny.

It was in the 15th century that a series of locally powerful families emerged within Gowrie. At the eastern end of the Carse of Gowrie and extending into southern Angus, the Grays controlled a network of estates centred on Fowlis Easter, Longforgan, where *Castle Huntly* became one of their chief strongholds, and Kinnaird. The family had been established in Gowrie in 1374 when the East Lothian knight, Sir Patrick Gray of Broxmouth, married the heiress to Longforgan. Closely associated with the Ogilvies and Lindsays, he formed part of the force which pursued Clann Donnchaidh and the sons of Alexander Stewart in 1396 after their raid into Angus, and was seriously wounded in the fight at Glen Brerachan. His successor, Andrew, set the family on their meteoric rise to power. Sir Andrew Gray's political influence was recognised in 1445 when James II's government elevated him to a lordship of parliament as Lord Gray. He remained a committed supporter of James II during the young king's conflict with the Black Douglases and, following James's murder of the earl of Douglas in the course of a heated political argument following dinner at Stirling in 1452 – in which both he and his son were active participants – Andrew was created Master of the King's Household. His son, Patrick, Master of Gray, is named in the chronicles as one of the nobles who were with the king on that fatal occasion, the *Auchinleck Chronicle* claiming that he attacked the earl immediately after the king had first stabbed him, striking him on the head with a pole-axe which he had, rather inexplicably, brought with him to the dinner party – and dashing out his brains! In the political turmoil which followed this brutal slaying, Sir Andrew received royal permission to build his new stronghold at Castle Huntly.

The 2nd Lord Gray, also named Andrew, established the family's later reputation for conspiracy in the 1480s. An opponent of James III's unpopular regime, he had become involved in the treasonous plots of the king's younger brother and was one of the hard-line lords who mounted a coup against the king in 1482. Gray's personal territorial ambitions in Angus and Perthshire ensured that he remained hostile to James III, amongst whose closest supporters were several men whose interests collided with Sir Andrew's. Thus, in the rebellion of 1488 which saw the defeat and death of the king at Sauchieburn by an army led by his own son, James IV, Lord Gray was prominent amongst the rebel command. His adherence to James IV's cause brought rewards: in 1492 he regained the office of Master of the King's Household, and also rose to the office of Justiciar.

Amongst Gray's rivals was Sir William Ruthven, whom James III had made a lord of parliament as Lord Ruthven. He was the descendant of a 12th-century knight of Anglo-Scandinavian ancestry who had acquired the lands of Ruthven on the Angus bank of the Isla. The family had made little social headway until the 15th century, but in the capable hands of Sir William began a rapid rise to prominence. Loyal service to James III brought a succession of property grants, including significant properties in lower Glenalmond, and the title of Lord Ruthven in 1488 was intended to preserve that loyalty in the face of rebellion. Ruthven survived the king's fall but was effectively excluded from power in the new regime.

Both the Grays and the Ruthvens played prominent roles in the turbulent politics of the 16th century, with the Ruthvens succeeding in gaining ground over their erstwhile rivals. Patrick, 3rd Lord Ruthven, was an early convert to Protestantism and played a leading part in the murder in March 1566 of Queen Mary's Italian secretary, David Rizzio. His son, William, an ultra-Protestant, held the commendatorship of Scone Abbey and in 1581 had this erected into a temporal lordship and was created Earl of Gowrie. His religious views put him in opposition to the government of James VI and in 1582 he kidnapped the 15-year-old king and detained him for ten months in captivity. A second bid for power in 1584 led to his execution. His younger son, John, 3rd Earl of Gowrie, appears to have harboured similar ambitions, or was at least suspected by King James of potential treason. In 1600, whilst visiting the Earl John at his townhouse, Gowrie House in Perth, James claimed that the earl was plotting to seize him. In the resulting confusion, the earl was killed by the king's attendants. As a result of this so-called Gowrie Conspiracy, the Ruthven family were forfeited and their name proscribed.

The Medieval Church

In tandem with the changes to noble society set in motion by David I and his successors, the 12th and 13th centuries also saw a thorough reorganisation of the Church in Scotland. This coincided with the great expansion of papal authority across western Europe, with the popes determined to impose uniformity in religious practice across Christendom. The reform movement which converted papal ambitions into reality was not always attractive to kings throughout Europe, for in part it sought to free the church from their controls. In Scotland, however, although there can be no doubting the genuinely pious motives which drove its kings to embrace the programme of reform, it is also clear that David saw his involvement in the process as a means of extending royal authority into a highly influential sphere. Foreign priests, well versed in the doctrines of reform, were appointed by the king as bishops when the native incumbents died and new monastic orders were introduced to Scotland from England or directly from the Continent. The existing Church structure was radically overhauled, with the communities of Celi De or Culdees at places such as St Andrews and perhaps Scone absorbed into or replaced by canons of the Augustinian Order.

Scone

The first new Augustinian priory was founded at Scone in *c.* 1115 by Alexander I, who introduced a colony of canons from Nostell in the West Riding of Yorkshire to staff it. Scone was a great success, sending out a colony to St Andrews in the early 1120s, where its prior, Robert, was nominated to the bishopric. A second off-shoot was planned at Loch Tay, but this appears never to have developed much beyond the planning stage. Scone built up a complex of estates in western Gowrie, stretching from Campsie on the Tay to the north, to Fingask in the Braes of Carse to the south. Control of parish churches, firstly of the right to nominate the parish priest, then later to divert the income of the parish to the direct uses of the monastery, with a paid vicar installed to minister to the needs of the parishioners, brought additional rights and revenues to Scone. By the later Middle Ages, Scone controlled eleven churches in this fashion, five of which were served by one of the community of canons of the monastery and the remaining six by chaplains. Most parishes controlled in this way lay close to the monastery and could therefore be served by the canons, but others lay at a greater remove, such as Kildonan in Sutherland, and required alternative arrangements. This acquisition of property and rights aided the rapid growth of the monastery and by 1164 it had developed to such an extent that it was elevated to the status of an abbey.

Cistercian monastery at Coupar Angus

Despite its position as the location of royal inaugurations, Scone was never able to capitalise on its close relationship with the Crown but lost out instead to monasteries of the orders of monks favoured by the kings. In particular, David I and his successors favoured the Cistercians, an austere order believed to be the most effective intercessors between God and humanity. Towards the end of his life, David had evidently been laying plans for the foundation of a Cistercian abbey in Gowrie. This was realised in 1164 when Malcolm IV founded Coupar Angus Abbey and colonised it from Melrose, the most important of the Scottish Cistercian communities.

The abbot of Scone must have been an envious onlooker as Malcolm transferred large parts of his demesne lands in southern Atholl and Gowrie over to the monks of Coupar Angus, thereby providing them with the core of what was to become one of the greatest complexes of monastic estates in the kingdom and which ultimately secured the position as the wealthiest Cistercian house in Scotland. Additional endowments were made by local landowners, the earls of Atholl prominent amongst them, in return for masses and prayers said for the benefit of their souls.

As major landholders, the Cistercians led the way in agricultural improvements, draining land to bring it into arable production and establishing *granges* or satellite farms like Carse Grange and Drimmie which provided food and fuel for the abbey. *Campsie* was granted to Coupar Angus by William the Lion in 1175 to provide fish, timber and pasture. By the 15th century, when the lay brothers who had provided the labour to cultivate the monastic estates were in short supply (the number of recruits began to fall away sharply in the later 13th century) – the land at Campsie had been leased to secular tenants but the buildings were retained as a rest-home for the abbot and monks.

In common with its sister-houses of Cistercian monks, Coupar Angus was a major developer of its landed property. In contrast to its modern appearance as a rolling arable landscape, medieval Strathmore and the Carse of Gowrie were considerably less attractive. Strathmore was peppered with areas of marsh and scrubland, while the lowlands of the Carse comprised watery estuarine marshes interspersed with isolated outcrops of better ground. In both areas, the monks invested heavily in drainage and land-reclamation projects, because all land won from waste was exempt from payment of teind. There was thus a strong financial incentive for the monks to focus on such projects. The expansion of agriculture around *Carse Grange* was typical of the efforts of the medieval monks of Coupar Angus and their lay-brethren. Not all bog land was drained, however, and some areas nearer to the abbey complex, such as the marsh of Meigle which was granted to them by the local lord, Simon de Meigle, provided peats for the monastic fires. Access to such fuel became increasingly important from the 13th century onwards, as other sources, especially of timber, became more difficult to obtain.

In the hill country to the north of the abbey, especially in Strathardle, Glenshee and Glenisla, the monks developed extensive sheep-runs. Much land in these areas was obtained through grants by local landholders but, where the abbey sought to build up consolidated blocks of property with exclusive grazing rights, they also bought land on the open market. This territory was still plagued by wolves in the Middle Ages – indeed, there are traditions of ravening wolf-packs and an especially huge man-killing wolf in the Mause area north of Blairgowrie into the 17th century – and the monastic tenants in the district were required to keep packs of hounds to curb their depredations.

Although there is little left of the abbey buildings, it is one of the best-recorded monasteries in Scotland. Its records survive as one of the finest *cartularies* (charter books) in the country, but this set of records chronicling the build-up of its landed estate is outshone by the tremendously detailed information preserved in its rental book, which covers the period 1448–1538. This provides wonderful information about the management of a major estate in the later Middle Ages and offers a series of snap-shots of daily life and the routine of work in the monastery and on its properties. It records extensive programmes of planting: broom for winter fodder for livestock, roofing material, the making of hurdle fencing and firewood; osiers and willows for wattling and basketry; ash for wood for tool handles, wheel spokes, furniture etc; and fruit trees for the domestic needs of the household. The abbey also practiced fish-farming in stanks or fish-stews, where eels and other fish were bred to supplement the salmon caught through the monastery's rights to take fish on the rivers Esk, Ericht, Isla and Tay.

Augustinian priory of St Fillan
There was only one other monastic community within medieval Atholl and Gowrie, the minor Augustinian priory of St

Fillan in Strathfillan at the extreme west of the region. It is probable that there had been an earlier Celtic community at or near this location, but it does not appear to have survived into the High Middle Ages. The priory owed its origins to the patronage of Robert I who, while fleeing westwards through Glendochart (the land of St Fillan) in the aftermath of his defeat at Methven outside Perth in June 1306, had been attacked again by allies of the Comyns, including the Macnabs of Glendochart, at Dail Righ near Tyndrum. The king may have attributed his escape from the rout to the saint's intervention, for he was said afterwards to have held him in special veneration. In 1317, he granted the churches associated with Fillan, Killin and Strathfillan, to the Augustinian abbey of Inchaffray in Strathearn, with the intention that these should provide the basis for the foundation of a colony. It never developed into an important community.

Dunkeld Cathedral

The only other major ecclesiastical foundation in the region, and one of the chief land-holders, was *Dunkeld Cathedral*. It was not a new foundation in the 12th century but had early Scottish or even Pictish origins. This accounts for its profusion of detached endowments across Scotland from Bunkle in Berwickshire to Loch Etive in Argyll. Its main possessions, however, lay scattered through Atholl, Gowrie, Angus, Fife and even into Lothian: Cramond on the western outskirts of Edinburgh was one of its important properties, the bishop having one of his main residences there. Like monks and canons of the major monasteries, the cathedral clergy were supported by revenues drawn from parish churches which had been gifted to them by the lay landholders who had originally founded and endowed them. Within the diocese of Dunkeld, seventeen churches contributed directly to the income of the bishop while a further twenty-three constituted the prebends which supported the canons of the cathedral chapter. The revenues of the church of *Abernyte* in Gowrie provided for four vicars choral, who sang the offices in the cathedral choir. By the 13th century the revenues of the cathedral outstripped those of the earls of Atholl. So, despite the creation of so many Anglo-Norman and native lordships in Atholl and Gowrie, it was the abbeys of Scone and Coupar Angus and the cathedral of Dunkeld which were the largest landholders in the region between the 12th century and the Reformation.

Parishes and 'free parsonages'

The reign of David I also saw significant moves towards the development of a national system of parishes, based on the pattern of secular lordships. David is believed to have set in place legislation which enforced payment of *teind* – a tenth of all the annual increase in flocks, herds, crops and revenues – throughout the kingdom, thus providing the revenues which would support the parish clergy. This income was very attractive to the monasteries and major religious institutions and, as they came to control more and more parish churches, much of it was diverted from the hands of the parson or rector into the coffers of the abbeys. This process was known as 'appropriation' and has been seen as one of the major evils of the pre-Reformation Church in Scotland. After all, by 1275 approximately 80 per cent of parish churches in Scotland had been appropriated to some monastery or cathedral, effectively starving the parishes of cash. As a consequence, few high-quality priests could be persuaded to enter the parish priesthood, with ill-educated curates on a meagre stipend serving in their place.

Not all parishes were appropriated. In Atholl, a series of parishes in the Highland zone – Ardeonaig on Loch Tay and Weem in Strath Tay, Blair, Kilmaveonaig, Lude and Struan in central Atholl, and Rannoch in the remote west – remained 'free parsonages' until the Reformation. This may have been a consequence of their remoteness from any major monastery, but in the case of the Atholl group is more likely a reflection of the continuing control over them of the earls of Atholl.

Medieval parish churches were most commonly simple aiseless rectangles, rubble-built with few small windows. The diversion of revenues from the parishes to appropriating monasteries was the main factor behind this lack of sophistication, but it also seems that, unlike England, few local nobles were prepared to win salvation for their immortal souls by contributing to the architectural embellishment of the parish church.

That phenomenon can be seen in Scotland in a few special instances in the late 15th and 16th centuries. Examples of these simple churches can still be seen at *Rait* and *Cambusmichael*. Most medieval churches were proprietorial in origin, meaning they were built and provided with land to support the priest by the local secular lord, who then retained the right to appoint the parish priest whenever a vacancy arose. It was this characteristic which made it easy for control to be transferred to a monastery. Examples of proprietorial churches can be seen at *Clunie*, Cargill and Kinnaird, which were built and endowed initially by lords for the use of their own family and retainers. In the late medieval period the endowment of collegiate churches – 'collegiate' in the sense that they were served by a 'college' or group of priests and chaplains rather than that they held any educational function – replaced the foundation of larger monasteries as the most cost-effective way of purchasing the saying of masses and prayers for your soul's ease. In many cases, parish churches were converted to collegiate use by local lords who provided sources of income to support several additional chaplains within the church, often also expanding the old buildings considerably. A particularly fine example of a collegiate church has survived at *Fowlis Easter*, with many of its medieval features, including the remains of the wooden rood screen and painted panels, possibly from the reredos behind the high altar.

The later Middle Ages also saw a proliferation of small chapels, often established to serve outlying centres of population in far-flung parishes. Few have survived in any substantial form, with most being commemorated simply by farm or field names, or marked by a spread of rubble or feature-less rubble walling, such as the example at *Over Kincairney* near Clunie. One outstanding survival, however, is at *Dron* in Gowrie, where a fine chancel arch of late 15th- or early 16th-century date remains from a chapel probably built by the monks of Coupar Angus. The chapel lies roughly mid-way along the ancient track which ran from the abbey through the Sidlaws to its properties in the Carse of Gowrie.

Medieval castles and lordship estates

Although the earthwork and timber motte-and-bailey tradition remained popular in Scotland into the early 14th century, it was not the only, nor, from the 13th century, the dominant tradition. In parts of northern and western Scotland, castle-building in stone made its appearance in the early 12th century, as is believed to be the case at Castle Sween in Argyll and is documented to be so at Cubbie Roo's Castle on Wyre in Orkney. Simple stone towers also appear to have been an early development in the northern mainland, as at Castle of Old Wick and Braal Castle in Caithness, but evidence for their construction elsewhere in the kingdom at so early a date is the subject of intense academic debate. As discussed above, the first stone castles in this region were probably built by the kings of Scots, who had both the resources and the desire to express their growing authority through such strikingly visual symbols of power. Little can be said for the early form of the castle at *Clunie*, but at *Kinclaven* Alexander II's great quadrangular *enceinte* constitutes a bold declaration of the might of one of Scotland's most aggressively militaristic medieval monarchs. The earls showed little inclination to follow this expensive tradition, probably not through lack of resources but more as a consequence of confidence in their own status and power. They did not need to make stone-and-mortar expressions of power in the heartlands of their domain.

Indeed, it is not until the mid 13th-century, by which date Anglo-Norman cultural traditions had saturated even the most conservative of the Gaelic nobility, that an aristocratic tradition of stone castle building emerges, with *Caisteal Dubh* at Moulin above Pitlochry representing the earliest survival of this form. Despite the traditional naming of the main tower at *Blair Castle* as Comyn's or Cumming's Tower, commemorating the first development of the castle by John Comyn of Badenoch in the late 1260s, no stonework in the building is likely to date so early.

Tower-houses

The devastation of the Wars of Independence saw the end of many of the early stone castles and, as a centre of anti-Bruce power in both main phases of the wars, it is likely that the chief power centres of the earls of Atholl were reduced to rubble. The royal castles at Clunie and Kinclaven met similar fates, neither being rebuilt when peace returned. The changes in lordship which followed the wars witnessed a dramatic burst of castle building as the new lords sought to establish their authority and proclaim their status for all to see. Thus, the Stewarts at *Blair Atholl, Garth* and *Grandtully,* the Menzieses at *Comrie,* and the Campbells at *Finlarig* and subsequently at Balloch (now superceded by 19th-century Taymouth Castle at Kenmore), proclaimed their might through their castles. Many lesser lords followed suit, like the Blairs, builders of the stark tower at *Balthayock* overlooking the Carse of Gowrie. Ecclesiastical lords were not slow to follow the fashion. In the late 14th century, following his kidnapping from his old, undefended and apparently timber-built residence at Dunkeld, Bishop Robert de Cardeny built a sophisticated new palace in stone comprising a towerhouse and adjacent hall block. This survived largely intact until the late 17th century but had disappeared entirely before the 1800s when the grounds around the cathedral were landscaped. His 16th-century successors constructed a second tower-house on the island in the Loch of *Clunie.*

The change in design evident in many castles was less a consequence of the increasingly sophisticated military technology of the era and more a result of demands for comfort and convenience coupled with defence. Certainly the upheavals of prolonged warfare and especially the development of heavy siege artillery necessitated the replacement of many earlier castles. But few men other than the king could afford – or were permitted – to possess an artillery train, and most castles were not built with anything other than short sieges and attacks by raiders in mind. Despite its strikingly defensive appearance, the towerhouse tradition which developed in later 14th-century Scotland was largely a reponse to the social and domestic requirements of their owners. Their starkness, moreover, is often misleading and is largely a result of the destruction of the complex of buildings of which they were only the largest and most prominent portion. Archaeology has revealed that rather than serving as the cramped accommodation of the entire lordly household, the tower-house was under normal circumstances simply the 'family suite' of the castle's owner with the remainder of the household living in the cluster of buildings ranged round the courtyard at the tower's feet.

It is beginning to be recognised that the Hollywood-style presentation of castles as gloomy, damp and uncomfortable fortresses fails to adequately represent the role or character of most of them. Few were fortresses, but served rather as family homes and the judicial and economic centres of landed estates. The larger castles of the greater nobles may have incorporated quarters for private retinues, but, more importantly, they functioned as the meeting places for law courts and councils.

The spread of function within such buildings can be seen in the layout of just the tower-houses. The basement generally comprised vaulted storage, where the bulk goods received as rents from the laird's tenants could be dry-stored. In larger castles, these might also include a pantry (French *panetarie*, bread store) and buttery (French *bouteillerie*, bottle – i.e. wine store), usually linked by stairs to the hall or laird's private chambers in the floor above. Kitchens, too, were often incorporated into the fire-proof basements. The main hall of the building was usually on the first floor, although separate hall blocks are now increasingly being recognised as vanished components of the castle complex. Traditionally, the hall has been portrayed as a venue for banquets, but would also have operated as the nerve-centre of the building, functioning as court and council chamber, principal public reception room and dormitory for the junior servants. The laird may have had a more private chamber opening off the hall, otherwise the upper floors contained the private rooms of the senior members of the household. In the later 15th and 16th centuries, the demands for greater comfort and privacy saw the development of flanking towers to provide more space. This first manifest itself in the so-called 'L-plan', where a single wing was appended to the main rectangular block. The wing often contained the main stair in its lower stages, with bed-chambers for the more important members of the family in its upper floors. Greater sophistication in planning led to the 'Z-plan', where towers were provided at diametrically opposed angles of the main block.

Throughout most of the Middle Ages, the chief defensive arrangements of most castles were concentrated at the wall-head. Parapet walks were provided with *crenellations* behind which defenders could shield themselves while reloading their weapons and *machicolations* through which missiles could be dropped on the heads of attackers who were approaching the foot of the wall. Machicolations were formed by carrying the parapet out beyond the vertical face of the wall on corbels. They remained a significant defensive feature into the 15th century, often being placed over the main doorway to the tower or other vulnerable areas. In the later 15th century, the corbelling which carried the parapet walks became increasingly decorative rather than functional, until in the 16th century its original defensive character was altogether lost. By that date, the introduction of fire-arms for the defence of castles had seen greater emphasis being placed on the wall foot, where strategically-sited gun-loops could create an overlapping field of fire around the tower-house. Further protection for the wall face was provided by gun-fire from the angle towers or from projecting roundels at the angles of the parapet. In general, however, the wallhead features became progressively more decorative, with roundels developing into corbelled angle turrets or *bartizans*, garret windows developing into elaborately carved dormer windows with fine stone pediments, and great chimney stacks breaking up the roof line. *Castle Menzies* is an excellent example of late 16th-century flamboyance, where a fairytale proliferation of turrets, pepper-pot roofs, crow-step gables, dormers, corbels and chimneys crowns the rigid symmetry of the Z-plan block.

The estates and tenure

The castle lay at the heart of an agricultural estate. Lordship estates, known in the earlier Middle Ages as *shires* or *thanages*, were redefined as *baronies* as 'feudalism' spread throughout the kingdom. In whatever form, these units of lordship were sustained by tenant farmers and labourers. The fundamental agricultural unit in the medieval and early modern period was the *toun* or *township*, and an estate of ten to twenty touns could provide for a substantial landholder. The township's arable land was cultivated in rigs or long strips, 3 m to 6 m wide, held in joint tenancy, each tenant holding a scattered share of the rigs. The cultivated ground was divided into *infield* and *outfield* land, the fomer being the prime arable land which was cropped and manured continuously while the latter was of poorer quality and only occasionally cropped. A head dyke or stone or turf bank or wall separated the cultivated ground from the rough-grazing hill land beyond. A particularly well-preserved example of this arrangement can be seen on the west-facing slopes of Glen Shee at *Spittal of Glen Shee.* During the summer months, stock were removed to *shielings* or summer pastures on the hill land where they were tended by women and children, allowing the outfield pastures to recover, and minimising the risk of cattle straying into the ripening crops. At the shieling sites were one-roomed living quarters, outbuildings for making and storing butter and cheese, and enclosures for livestock, all commonly built of turf and drystone walling. Other work took place beyond the head-dyke, including iron-smelting on once wooded areas like Rannoch Moor. Here, *bloomery* sites survive as grass-covered mounds of slag. These crude charcoal furnaces were often nothing more than shallow cavities scooped out of the ground to produce *bloom* or lumps of iron which were then hammered to remove any impurities.

A small minority of tenants in late medieval Scotland were freeholders who held their land from their lord with full security in return for a fixed amount of service or yearly payment. The majority, however, rented their land on short-term tenure, negotiable annually. *Husbandmen* were substantial peasants, cultivating their arable lands with eight-ox plough teams. *Cottars,* sub-tenants of husbandmen, had less land which they cultivated with spades rather than ploughs and often had to eke out their livings with other occupations like weaving. A unit of the estate could be leased or *tacked* to one individual, the *tacksman,* who then sublet various farms on it. In addition to receiving rents from their tenanted lands, landlords also owned personal or demesne land, often called *boreland, bordland* or *mains* in Scotland.

Burghs of barony and royal burghs

Although medieval Scotland was essentially rural, the period saw the growth of small towns and small-scale industry. Burghs were created by royal jurisdiction with their own laws, privileges and institutions. These burghs enjoyed monopolies as market centres for the agricultural surplus of the surrounding communities and often became centres of royal administration. As a result of these monopolies and privileges, specialist occupations developed in the burghs, in trade, commerce and manufacture. Keithick, for example, became a burgh in 1492 and *Dunkeld* some time before 1511 – the former at the behest of the abbot of Coupar Angus, the latter with the bishop as its immediate lord. These, however, were both what are referred to as *burghs of barony* rather than royal burghs, where the Crown has permitted a local landholder to establish a privileged community along the lines of a royal burgh, but lacking its franchisal liberties and trade monopolies. Royal burghs were always wary of the development of such lesser markets and fought vigorously to defend status and attendant privileges. The burgesses of the royal burgh of Dundee, for example, were permitted to send sheriffs to Alyth and Coupar Angus, where a second community dependent on the abbot was developing at the gates to the abbey precinct, to ensure that 'nobody might hold a market of things for sale in these places or have access to them for buying and selling'.

POST-MEDIEVAL PERIOD

c. AD 1600 to *c.* AD 1900

Rebellion and repression

The fall of the Ruthvens in 1600 marked the beginning of a period of change in the patterns of landholding and power in Atholl and Gowrie. New alignments emerged from the wreckage, with the Grays, for example, continuing to extend their influence westwards through the Carse of Gowrie into territory that had once been dominated by their former rivals. No clearly planned steps were taken by the Crown immediately to provide a replacement locally for the strong lordship which the Ruthvens had exercised since the 15th century. It was not until after his succession to the English throne in 1603 and consequent move south that James VI provided any successor for this lost social leadership. The erection in 1606 of the lands of Coupar Angus Abbey into a temporal lordship for James Elphinstone, younger son of John Elphinstone, Lord Balmerino, James VI's former Secretary of State, created a significant new power within Gowrie which went some way towards filling the vacuum created by the disappearance of the Ruthven earldom. And in the same year, the king re-granted the lordship of Scone to David Murray of Gospertie, his comptroller (created Viscount Stormont in 1621) – but neither Scone nor Coupar Angus achieved the local dominance of their predecessor. There were more local changes in landholding also, with, for example, Fingask passing into the hands of the Threiplands, a family originally from Peeblesshire. They became established quickly in the local political scene, emerging as an influential family in the burgh affairs of Perth. Change was in the offing in Atholl too, but without the political, social and economic upheaval which accompanied the forfeiture of the House of Ruthven. There, the succession of Stewart earls ended in 1629 when the title passed, as the result of marriage, into the hands of the Strathearn-based Murrays of Tullibardine, with whose descendants the title remains.

These changes occurred against a background of rumbling political and religious dissent in the kingdom as a whole. James VI's religious policies had seen the introduction of an episcopalian style of Church government in the face of strong opposition from a hard core of ultra-Presbyterian ministers and their lay supporters. This had been one of the many contributing factors to the stormy relationship between the king and the Ruthvens in the late 16th century. James triumphed, however, and a meeting of the General Assembly of the Kirk at Perth in 1618 acquiesced to the introduction of a series of rites and observances which brought a more strongly episcopalian character to the Scottish Church. Ever the pragmatist, James knew that he could not push through too radical a programme too swiftly. His son Charles I, however, lacked this lightness of touch. Wholly unfamiliar with a kingdom which he had left as a three-year-old child and surrounded by 'advisors' who were either equally out of touch with Scottish sentiment or were wholly discredited within Scotland, Charles pressed on with policies which antagonised most Scots. Well-meaning but badly presented policies concerning property holding, growing demands for manpower and money for foreign wars, and disastrously ill-judged changes to the Church to bring it more into line with Anglican forms brought mounting opposition. Economic and political grievances, fuelled by religious controversy, spilled over in 1638 with the drawing up of the National Covenant, a document which professed loyalty to the king but preached open rebellion against his government, councillors and their policies. By 1641 Charles's attempts to bring the Covenanters to heel had foundered and he was forced, against a background of growing hostility to his government in England, to accept their political and religious manifesto.

Many moderate lords quickly became alienated from the cause of the Covenant as they saw it become progressively dominated by radicals and by men who regarded it as a useful vehicle for seizing political power and settling scores. In particular, James Graham, marquis of Montrose, had become disenchanted with Archibald Campbell, 8th Earl of Argyll's cynical manipulation of the power which his role as one of the chief military backers of the Covenant had given him. In 1640, Argyll had led his clansmen through southern Perthshire into Angus in a direct assault on the lands and interests of the Royalist Earl of Airlie, one of his personal opponents. Coupled with attacks by Argyll's followers on some of Montrose's dependents, this unease produced a clear breach between the two men. In 1643–4, as the Scots became drawn into the confrontation between Charles and Parliament in England, Montrose emerged as the military leader of the Royalist cause in Scotland.

To begin with, the Royalist 'army' numbered only a few hundred men, mainly dependents of Montrose. In August 1644, however, Montrose with his small band of followers rendezvoused in northern Atholl with a force of 2000 Catholic Irish led by Alasdair MacColla, a bitter enemy of the Campbells. Marching south, they confronted and routed a Covenanting army at Tippermuir to the west of Perth on 1st September, opening what was to be a year of remarkable Royalist victories in a campaign which carried Montrose into the North-East, Argyll and the Borders. Despite these victories, however, few men rallied to the Royalist banner, even amongst the Perthshire families who owed so much to the Stuarts, and it was a pitifully small force which the Marquis commanded in the final battle of the campaign, the rout at Philiphaugh near Selkirk in September 1645. The defeat effectively ended active support for the Royalist cause in Scotland until 1649, when the execution of Charles I swung most Scots behind his son, whom they proclaimed as Charles II.

In June 1650, Charles arrived from his continental exile, landing in Moray. From there, having signed the Covenant as a prerequisite of his acceptance as monarch by his subjects, he was escorted southwards to Scone where, on 1st January 1651, he was crowned. The Scots, however, had already been defeated in the field by the English army of Oliver Cromwell and by the autumn of 1651 Scotland was occupied by the Cromwellian army. Although Cromwell moved swiftly for an incorporating Union of Scotland with England, his regime in Scotland faced continued opposition. In 1653–4 a serious rising led by William Cunningham, Earl of Glencairn, erupted in the Highlands. Cromwell's army in Scotland criss-crossed the region in an effort to put down the rising, in 1653 battering *Blair Castle* into submission with a devastating artillery barrage. In the end, however, it was internal bickering amongst the rebels rather than military defeat which brought about the collapse of Glencairn's rising.

On his restoration to his throne in 1660, Charles II revealed his implacable hostility to the Covenant which he had been forced to sign ten years before. His reaction saw the re-introduction of episcopacy and the harrying of those whom he regarded as the prime movers in the rebellion against his father after 1638 and in the defeat of the Royalist cause. Argyll, by whom he had been crowned but who had come to terms with Cromwell's government, was the most prominent casualty. His execution in 1661 was mourned by few outside his traditional powerbase. Over the next fifteen years, Charles's policies in Scotland veered sharply between conciliation and repression as he sought to impose his form of Church government on a largely reluctant populace and to establish a secure political regime in a country where faction and personal feud bedevilled strong government. There were, however, many willing supporters who saw the opportunity for political advancement in royal service. These ranged from the greatest in the land, such as John Murray, earl of Atholl, who served Charles II as Justice-General from 1670 to 1678, and whom the king pushed forward as an alternative in the Highlands to the power and influence of the Campbells, to lesser men. Prominent amongst these was Patrick Threipland of Fingask, who had been provost of Perth in 1666. In 1674 he was knighted for his loyal service to the king in suppressing 'conventicles', the illegal religious meetings of those who refused to accept episcopalian-style worship. Threipland's loyalty was further rewarded in 1687 when James VII created him a Baron of Nova Scotia, but his fall followed swiftly. A supporter of the exiled Stuarts after 1688, he died a prisoner in Stirling Castle in 1689.

While most of the foregoing had little direct impact on people of Atholl and Gowrie, the overthrow of James VII in the English revolution of 1688 opened the long saga of

Jacobitism which was to touch many of them personally. *Jacobites*, from the latin *Jacobus* (= James), were the supporters of the exiled James VII and his descendants. In May 1689, John Graham of Claverhouse, Viscount Dundee, raised the standard of rebellion in the name of the exiled king. His principal support came from the Highland clan chiefs, with many of whom James VII had established strong personal ties. In July, Claverhouse marched south out of Badenoch into Atholl at the head of a strong force of Highlanders, garrisoned *Blair Castle*, and continued his route towards Perth. On 27th July, just south of Blair Atholl, however, where the River Garry flows through the *Pass of Killiecrankie*, he encountered the government army commanded by General Hugh Mackay. The Highlanders routed Mackay's army, but Claverhouse was mortally wounded in the battle and was carried back to Blair Castle to die. His body was buried in the old church at Blair, where his memorial can still be seen. Deprived of his unifying leadership, the Jacobite campaign faltered and it was only in mid-August that the southward march resumed. This, however, was checked at *Dunkeld*, where the Cameronian regiment under the command of William Clelland had fortified the burgh. The Jacobites attacked the burgh but, on 21st August, were repulsed with heavy losses and withdrew back into the Highlands. The defeat of the remains of Claverhouse's army at Cromdale in Strathspey in May 1690 ended this first Jacobite Rebellion.

Jacobitism took deep root in Atholl and in Gowrie. In Gowrie, the Threiplands of Fingask, who had strong traditions of loyalty to the Stuarts, were prominent amongst several local noble families who maintained those links. Sir David Threipland joined the Earl of Mar's 1715 Rising in support of the Old Pretender, James, son of James VII, and entertained the would-be king at Fingask. When the rising collapsed in early 1716, Threipland was forfeited and Fingask was sold to the York Building Company, a notorious asset-stripper. Fingask was saved, however, when it was re-purchased by the exiled Sir David's wife. Despite their experience in 1715, in 1745 the Threiplands again rallied to the Stuart standard, the heir to Fingask, David, dying in the

Jacobite victory at Prestonpans, while his younger brother, Stuart, accompanied the Young Pretender throughout his campaign and in his subsequent wanderings around the Highlands and eventual escape into exile. This time forfeiture was more lasting, the baronetcy not being restored until 1816.

Families were also divided in their loyalties. The Murrays of Scone, who had been created Viscounts Stormont in 1621, had avoided the political limelight for most of the 17th century. In 1715, however, James Murray, second son of the 5th viscount, declared his support for the Old Pretender and joined the Jacobite army as it advanced on Stirling. On the collapse of the rising, he managed to escape to France to join the court-in-exile at St Germain and rose swiftly in the Pretender's service, negotiating his marriage to Clementina Sobieska, and receiving the title of Earl of Dunbar from his grateful master. In 1724, he was appointed governor of the 'Prince of Wales', the young Charles Edward Stuart, but remained on the Continent when Charles launched his ill-timed rebellion in 1745 and died in exile there in 1770.

In Atholl, it was the senior branch of the Murrays who were riven by conflicting loyalties. John Murray, whose service to Charles II had seen his elevation in 1674 to the Marquisate of Atholl, had been a strong supporter of James VII in the 1680s. In 1685, he had led an Atholl force into Argyll as part of the suppression of the Earl of Argyll's rebellion in support of the Duke of Monmouth's bid for the throne, and had occupied Inverary, the very heart of Argyll's power. Atholl, however, stood back from the events in 1688–9 which brought the deposition of James VII. He played a highly ambivalent role in the settlement which followed, supporting the new regime of William III and Mary but opposing the policies of John Campbell, earl of Breadalbane, whom the new king had chosen to head his efforts to bring over the Highland chiefs to his cause. Breadalbane, of course, was a local rival and a threat to the Murrays' hard-won political dominance in the central Highlands. Breadalbane's implication in the issuing of orders which led to the Massacre of Glencoe in February 1692 provided Atholl with a powerful lever to use against his rival and his loud criticisms of the earl's involvement led to his appointment as the head of the commission which investigated the atrocity.

Atholl's prominence in government was maintained by his son, also called John, who succeeded to the marquisate in 1703. In the same year he was created Duke of Atholl by Queen Anne. He had served as Secretary of State in the 1690s and in 1703, supposedly in recognition of the influence which he had with the Jacobite faction in Scotland, was appointed Lord Privy Seal in the queen's new administration. Despite this favour, continued rumours of Jacobite sympathies dogged him and in 1707 he became involved actively in the Old Pretender's schemes for a Stuart Restoration. Throughout the same period, he was a consistent opponent of the proposed parliamentary Union with England but when his loyalties were finally put to the test in 1715 he opted to support George I rather than the Old Pretender. His sons, William, Marquis of Tullibardine, heir to the dukedom, and Lords Charles and George Murray, however, were less ambivalent and joined the 1715 rising and the less well-known Jacobite effort of 1719. Only his second-surviving son, James, followed his father's stance. William was prominent in the Jacobite court-in-exile, being created Duke of Rannoch by the Old Pretender in 1717. His Jacobitism, however, led to his attainder for treason and exclusion from the succession to Atholl, which passed on their father's death in 1724 to his younger brother, James. In 1745, Duke James again adhered to the government cause while his brothers, William and George, served prominently in the Young Pretender's army. Lord George Murray proved to be a general of some capability and was appointed by the Prince as his Lieutenant-General.

The degree of bitterness between the brothers was revealed in 1746 as the retreating Jacobites headed north. Duke James, who had discreetly removed himself from Scotland in 1745, had admitted a government garrison into *Blair Castle* to command the road north, and Lord George turned the Jacobite guns on his family's seat. Despite a heavy artillery barrage which inflicted significant damage to the old building, the castle held out. It was to be the last violent episode in the long history of rising and repression which followed 1600. William and George took part in the final chapter of the Jacobite rising at Culloden on 16th April 1746, a battle fought against the advice of George. Following the defeat, William surrendered to the Government forces and died in prison soon after. George, however, took to the hills and escaped to the Continent where he died, bitterly disillusioned with his former master, in 1760. It was the passing of an age.

The Church

Despite the 16th-century Reformation of the Church in Scotland, there were, as we have seen, few significant changes to the social, political and agricultural landscape of Atholl and Gowrie in the 17th century. Eventually, architecture would take account of the liturgical and sacramental requirements of the Reformed Church but for the first 100 years, when the nature of the Church swung repeatedly between extremes of Presbyterianism and Episcopalianism, adaptation of the small medieval churches sufficed. These medieval buildings were purged of overtly 'Popish' features, such as statues, ornaments for the altar, stained glass, wall-paintings and most carved woodwork, such as rood screens, choir stalls and the like. Services were now held in Scots rather than in Latin and the emphasis was on readings from scripture and preaching. This resulted in a shift in the liturgical focus of the church away from the altar in the east end to the pulpit, often with the addition of a reader's desk. Often, the medieval chancel in which the altar had been located was abandoned and dismantled and the chancel arch built up, its remains sometimes being taken over by the leading local family as a burial aisle.

Furthermore, the orientation of the building was decisively shifted by the placing of the pulpit midway down one of the long walls of the former nave. This also signalled a change in communion practice. Whereas in the Middle Ages it was often only the officiating priest and important members of society who would fully partake in the Eucharist, the rest, if permitted, receiving only the Body and not the Blood of

Christ, communion was now received by all full members of the Church in both kinds. Full participation of the congregation was required now, the minister acting as guide and leader in the rite rather than simply functioning as the intercessor or intermediary. This was reflected symbolically in the siting of the communion table and the minister's position in respect to the congregation. Instead of standing in the style of the pre-Reformation officiants, remote in the chancel with his back to the congregation (in effect placing himself between God and the congregation), he now faced them across a table which was located centrally in the church and around which the congregation was ranged, like participants in the original Last Supper.

The more idealistic of the Reformers fought for a Church that was free from earthly controls, but before the end of the 16th century they had lost the battle to secure control of the revenues that had once flowed to the pre-Reformation hierarchy and which was essential for the establishment of a financially sound, independent entity. They had also lost the battle to free the Church from the influence of lay patrons. In many instances, the control of parish churches which had been exercised by the old abbeys and cathedrals simply passed into the hands of the noblemen who secured control of the former monasteries and their properties. Thus, for example, the Gowrie-based Ruthven family acquired the abbey of Scone, which was converted into a temporal lordship for the 4th Lord Ruthven in 1581 and formed the primary landed basis for his earldom of Gowrie. Likewise, Coupar Angus passed to the Elphinstone family, for whom it was erected into a temporal lordship in 1606.

As a consequence of these events, the right to appoint the ministers of the churches which had once formed part of the monastic lordships attached to those abbeys passed into the hands of their new lords. The new patrons frequently developed burial aisles for their families at the parish church, often incorporating them into the private lofts or galleries which they built for themselves. A good example of this can be seen at *Weem*, where the local Menzies lord constructed a 'laird's loft' with private retiring room for use between the

Sunday services within the medieval transeptal chapel on the north side of the church.

Small and plain in most instances, the old medieval churches required little structural modification to adapt them to the needs of the new order. Often the only trace of alteration in the external fabric of the building is the enlargement of the windows to allow more light into the dim, mystery-inducing pre-Reformation churches. Cathedral churches were more difficult to adapt in their entirety, as they were generally much larger than would be needed by the population of the communities within which they were located. At *Dunkeld*, as elsewhere in Scotland (e.g. Dunblane) only the choir of the medieval structure was maintained, the nave being left to decay.

There was no place for monks in the Reformed Church and monasteries, which had been in slow decline throughout the later Middle Ages and were generally permitted to moulder away. At Scone, the abbey buildings had been plundered by a Protestant mob in 1559 and were largely reconstructed in the later 16th century when the Ruthvens converted the complex into a private residence. A new parish church was built outwith the precinct to serve the local community which had worshipped in the nave of the old abbey, it being in this structure that Charles II was crowned by the Scots in 1651. Coupar Angus shared the same fate. While the cloister was converted post-Reformation into a private residence for James Elphinstone, lord Coupar, at least part of the old abbey church was maintained for parochial use. Elphinstone's house was sacked in 1645 by members of the Royalist army commanded by the Marquis of Montrose, who killed the minister, Robert Lindsay, as he attempted to defend his church against the Roman Catholic Irish of the raiding party. Thereafter it was systematically plundered for stone by the townsfolk of the burgh which had grown up at its gates, being described by 1682 as 'nothing but rubbish'. Pieces of decorative stonework from the abbey buildings have been found built into houses and post-Reformation churches throughout the surrounding district. The parishioners appear to have continued to use the neglected fabric of the abbey church until 1686, when work commenced on a new building and the demolition of the old church proceeded apace. This evidently stood on the site of part of its medieval precursor, probably the nave. It was substantially enlarged and rebuilt in 1780 and entirely replaced by the present building in 1859.

As the case of Coupar Angus nicely illustrates, there was no great church-building movement in Scotland until after *c.* 1690 when, following a lengthy period of episcopacy, the Church in Scotland finally emerged as Presbyterian in organisation and doctrine. Many of the simple medieval churches evolved into T-plan buildings with the addition of a transeptal aisle, sometimes with a tower on the opposite side. In many cases, however, the old medieval buildings did not survive for long after 1690. Often, indeed, the only indication of the sophistication of some of these vanished structures are the carved fragments still to be seen in the churchyards of their 18th and 19th-century successors, as for example at *Kettins*, where the predecessor of the present building appears to have been embellished with materials plundered from the abbey at nearby Coupar Angus. At *Errol*, the only indicator of the former richness of the medieval parish church, which benefitted from the patronage of the Hays of Megginch, was a magnificent tomb effigy of a knight in full plate armour of the earlier 15th century, found in the 19th century and built into the post-Reformation kirkyard wall. The new churches of the 18th and 19th centuries were designed largely in Georgian neo-classical and Gothic Revival styles and the long, low churches of the medieval period were replaced by high, wide-bodied buildings.

Not all medieval ideas disappeared with the Reformation, however. Some found new outlets. Burial aisles, like that at *Kinfauns*, for example, replaced the medieval chantry chapels, collegiate churches and other endowments and a new taste emerged for elaborate commemorative monuments, such as that at *Weem*. The *Kirk Session*, a body of lay elders, was responsible for maintaining religious and moral discipline and at Weem and Dowally the *jougs* or neck collars used to punish miscreants have survived. Later, the threat of body snatchers who supplied cadavers for anatomical research, led to the widespread use of *mortsafes* or iron grids which secured the coffin until the decomposed corpse was no longer at risk. Three well-preserved mortsafes survive at Logierait.

Agricultural reform

Major reform also occurred in agriculture in the 18th century. Improving landowners provided the impetus, keen to maximise profit, but it was most often the estate grieves, factors, surveyors or labourers who were the actual agents of 'improvement'. They already possessed the technical skills to provide an infrastructure for agricultural reform with improvements such as road-building and corn mill design and land improvements like liming and drainage. Limestone was quarried and burnt from the 17th century onwards to provide lime for both building mortar and, principally, for improving the acid soils of the reclaimed lands. Early lime-burning was in clamp kilns – mounds of turf and stone – but during the 18th century more sophisticated draw kilns were introduced and it is these which survive on many farms in Perthshire. Round or square, they were often built into slopes so they could be loaded with stone and fuel at the top and the lime extracted from the bottom. A particularly large and partly-restored example can be seen at *Tomphubil* at the summit of General Wade's military road from Aberfeldy to Tummel Bridge (B846).

During the 18th century, several other agricultural processes were mechanised, including corn-threshing. Traditional methods of corn-threshing by hand using a flail to separate grain from straw were extremely labour intensive and time-consuming. In 1786 Andrew Meikle invented the powered threshing machine and by 1794 already sixty-one such machines were in use in the Carse of Gowrie alone. The commonest method of powering them was by two or more horses which walked in a circle around *horse gins*, open on smaller holdings but housed in distinctive circular or polygonal buildings on larger farms. These conical-roofed structures, their walls broken by large openings to admit carts, though now disused, are common features of many farm steadings throughout Perthshire. Several good examples can be seen at the farms which flank the A9 between Perth and Pitlochry.

Meal mills also became increasingly efficient with water-powered wheels mounted with blades or buckets in the vertical plane, driving the mill-stones through gearing. A feature of all the larger mills was the kiln, a funnel-shaped structure surmounted by a ventilator, where grain was dried before it was ground. Individual corn-drying kilns were in use at fermtouns up to the late 18th century when better seed and earlier sowing and harvesting times made them obsolete. Many can still be seen at deserted settlements in Atholl and Gowrie, most often as circular depressions at a safe distance from the other buildings, like those in Glenshee. Corn was laid on a grid in these small kilns, half-way up the chamber, and a fire was lit at the outer end of the flue. The heat, inducted inwards, dried the grain without risk of fire. When they were no longer required, several, like those at *Allean Forest*, were converted to burning limestone by lengthening and narrowing the flue to increase the draught.

Not all of the improving innovations which brought such great benefits to the landowning class were found as beneficial by the tenants. With the late 18th-century improvements, the multiple-tenancy fermtouns and cottartouns were replaced by single-tenant farms. Landowners waited until the leases for the various shares fell due and then, with the legal authority of the sheriff courts to back them up, simply refused to renew them, consolidating and amalgamating them into larger and larger units. The desertion of *Glenshee* was instigated in just this manner and was completed by 1862.

Mansions and estates

Increasing profits for the landed aristocracy financed their great mansions, palaces and houses of the 18th and 19th centuries. With the need for defence removed and with accompanying changes in lifestyle and taste, the stacked vertical towerhouse of the 16th century gave way to classical country houses from the 17th century onwards. By the later 17th century, some older towers were already being remodelled to bring them into line with new fashions in architecture. At Tower of Lethendy near Blairgowrie, for example, the Heron family undertook a refurbishment of the 16th-century towerhouse in 1678, at which time angle turrets and wallwalks were removed and the wallhead finished instead with pedimented dormers.

Palladian architecture from Italy reached Scotland via English architects like Christopher Wren and Inigo Jones. The first major exponent of this style in Scotland was Sir William Bruce (*c.* 1630–1710). He and other Scottish architects like John and Robert Adam were commissioned by the Scottish aristocracy to design houses befitting wealthy cosmopolitan families. One of the finest of these new mansions was Dunkeld House, built for the Duke of Atholl in wooded grounds to the north of the cathedral. This huge quadrangle towered above the medieval church and the burgh until the early 19th century when it was torn down to make way for an even larger neo-Gothic palace which, perhaps fortunately for the finances of the Dukes, never proceeded beyond the laying of foundations. The Atholls also remodelled their older house at *Blair Atholl* to bring it into line with classical tastes. Between 1747 and 1758 a programme of works under the direction of James Winter saw the slicing off of two storeys of the lofty towerhouse, the removal of all parapets and bartizans, and the hammering through of the thick, late medieval walls to open up large rectangular windows at regular intervals. The result was a severely plain Georgian house, re-named Atholl House.

Towards the end of the 18th century, the neo-Gothic style, which adopted motifs from European medieval architecture, largely replaced the classical detailing which had drawn on the architecture of the Greeks and Romans. The earliest and finest of these buildings is *Scone Palace*, built 1803–12 for the Earl of Mansfield to plans prepared by the able English architect, William Atkinson. Here, the late 16th and early 17th-century palace of the Ruthvens and Murrays, which had evolved out of the medieval abbey buildings, was swept away and replaced with one of the earliest asymmetrically-planned houses in Scotland. The rebuilding scheme also extended to the grounds of the house, where the old burgh of Scone and its parish church were demolished and replacements built at New Scone, outwith the new walled *policies* of the mansion.

Atkinson also provided plans for Lord Kinnaird's new mansion at Rossie Priory near Inchture. Built in 1810, it was one of the largest mansions in Gowrie, but much of its main block was demolished in the 20th century.

Perhaps the most eye-catching of the neo-Gothic 'castles' of the area lies at the opposite end of the Carse from Rossie Priory. *Kinfauns Castle*, built 1820–4 to designs by Sir Robert Smirke for the 14th Lord Gray, is a wonderful concoction of battlements and towers on an elevated site overlooking the Tay at the foot of the dramatic folly-crowned crags of Kinnoull Hill.

The finest of the neo-Gothic houses of Atholl is *Taymouth Castle*, which developed out of an original Adam house built for the Marquis of Breadalbane.

From the neo-Gothic style developed the fully-blown Scots Baronial of the Victorian and Edwardian eras. This borrowed and adapted Scots vernacular motifs, incorporating many of the features of medieval Scottish architecture, in particular from the towerhouse. Championed by Queen Victoria and Prince Albert – who, ironically, demolished an existing 16th-century tower to build the epitome of the style at Balmoral – it quickly became the accepted form of architecture for the houses of gentlemen of all ranks. At *Blair Atholl*, where in 1844 Queen Victoria had complained of the 'large plain white building', the 7th Duke of Atholl employed David and John Bryce in 1869 to re-castellate it. The wonderful asymmetry of the current building and the exuberance of its roof-line, therefore, is the product of 19th-century romanticism.

Landowners enjoyed other comforts like a ready source of fresh and frozen meat throughout winter, provided from well-stocked doocots and ice-houses. The doocots of Perthshire are mostly lectern-shaped and rectangular with sloping roofs, such as the excellent example at *Knapp* in the Carse of Gowrie, where the building was subsequently converted into a cottage. Internally, the doocots had some 500 to 2000 boxes or ledges on which the birds nested and roosted, which would have been accessed by ladders. One distinctive feature of the exterior of the buildings is a broad string-course or 'rat-ledge' below the level of the birds' access holes to prevent rats from climbing in and destroying the eggs.

Icehouses were the precursors of the deep-freeze for the wealthy. They were usually built at least partially underground with an opening into which blocks of ice were stowed – cut from local ponds or, later, imported from Scandinavia. A fine example of an icehouse survives in the grounds of Dunkeld House. That example was for domestic use by the ducal household, but the fine barrel-vaulted structure on the Tay at *Seggieden* was a commercial development connected with the salmon fishings on the tidal reaches of the river.

Humbler homes

Housing for the majority of the population of Atholl and Gowrie changed less significantly in the post-medieval period, though here too agricultural reform had some impact. Traditional Scottish housing was couple- or cruck-framed, that is the roof was supported not by load-bearing walls but by a framework of braced timbers, the *couples* or *crucks*. Originally, when walls were built of turf and rubble, this framework was essential, but even when more solid walls appeared they remained a traditional feature. Though the timbers themselves have mostly long gone, cruck-slots in the walls can sometimes still be identified – for example at the restored *Allean Forest* settlement.

The availability of clay in the Carse of Gowrie resulted in the development there of the most sophisticated clay buildings in Scotland and some two- and three-storey clay houses survive in Errol and nearby villages. Clay-walled buildings, or buildings of 'clay-and-bool' construction (where large water-worn pebbles are bonded together with clay) – were once more widespread in the area, but, once the roof is lost they become very fragile and quickly erode into tumbles of rubble or clay mounds. Some of the earliest improved settlements were built using these impermanent techniques, with the result that they have left little of substance by way of structural remains. At Pitmiddle in the Braes of Carse above Kinnaird, for example, the village survives only as series of spilled rubble walls and slumped earthen banks.

Planned estate villages

The improving movement introduced a new element to the village pattern of Atholl and Gowrie: the planned estate village. In the late 18th and early 19th centuries over 300 planned villages were established in Scotland to accommodate those who had moved off the land as well as the increased number of workers both on landed estates and in the new, large-scale manufacturing industries which were emerging. These villages like *Inchture* feature standardised housing on regular street plans. One of the earliest was New Scone, founded by the Earl of Mansfield to replace Old Scone, the straggle of houses which had grown up originally at the gates of the abbey precinct, in the course of the remodelling of his palace between 1803 and 1812. Similar ideas for the aesthetic improvement of the environs of the houses of the nobility led to the development of Kenmore at the gates of Taymouth Castle after the older settlement – which had stood closer to the Campbell of Breadalbane tower of Balloch, from which Taymouth was developed – was swept away. A later example of an estate village can be seen at nearby Fortingall in Glen Lyon. There, the houses built in the period 1886–90 follow various earlier vernacular traditions imported from Lowland Scotland.

Farm buildings continued to be developed throughout the 19th century, particularly in the rich agricultural districts of Gowrie. Both farmhouses and the accommodation for the farm labourers grew more sophisticated as the century progressed. The thatch-roofed Balnald Cottages at Fortingall represent a late 19th-century essay in architectural revivalism. More typical are the rows of labourers' cottages to be seen throughout the region, such as the fine sandstone houses of the Rossie Priory estate of Lord Kinnaird (for example those at Baledgarno at the western gate of the policies).

Experimentation in design continued in to the 20th century and it would be wrong to think of the planning of estate buildings as a homespun industry. Some of Scotland's greatest architects contributed significantly to the rural architecture of the region. One of the finest surviving examples of such work is Sir Robert Lorimer's superb ogee-roofed dairy and attendant scullery building at the entrance to Kinfauns Castle, where it forms part of an earlier Home Farm complex. This was erected as recently as 1928.

Industrialisation

The Agricultural Revolution, with the mechanisation of processes like saw-milling and lime-burning, itself stimulated industrial growth and in Perthshire the greatest opportunities were to be found in the textile industries. Most textiles were manufactured by hand up to the 18th century. The exception was the fulling or beating of cloth whereby the fibres were matted using fuller's earth. Originally this *waulking* was done with bare feet until the process was mechanised at waulkmills using water power. The next process to be mechanised was the scutching of lint or flax for the linen industry. *Scutching* removed the woody material from the stems of flax by bruising and beating it and in the 1720s powered rollers and revolving blades were developed to achieve this. The circular lint mill at *Invervar* in Glen Lyon is one of the most complete examples to survive in Scotland.

Rural Perthshire's place in the industrial revolution was secured by its abundance of water, so necessary for powering the machinery and a vital ingredient in several manufacturing processes. Bleaching, for example, was another important process in linen manufacture, originally dependent on the availability of large amounts of water for washing, rinsing and moistening the cloth and plenty of space for bleaching it in the sun. In the early 18th century lack of care in bleaching was identified as a major factor in the low quality of Scottish linen and by the 1720s large numbers of bleachfields were established where the processes could be controlled and supervised. In the 1750s the cloth needed four months' exposure for bleaching, providing employment for many migrant Highland workers as well as local people. With the introduction of new chemical methods, however, the bleaching process was completed in considerably less time and no longer required natural sunlight.

The abundance of fast-flowing rivers in Atholl and Gowrie also accounts for the establishment there of large water-powered spinning mills. Several new cotton mills were established in 1785 and afterwards by Sir Richard Arkwright and his associates, including that at *Stanley* where the Bell Mill is one of the finest surviving early cotton mills in Scotland. Spinning required a linear layout of machinery and aisles, resulting in the characteristic long, multi-storeyed buildings with regular, large windows to provide good, natural light. With the advent of steam-power, engine houses and factory chimneys became a familiar feature.

During the mid-19th century the hemp and jute trade extended the use of textile technology with the manufacture of canvas, bagging and ropes and several cotton and flax mills switched to spinning jute. One of the most remarkable groups of jute and flax mills is at Blairgowrie where water-wheels survived to power the textile industry on an unprecedented scale.

The same abundance of water, and its high quality, also made Perthshire particularly attractive for whisky distilling. Until the late 18th century, private distillation for home consumption was common but excise controls meant that illicit, small-scale distilling had to be carried out in secluded bothies, like that at *Invereddrie*, where water was easily available, using copper pot-stills and pipes which could be easily dismantled at a moment's notice. By 1880 there had been over 14,000 successful raids on illicit stills and the legalised industry began to gain a firm foothold. The principal buildings at these legitimate distilleries were the multi-storeyed malt barns, warehouses and distillation blocks. Several distilleries like *Edradour* at Pitlochry were required to guard against drought by the use of dams.

Salmon fishing also became an important industry on

the River Tay during the late 18th and early 19th centuries, in particular in the parish of Kinfauns, controlled by the wealthy local merchant, John Richardson of Pitfour. Early in the fishing season, when the weather was still cool, fish could be shipped raw to London in a variety of chests, boxes and baskets. With the introduction of the use of ice to keep this early fish supply fresh, ice-houses like that at *Seggieden* were built for storage. Later in the season, the market shifted to the continent and the fish were pickled with Portuguese salt or French vinegar and exported in barrels to ports in the Netherlands, France, Spain, Portugal and Italy.

Attempts – not all successful – were also made to exploit other natural resources in Atholl. Lead was discoverted at Tyndrum in 1741 and the mining operations began a couple of years later. Initially, the lead was carried out by pack-horses to be smelted at the bottom of Glen Falloch but later smelting operations were completed at the mines themselves until they were abandoned at the end of the 18th century. During the following century the Marquis of Breadalbane established a copper mine and associated chemical works on the south shore of Loch Tay.

Communications and infrastructure
Increased surpluses and trade brought about by the Agricul-tural and Industrial Revolutions required an improved infra-structure of roads, bridges, ferries and railways. In the 18th century, the stimulus for road building came from revolu-tion of a different sort. After the Jacobite rebellions of 1715 and 1719, the government determined to bring the High-lands to heel by establishing military bases there, accessed by roads from the south. General George Wade (1673–1748) was appointed commander of the scheme and charged with the task of extending northwards the existing roads which ended at Crieff and Dunkeld. The resulting road north from Dunkeld was the forerunner of the A9, while the route from Crieff pioneered the line now followed by the road north through the Sma' Glen to Amulree and on to Aber-feldy. There it crossed the Tay by the superb Adam bridge, climbed from Keltneyburn over the ridge to Foss and down

to Tummel Bridge, from where it again climbed over the hills to Trinafour and the junction with the Dunkeld route at Dalnacardoch. Temporary camps were established every ten miles to accommodate the labouring soldiers and at these locations 'King's Houses', inns or hostelries developed subsequently. Good examples can be seen at Amulree in Strathbraan and at Dalnacardoch, where the present shooting lodge, partly screened by trees to the west of the modern A9, was developed from the earlier inn. Built in 1744, it housed Prince Charles Edward Stuart on his southward march in August 1745 and on his return north in February 1746. A few miles further north, near a lay-by on the south-bound carriageway of the A9, is the so-called Wade Stone, an eight-foot pillar of rock erected in 1729 to commemorate the completion of this stretch of roadway northwards to Drumochter. Well-preserved stretches of Wade's road can be seen at *Dunkeld* and *Glen Cochill*, and a particularly good stretch can be seen clearly from the modern A9 north of Calvine. Of his bridges, the William Adam structure at Aberfeldy is without doubt the finest, but several less sophisticated examples survive along his roadways. A further 1200 km of road and 1000 bridges were built by Wade's former assistant and eventual successor Major William Caulfield, following the 1745 rebellion.

Road rage and railway mania
In rural Perthshire long-established drove roads, like that down Glen Tilt, were the primary network of communication into the 18th century and the routes from Rannoch into Glen Lyon and southwards to the great cattle trysts at Crieff and later Falkirk continued to be used by droving traffic into the early 19th century.

With the threat of uprising removed in the Highlands, the government no longer saw a need for maintenance of roads or road-building programmes and privately-funded Turnpike Trusts emerged in the early 19th century. These recouped their income from tolls collected in toll houses which were leased out to toll-keepers. All traffic except the Royal Mail coaches and Public Stage Coaches had to pay a fee until the system ended in 1878. One of the finest products of this period of development is the superb bridge at Dunkeld built by Thomas Telford in 1809 for the Duke of Atholl. Designed as a toll bridge, the collection of tolls by the Duke's agents was a source of hostility from the first, particularly from the people of Dunkeld. The toll of a 'bawbee', or ha'penny was collected for almost fifty years before serious opposition was encountered. This stemmed from a misapprehension that the charge had been to pay off the building costs and that the capital outlay must surely have been recouped, but was fuelled by the resentment of the townsfolk at having to pay every time they crossed the bridge to get to the railway station at Birnam, which opened in 1856. The result was over twenty years of protest, headed by a local merchant named Alexander Robertson of Dundonachie, which involved riots, gate-smashing, and even the threat of military intervention. Although Dundonachie himself was financially ruined in the process and spent several spells in prison, the dispute became something of a *cause celebre* and contributed significantly to the 1878 Roads and Bridges Act which superseded the turnpike legislation. The Duke, however, did not simply lose his right to levy tolls, receiving £18,000 in 1879 when the ownership of the bridge was taken over by the county council.

One of the chief reasons for the 1878 Act was the dramatic change in the transport system as a whole which had been brought about by the arrival of the railways as media for mass movement of people. In northern Perthshire the principal enthusiast for rail development was John Campbell, 2nd Marquis of Breadalbane, the second greatest landowner in the country and one of its wealthiest men. The Breadalbane Campbells had embarked upon a systematic commercialisation of their far-flung estates in the late 1700s, initiating one of the most widespread programmes of clearance in the Highlands. In Glenorchy, for example, the population fell from 1806 to 831 between 1831 and 1841. The Marquis, however, was not merely a ruthless evicter of the unprofitable poorer tenants; he was prepared to invest heavily in improvements to his estates. His agricultural improvements were matched by other commercial enterprises, most notably by plans to exploit the mineral resources of his land. In 1838 he re-opened the Tyndrum lead mines.

An unexpected off-shoot of his mineral prospecting was the discovery of a mineral spring at Moness on the hillside above Aberfeldy, which he planned to develop as a spa. The possibilities of tourist income immediately sparked the idea of a rail link, which would also provide transportation for the sheep and cattle reared on his properties or traditionally driven through them. In 1845–6, at the peak of the so-called 'railway mania', therefore, the Marquis started to promote two railways on his estates. The first – the Strathtay and Breadalbane – was a small concern intended to form a branch from the projected Perth-Inverness railway up Strathtay from Dalguise to Aberfeldy. The second was one of the grandest schemes of the period, the Scottish Grand Junction Railway. It was proposed to start at Callendar, where it would link up with the line from Dunblane and thence into the main Scottish network, providing a main line to Oban. A branch was proposed which would run from Crianlarich through Glen Falloch to the head of Loch Lomond, where it would link with the steamer service on the loch. A second branch was proposed running north-east from Tyndrum across Rannoch Moor to Loch Ericht and thence to Dalwhinnie, where it would link with the Perth–Inverness line. A third spur was to run from Lix in Glen Dochart down to Killin and it was even proposed to extend this line via Glen Lochay to join with the Tyndrum–Dalwhinnie line. Most of this ambitious scheme was never authorised, let alone saw any building work, and it was not until after the Marquis's death that the line from Callendar to Oban was completed.

Although waterways are abundant in both Atholl and Gowrie, there was little use of them for transport purposes as much of it is incapable of navigation. Passenger steamer services were established in the 19th century on Loch Tay and Loch Rannoch, the former by the Marquis of Breadalbane, but otherwise it was only on the Tay below Perth that the river system of the region saw much water-borne traffic. There were plans, however, for a more elaborate system of waterways, but these never got beyond the drawing board. In the aftermath of the Napoleonic Wars, when large numbers of unemployed servicemen returned from the army, it was proposed to soak up their surplus labour in a scheme of canal building. Ambitious proposals were made for a canal which would link the Tay with the North Esk, possibly with an extension on to Aberdeen.

With the coming of the railways in the second half of the 19th century, Atholl and Gowrie developed a tourist industry which continues to thrive. Though the lint, cotton and jute mills are now out of production, several continue to contribute to the economy of Perthshire as tourist attractions. And water remains a vital resource for Perthshire industries such as distilling, and continues, as it has always done, to provide inexpensive, safe power to domestic and industrial users via schemes like the Pitlochry Hydro-Electric station, which bears the fitting motto 'Strength of the Glens'. But with the introduction of new crops like raspberries and straw-berries in Gowrie, it is agriculture which remains the main-stay of the economy and identity of Atholl and Gowrie, as it has done for over 6000 years.

TOURISM – AN EPILOGUE

Royal endorsement of Atholl by Queen Victoria and her physician who recommended the health-restoring qualities of the local air and climate during a visit in 1845, provided the impetus for tourism as a new and important development in the region, focused initially on the town of Pitlochry. Until the royal visit, Pitlochry had been a small distillery village with a coaching halt at Fisher's Hotel, established in 1839. The arrival of the railway line from Dunkeld brought an even greater influx of visitors, and Fisher's Hotel was supplemented by two curative, hydropathic hotels, the Atholl Palace Hydro, designed by Andrew Heiton in 1878, and the Pitlochry Hydro, built in 1890. At first, holidays were principally for the wealthy who could enjoy the ease and comfort of travel offered by the railway companies. Industrial and banking families from Glasgow and Edinburgh commandeered whole houses for long vacations, though hardly on a self-catering basis. The Archibald Coats family of Paisley, for example, took over Balnakeilly House near Pitlochry for two months in 1896, arriving with their household staff and horses by a special train laid on for the occasion.

Soon middle-class families were renting smaller houses and villas in the area, the owners retreating to makeshift accommodation elsewhere. Railway stations were opened in Killin and Tyndrum as part of the Callendar to Oban railway, completed in 1880, and before long round-trips were available by rail, coach and steamboat, departing from Glasgow and Edinburgh. The enterprising 3rd Marquis of Breadalbane established the Loch Tay Steamboat Company and eventually there were two passenger steamers, *Queen of the Lake* and *Lady of the Lake*, which gave his tenants on the lochside estates access to outlets for their farm produce in the large towns to the south and also brought in tourists. Some of the piers for the steamboat service still survive around the loch. When the Callendar and Oban railway declined to provide a spur line from Lix to Killin to connect with the steamer service, the Marquis went ahead and established the

Killin branch-line, including a station on Loch Tay to serve the boats.

Sporting holidays had been the preserve of the wealthy since the establishment of the medieval royal hunting forests. In the late Victorian and Edwardian periods, sporting estates were established in Atholl and Gowrie and they too benefitted from the improved road and rail network. Some estates even built their own private railway lines. Between Dalmunzie Lodge and Glenlochsie Lodge, near Spittal of Glenshee, for example, a light railway, including zig-zag reverses, was built in 1920. First used to convey stone for building work, with the task completed it then transported shooting parties to and from the lodge, and was still in use by tourists in the 1950s.

Atholl and Gowrie remain popular tourist destinations, not least because of their wealth of archaeological sites which provide a window on the evolution of the modern landscape.

PART II

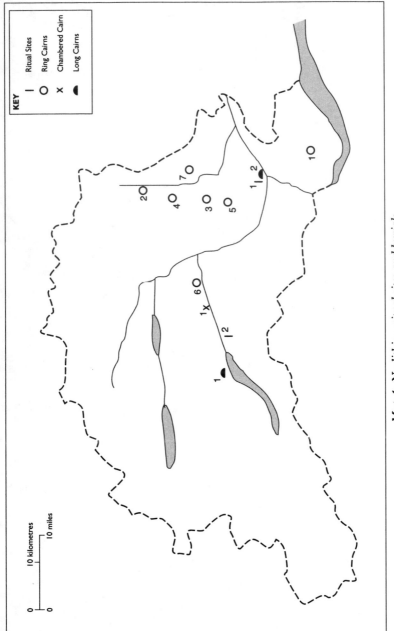

Map 1: Neolithic – ritual sites and burials

10 kilometres

10 miles

GAZETTEER OF SITES AND MONUMENTS

NEOLITHIC SITES

RITUAL

1   Cleaven Dyke, Meikleour   NO 175 397 to NO 154 409

The 1.73 km-long section which runs through North and
South Wood, north-east of Meikleour, is the most accessible and best preserved length of this 2.3 km-long *cursus* or
avenue which is aligned from north-west to south-east. Until
recently it was classified as a Roman monument connected
with the nearby legionary fortress at Inchtuthil but it has no
real parallels from the Roman period and is more likely to
be of Neolithic date. It has been identified as a *cursus*, a class
of monument more usually associated with the south-east of
England but increasingly recognised in Scotland from cropmarks. The function of these avenues is uncertain but they
have been linked to funerary and ritual sites.

The Cleaven Dyke consists of a bank up to 1.8 m high and
averaging 9 m wide, flanked by two ditches which have been
dug in short segments. On either side of the bank there are
broad terraces, giving the avenue a total width of 40–50 m
within the ditches. The bank itself, which is not entirely
straight, has been constructed of sand and gravel revetted
with turf.

Essential Viewing

2   *Croft Moraig, Kenmore**   *NN 797 473*

*At the farm entrance on the A827, 3.5 km north-east of
Kenmore, there is a small gate leading to this remarkable stone
circle. On excavation in 1965 it was discovered that it was
constructed in three different phases and in its earliest phase
was not a stone circle at all but a timber circle. At least fourteen
upright timbers, around 2 m high, had been positioned in a
pennanular or horseshoe shape, 8 m by 7 m, with a flat stone*

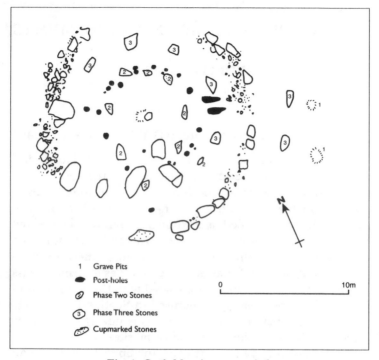

Fig. 1: Croft Moraig – stone circle

containing a charcoal-filled hollow, probably a hearth stone, in the centre. The horseshoe was open to the south-west and immediately to the south-east was a pair of elongated post-holes which each originally contained three upright timbers.

This timber horseshoe was later replaced by eight upright stones arranged in an oval shape, 7.6 m by 6 m, with an arc of three outliers to the south on the same axis as the earlier monument. The massive recumbent stone on the S-S-W axis of the kerb may have had special significance as it has twenty-three cupmarks, two surrounded by partial rings, on its upper surface. Associated with this phase is the roughly circular outer bank edged with boulders and broken on the north-west and south-west like a henge monument. Neolithic pottery and water-worn and angular fragments of white quartz were recovered from the flattened ground surface.

In the third and final phase, a further ring of nine large stones was added, 12.2 m in diameter, with a pair of massive outliers, 2.28 m and 2.18 m high, marking the entrance in the south-east and incorporating the earlier outliers. In front of each of the entrance stones was a deep grave-pit typical of inhumation graves for crouched burials characteristic of the early 2nd millennium BC.

Croft Moraig in its second and third phases may have been a variant of the more northerly recumbent stone circles, with their massive recumbent stones, south-west orientation, outer stony banks, scatterings of quartz pebbles and graded stones.

BURIALS

RING CAIRNS

1 Culfargie, Balbeggie   NO 224 298

This heavily-robbed ring cairn lies on moorland 1.5 km south of the B953 Abernyte–Balbeggie road. It is 10 m in diameter and 0.3 m high with a 5.5 m-wide central court, of which three small boulders from its kerb survive. The outer kerb includes three large displaced boulders on the south-west which may have been graded in height. Its poorly preserved north-west quadrant is obscured by an overlying shieling hut. Some 60 m south is another cairn (see p. 112).

2 Lair, Glen Shee   NO 139 637

A landrover track north of Lair leads west from the A93 Rattray Spittal of Glenshee road to this ring cairn which is 500 m north-west of Lair farmhouse. Lying on a low, heather-covered knoll, on the edge of a narrow terrace overlooking lower ground to the south and west, it is circular, 15 m in diameter and 0.3 m high. At least twenty-six stones of its outer kerb are in situ but its inner kerb, 4 m in diameter, is poorly preserved with only one boulder in its original position. This inner court is not quite central to the outer kerb, lying slightly off-centre to the south-east. The cairn has been robbed for building the faintly-discernible adjoining

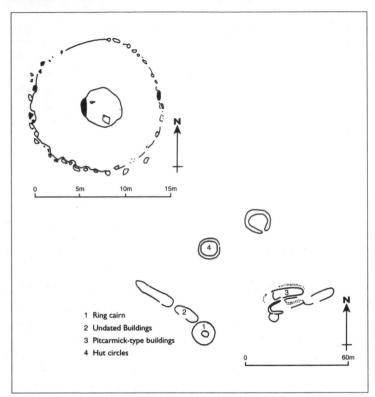

1 Ring cairn
2 Undated Buildings
3 Pitcarmick-type buildings
4 Hut circles

Fig. 2: Lair – ring cairn and site plan

sub-rectangular structures on the west. Nearby there are two hut circles (NO 139 638) and early medieval Pitcarmick-type buildings (see p. 172).

3 Middleton Muir   NO 118 482

Two and a half kilometres west of Middleton and the unclassified Kinloch-Middleton road, 300 m beyond the Buzzart Dykes enclosure (see p. 219). This is a small cairn of only 4 m in diameter with an inner court, built over a bank 1.1 m thick. The bank is revetted by a boulder kerb up to 0.25 m high on the south-west. Characteristically, the inner-facing stones of the court and the boulders of the outer kerb are graded with the largest stones on the south-west. The south-west, south-east, and north-east sides of the court are roughly rectilinear.

4 Muir of Merklands, Strathardle   NO 101 571 and
NO 103 568

This extensive area of settlement, ritual and burial activity provides an excellent introduction to Late Neolithic and Bronze Age sites. Although most of the domestic sites are hut circles of the late Bronze Age (see p. 140), the two ring cairns suggest that the land here was already settled in the Late Neolithic period. They lie about 750 m north-east of Stylemouth Farm, to the east of the A924 Kirkmichael-Bridge of Cally road. A landrover track leads between two forestry plantations up on to the pasture land beyond the prominent Grey Cairn (see p. 114).

The smaller of the two ring-cairns is 90 m north-east of Grey Cairn. It has a diameter of 6.5 m and is 0.3 m high, with an internal court 3 m in diameter. There are still some small outer kerbstones on the southern arc and four larger stones, one displaced, form the south-western arc of the inner kerb. Excavations in 1865 revealed only an area of rough paving at the centre and great quantities of white quartz pebbles so often associated with Neolithic and Bronze Age burial and ceremonial sites.

The second ring cairn lies 300 m to the south-east, beyond a scattering of small cairns. It is roughly oval with a bank 7.5 m by 6.8 m in diameter over a boulder kerb graded with the largest stones in the south. The 3 m square central court is also bounded by a kerb, its stones laid lengthwise and flush with the crest of the bank.

5 Ninewells   NO 075 436

In a plantation near the entrance to Ninewells farm, off the unclassified road between Loch of the Lowes and Glendelvine, east of Dunkeld. This cairn is 10 m in diameter and 0.75 m high within a stony platform which is almost intact, consisting of twenty-five large boulders and slabs set on edge, graded with the largest stones on the south-west. In the western arc, the three largest slabs have been set on edge. Most of the cairn infill has gone but is reported to have included white quartz at the centre. Although there is no evidence of an internal court, this cairn, with its external platform, is similar to the Late Neolithic Clava ring cairns and passage graves of the Inverness area.

6 Pitnacree, Strathtay   NN 928 533

This mound, landscaped with trees by the Victorians, and measuring 27.5 m by 23.5 m and 2 m high, with a small standing stone on top, can be seen immediately south of the A827 Aberfeldy–Ballinluig road, 100 m south-east of its junction with the unclassified Strathtay–Weem road. Excavations at this site in 1964 revealed a penannular ring cairn bounded by a kerb with turf and stone infill material. Interestingly, as at Croft Moraig (see above), there was post-hole evidence here for the use of timber in this Neolithic structure.

Within the cairn, a blocked dry-stone entrance led into a stone rectangular mortuary enclosure over four cremations, dated to around 2860 BC. Excavations also revealed two post-holes from an earlier timber structure below the standing stone and a cremation from beneath the stone was dated to 2270 BC. Pottery recovered from the old land surface beneath the cairn was also dated to the Neolithic period.

7 Smyrna, Forest of Alyth   NO 184 528

South of the unclassified Alyth–Glen Shee road, on a low rise to the north of Olies Burn, 550 m south-south-west of Smyrna cottage. This poorly-preserved ring cairn measures 5.2 m in external diameter and 0.3 m in height. Only six of the inner kerbstones can be seen and there is little evidence of the outer kerb.

CHAMBERED CAIRN

1 Derculich, Strathtay   NN 886 525

On a gentle slope on the north side of the Tay valley, 250 m north-west of Derculich farmhouse which was developed as a model steading in the 1920s, this is the only known surviving example of a chambered cairn in Atholl and Gowrie. The cairn material has been largely removed except for a heap of stones 1.5 m high in the corner of a modern wall. Its main feature is a group of three upright contiguous slabs which have formed the back of the chamber.

LONG CAIRNS

1 Bridge of Lyon, Fortingall   NN 729 465

180 m south-east of Bridge of Lyon, in a field with a number of other, later monuments (see pp. 129, 197). This very prominent long, narrow mound of earth and stones is 32 m in length on an ENE–WNW axis, 1.5 m high and 9.1 m wide at its east end and 11.7 m wide at its centre and west end. There may be a ditch on the south side.

2 Herald Hill, Hallhole   NO 187 396

Six hundred metres north-east of Hallhole steading, this was considered a natural mound until recent excavation revealed it to be a Neolithic long cairn. It lies on the crest of Herald Hill and measures 60 m east-west and is 18 m wide at the east end, where the terminal is particularly impressive, and 9 m wide at the west end. Field-gathered stones have been added to the field more recently.

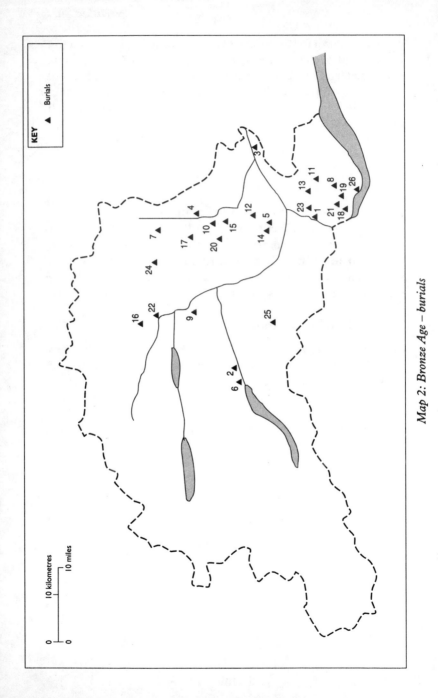

Map 2: Bronze Age – burials

BRONZE AGE SITES

BURIALS

1 Ardgilzean, Stormontfield   NO 126 295

East of the A93 Perth–Meikleour road and 70 m south of the
private drive to Ardgilzean are the remains of an oval cairn,
32 m by 27 m and 2.5 m high. It was probably smaller originally but field clearance stones have been added to it.

2 Balhomais   See p. 119

3 Belliduff, Belmont, Meigle   NO 289 442

Near the estate boundary, 380 m north-east of Belmont
Castle and west of the B954 Meigle–Newtyle road, this round
barrow is 15 m in diameter and 1.8 m high. When it was excavated in 1855 a short cist was found at its centre, 0.6 m below
the surface, now marked by a hollow. Some of the stones at
the north edge of the cairn may have formed part of the cist.

4 Cairn Gleamnach, Forest of Alyth   NO 158 554

The jagged kerbstones of this cairn can be seen on the crest
of a low knoll below Hill of Kingseat as it is approached from
the unclassified Glen Shee-Alyth road, opposite the entrance
to Corb farm. It measures 19.5 m in diameter over a boulder
kerb and up to 1 m in height. About sixty kerbstones have
survived, though not all are in their original positions. The
two largest stones are on the south and south-west. Within
the retaining kerb, the cairn material has been heavily robbed
and the centre dug out.

5 Cairn Muir, Caputh   NO 098 423

This overgrown cairn lies 350 m east of the unclassified Glen-
delvine-Kincairney road, on the edge of a terrace 175 m
north-west of Cairnmuir Cottage. It is 32 m in diameter and
has stood to at least 4.2 m high but now appears as a low

amorphous mass of rubble, having been heavily robbed in the 19th century.

6 Carse Farm, Dull   NO 796 483, NO 797 484 and NO 799 485

These three barrows, overgrown and planted with trees, are 20 m in diameter and 2 m high, 23 m in diameter and 1.2 m high, and 16 m in diameter and 1 m high respectively. They can be seen from the B846 Aberfeldy–Keltneyburn road. Nearby there is a four-poster and a stone circle (see pp. 119, 123).

7 Craigies, Ashintully   NO 123 621

Off the Lair-Kirkmichael footpath, 20 m south of the deserted farmstead (see p. 238), there are the remains of a cairn 6.3 m in diameter and 0.8 m high. On the southern edge, six kerbstones survive up to 1 m in length and 0.3 m high. There is a second cairn 50 m to the S-S-E where erosion has revealed water-worn boulders and stones.

8 Culfargie   NO 223 297

On the high ground on the north side of the Carse of Gowrie, 1.5 km south of the B953 road and 60 m west of the ring cairn (see p. 105), this cairn is 9.6 m in diameter and 0.5 m high. The centre has been robbed out but there is a kerb of twelve boulders with a diameter of 7.5 m at a higher level than the cairn, probably representing a secondary phase in the use and construction of this monument.

9 Dunfallandy   NN 947 570

Visible from the unclassified Pitlochry–Logierait road down on the flood-plain of the west bank of the River Tummel, this large round cairn of earth and stones is 16 m in diameter and 2 m high, planted with trees. It has had a kerb of stones around it and lies within an elliptical stony bank 3.5 m wide which is contemporary with the mound and best preserved on the north-west. Some small cists were found in the mound.

10 Hill of Cally, Bridge of Cally   NO 133 521

At the junction of four fields to the south-east of the summit
of the hill, 1 km north-west of Bridge of Cally. It is 0.7 m
high, 20 m in diameter, over a kerb of forty-five boulders
with the largest in the south-east arc. Immediately north-
west of the centre of the cairn there is a broken slab on edge,
probably from a cist. A quern, since lost, was discovered
when the cairn was robbed to build dykes.

11 King's Seat, Collace   NO 231 330

On the summit of the hill, 1 km north of the B953 Abernyte–
Balbeggie road, surmounted by an OS triangulation pillar. It
measures 20 m in diameter and is 1.8 m high. Although the
centre has been robbed and the north side disturbed, several
of the kerbstones on the south-west arc in their original positions.

12 Kinloch   NO 141 448

Immediately south of the A923 Blairgowrie–Dunkeld road,
4 km west of Blairgowrie, this overgrown cairn is 2.5 m high
and over 30 m in diameter. The summit has been flattened
and disturbed and ploughing and tree growth have made its
boundaries indistinct.

13 Macbeth's Law, Lawton   NO 201 324

Within the garden of Lawton House, 2.5 km north of Kirkton
of Collace, this conical, flat-topped mound, much mutilated
by landscaping, is probably a burial mound rather than a
medieval motte. It is 32 m in diameter, 5 m high and its base
is partly surrounded by a low terrace.

14 Mains of Fordie, Caputh   NO 089 418

This large, conical cairn lies 400 m east of Mains of Fordie,
off the unclassified road between Clunie and Caputh. It is
3 m high and up to 25 m in diameter. Some field-cleared
stones have been added to its summit and a field bank runs
across it.

15 Middleton Muir NO 127 488 and NO 129 484

There are at least four burial cairns among the hut circles and field systems on Middleton Muir (see p. 138), most on the crests of ridges overlooking Strathmore to the south-east. Some of the smaller cairns may also cover burials.

The first cairn lies 2 km north-west of Middleton steading, on the summit of a low knoll within field systems around hut circles. It is 9.8 m in diameter over a boulder kerb and up to 0.3 m in height. In the centre there is a thin slab, 0.75 m long, possibly part of a cist.

A second cairn lies 250 m south-east of the first, within a group of small cairns to the W-N-W of another group of hut circles. It is 0.4 m high and 12.5 m in diameter over a boulder kerb of which thirty-two boulders are in their original position. They are not uniformly graded but the largest are in the south-west arc.

16 Monzie, Blair Atholl NN 902 680

The unclassified Old Bridge of Tilt road leads north-east out of Blair Atholl to Monzie. The cairn lies 250 m W-N-W of Monzie steading, by the east bank of the Fender Burn on the end of a glacial hummock. It has been constructed from large, quarried stones and at the east end of the summit there is a stone set on edge, possibly the slab of a cist. The cairn measures 25.6 m by 23.8 m and is 2.5 m–4.5 m high.

17 Muir of Merklands, Strathardle

Amongst the hut circles and small cairns to the east of Stylemouth (see p. 140) there are at least four large burial cairns. Most of the smaller cairns in the area are probably heaps of stones and boulders cleared to allow the cultivation of the fields.

17.1 Grey Cairn NO 101 570

Grey Cairn is extremely conspicuous as a heap of large grey stones and boulders between two shelter belts, 750 m north-east of Stylemouth steading. It is 29 m in diameter and 1 m high, reduced from a former height of at least 7 m, having been greatly disturbed during 19th-century excavations. The first excavation revealed a passage leading to the centre of the cairn but no trace of a chamber and in 1865 the whole cairn was turned over, revealing burning at the centre beneath large boulders. The only recorded finds were a small cupmarked boulder and a perforated stone disc.

17.2   NO 101 569

This cairn, constructed of boulders and slabs, lies 50 m S-S-E of Grey Cairn. It is 10.5 m in diameter and 0.5 m high. The 19th-century excavation trenches, from which fragments of white quartz were recovered, are still visible.

17.3   NO 105 570

On a low ridge, 400 m east of Grey Cairn, this cairn is 12 m in diameter over a kerb of boulders of which fifteen stones are still visible. A large cist has been exposed at its centre by 19th-century excavators – the notch in the top of the broken west slab marks where a crowbar was inserted. The cist was originally no deeper than 0.55 m, 0.8 m wide, and with a maximum length of 1.15 m. It had already been emptied before the 19th-century antiquaries opened it.

17.4   NO 102 571

On the crest of a knoll, 180 m north-east of Grey Cairn and overlying the outer bank of a hut circle, this cairn is 6.5 m in diameter and 0.4 m high. During excavations the centre was dug out and a pit with burnt bone and charcoal uncovered.

18 Murrayshall Hill   NO 165 253

On the summit of the hill, 450 m west of the unclassified Bonhard–Pitroddie road. A 19th-century memorial obelisk has been inserted into the cairn which measures 14.5 m in diameter and 1.5 m in height.

19 Pole Hill, Evelick

NO 196 261

This cairn, 3 m high and almost 20 m in diameter, lies on the summit of Pole Hill within a plantation bank and surmounted by an OS triangulation station, 500 m north-west of Evelick fort (see p. 150). Its stepped profile suggests that it has been built in three stages. The bottom tier is 19.5 m in diameter and 0.6 m high; the central tier is 13 m in diameter and 1 m high; and the upper tier is 7 m in diameter and 0.6 m high. Stony material is visible on the surface of the mound and an earth-fast stone to the south may indicate the line of a kerb.

20 Ranageig, Forest of Clunie

NO 113 492 and
NO 113 491

There are two cairns on either side of the track along the crest of the east-west ridge 900 m east of Ranageig farmhouse. The first is a robbed cairn on a low rise immediately north of the track. It is 11.8 m in diameter over a kerb of boulders and 0.7 m high. In the centre are the north and west slabs of a cist, 1.2 m by 0.6 m and 0.5 m deep.

Forty metres south-east, clipped by the south side of the trackway, is another robbed cairn. It is 18 m in diameter and up to 1 m high, and at least fifteen kerb stones survive. A cist has been exposed at the centre where there is a floor-slab in situ and a broken capstone lies immediately south of the cist.

21 Shien Hill, Arnbathie

NO 174 267

One kilometre north-west of Arnbathie Farm, on the west shoulder of Shien Hill, this cairn can be approached from the track across Dalreichmoor. Like Pole Hill (see above), it has been built in distinct phases. The lower tier is 32.5 m in diameter and 2 m high, constructed of stones and small boulders. The remains of a modern cairn sit on top of the mound.

22 Strathgroy, Blair Atholl

NN 899 649

Five hundred metres N-N-E of Strathgroy steading, off the Blair Atholl service road, this huge cairn sits on a spur above the River Garry, with extensive views down the glen. It is

38 m in diameter and 5.5 m high. The remains of a cist and secondary peristalith or ring of stones protrude near the centre.

23 Tammieteeth, St Martins   NO 144 311

One hundred and fifty metres west of the unclassified road between St Martins and Guildtown, this is a tree-covered mound, 12 m in diameter and 1 m high. A protective bank was built round the mound in 1791.

24 Tulloch, Straloch   NO 054 638

On the edge of a terrace, 480 m north-west of Tulloch Cottage, north of the A924 Rattray–Pitlochry road, this cairn is 27 m in diameter and 4 m high. Its flat top is 10.5 m in diameter. Though identified as a motte, this largely artificial mound is more likely to be a burial cairn. Two hundred and forty metres N-N-W there is a second cairn which measures 9 m in diameter and 0.6 m in height. Although it has been much disturbed by ploughing, traces of a boulder kerb around the cairn are still visible.

25 White Cairn, Glen Cochill   NN 907 412

This cairn lies on open moorland, 150 m west of the A826, commanding the glen to the south-east. It is 20 m in diameter over a boulder kerb which is up to 0.8 m high. An outer ring can be traced on the south side, 2.2 m from the kerb. In the centre a short cist has been excavated and the displaced capstone lies to the north. The only finds from the excavation were fragments of a long-necked beaker.

26 Witch Knowe, Inchyra   NO 189 212

One hundred and ten metres south-west of Inchyra House, 500 m north-east of St Madoes, clearly visible from the private drive. This is a grass-covered barrow, 18 m in diameter and 2.5 m high, from which cremated bone and several urns were removed around 1830, along with much cairn material when the mound was landscaped.

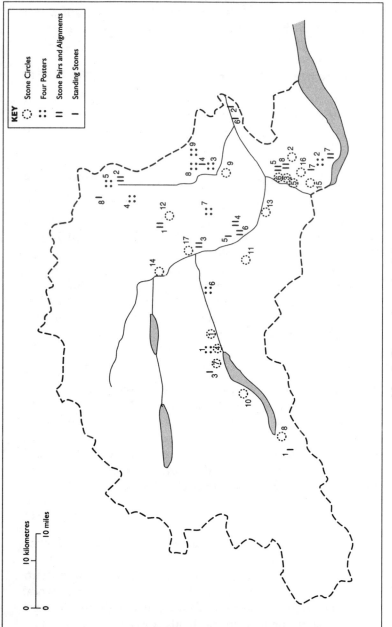

Map 3: Bronze Age – ritual sites

RITUAL

STONE CIRCLES

1 Balhomais, Dull   NN 823 493

One hundred and forty metres south of Balhomais steading, by the farm entrance immediately north of the B846 Weem–Keltneyburn road. An earthen barrow, 14 m in diameter, 1.5 m high and topped with conifers, is surrounded by the remains of a stone circle which has originally been up to 22 m in diameter. Two stones are in their original positions 4 m beyond the base of the mound, and a stone on the boundary to the south-east is probably also in situ.

2 Bandirran, Collace*   NO 209 310

Off the B953 Balbeggie–Abernyte road, 200 m east of Bandirran and featured in the *South-East Perthshire Stone Circle Trail*. There are ten stones in this elliptical 'circle', at least four of which stood to a height of about 1.5 m, on a diameter of 7.5 m by 8.8 m, but only two of them are still upright. Characteristically, the two largest boulders are on the south-west. An early plan shows a large central stone – which suggests interesting parallels with circles of that plan type in Galloway – but there is no trace of it now.

3 Blackfaulds, Guildtown   NO 141 317

Four hundred metres south-west of Blackfaulds steading, in a wood to the south of the drive. There are ten stones in this circle of 7.5 m diameter, though eight of them, 0.7 m–1.8 m in length, are now fallen. The largest stone, broken in four segments, is in the south-west quadrant and is flanked by two small stones. The stones on the north-west are all of similar size, 1.4 m–1.5 m, and the three on the south-east, from 1.2 m–1.8 m, appear to be graded.

4 Carse Farm, Dull   NN 802 485

Two hundred and fifty metres south of the B846 Weem–Keltneyburn road and 200 m south of a four-poster (see p. 123).

This site has been disturbed by ploughing down the centuries and there is now only a single upright stone, 1.8 m high, and two part-buried recumbent slabs, both cupmarked. A small amount of cremated bone and a circular river pebble, flattened on each face with a hollow worked in one of them, were recovered from the site.

5 Colen, St. Martins *   NO 111 312

This poorly-preserved stone circle lies on the edge of a plantation, 200 m east of the unclassified Old Scone–Cambusmicheal road, 740 m N-N-E of Colen farm and is signposted as part of the *South-East Perthshire Stone Circle Trail*. Only eight stones remain in the 7.7 m diameter circle and they are unusually short, with the three largest cupmarked stones on the south-west only 1 m high. The recumbent stone on the west is decorated with over twenty-five cupmarks and there are four cups on the only stone still standing.

6 Druid's Seat Wood   NN 125 313

This stone circle with an internal diameter of 7.8 m lies in a clearing in a conifer plantation, south-west of Guildtown and 900 m west of the A93. There are nine stones, taller ones up to 1.4 m high, alternating with short ones less than 0.8 m high. The largest boulders are on the south-west and the two shortest stones, 0.6 m high, have been set exactly opposite each other on the north and south.

7 Fortingall   NN 745 469

Park near the hotel and walk 400 m east along the unclassified Fortingall–Keltneyburn road. The stones can be seen in a field just south of the road. The three settings look like four-posters with stones missing but excavations in 1970 revealed otherwise. Two of the settings have actually been eight-stone 'rectangles', the largest stones at the corners. Charcoal and cremated bone were recovered from them as well as a Victorian beer bottle, indicating that they had been disturbed at least once before. The third setting has probably been an alignment with a massive boulder in the middle flanked by two smaller stones, 1.2 m–1.5 m high.

8 Kinnell Park, Killin   NO 577 328

This fine circle of six stones, five in their original position, lies in a flat field surrounded by wooded hills above the River Dochart, 100 m south-east of Kinnell House drive, east of Killin. It measures 10 m by 8.4 m and is graded to the S-S-W where there is a massive stone, 2 m high. Each stone has been erected with its broad face on the line of the circle's circumference.

9 Leys of Marlee, Kinloch   NO 160 439

This circle straddles the B947 Blairgowrie–Lethedy road. Six stones form an ellipse, 16 m by 11.5 m internally, but only four are likely to be in their original positions. The three stones on the west in a straight alignment may belong to a rectilinear setting.

10 Machuim, Lawers   NN 682 401

To the west of the A827, 250 m north-east of the entrance to Machuim farm. There are six massive stones in this oval, 6.7 m by 5.8 m, four of them still upright and two partially buried, all linked by traces of a kerb. It is graded to the south where the largest stone stands 1.5 m high. The turf-covered, sub-circular surrounding mound is 10 m in diameter and 1 m high and is probably contemporary with the 'circle'.

Essential Viewing

11 Meikle Findowie, Strath Braan   *NN 959 386*

On a terrace on the north-west flank of Airlich Hill, 350 m south of Meikle Findowie farmstead, south of the A822 Crieff–Dunkeld road and overlooking the River Braan below. This circle of small stones comprises an outer ring, 8 m in diameter and an inner circle, 3.3 m in diameter. Six of the nine stones of the outer circle are still upright, graded to the south-west, with the largest only 1 m high. The inner circle is built of eight smaller stones and possibly represents the kerb of a low central cairn. The whole circle is on a bank 7.6 m in diameter and two low stones to the west suggest the bank masks an outer kerb.

12 Muir of Merklands, Strathardle   NO 102 570

Eight hundred metres north-east of Stylemouth Farm, east of the A924 Kirkmichael-Bridge of Cally road, up a landrover track, 140 m S-S-E of Grey Cairn (see p. 114) in an area of extensive Bronze and Iron Age settlement (see p. 140). All nine stones of this 7 m diameter circle are now fallen, with the largest on the W-S-W. An outlying standing stone lies 10 m to the N-N-W. Along with several other sites on the Muir of Merklands, the circle was excavated in the 19th century and the trenches from the excavation are still visible. Charred wood was recovered from the centre of the circle and burned bones from its south edge.

13 Murthly Hospital   NO 103 386

In the hospital grounds, east of the B9099 Stanley–Murthly road, this circle is 10.1 m in diameter and graded to the south-west. A collared urn was excavated from its interior. Although the circle has been landscaped, the stones are probably in their original positions. Five of the original stones remain, ranging from 0.9 m to 2.4 m in height. In the 19th century, cinerary urns, since lost, were found near the circle, some in groups of two and three with one group reportedly arranged in a circle. One urn, buried alone, contained partly-burned bones together with a perforated bone object.

14 Pitlochry   NN 930 588

By the A9(T), this circle is 6.4 m in diameter and seven straight-sided stones remain, ranging from 0.3 m to 1.6 m in height. There have probably been another two stones on the north-east and south-west.

15 Sandy Road, Scone   NO 133 264

This 5.5 m diameter circle has been preserved within a housing scheme on the west side of the village. It comprises seven stones, with a buried socket for an eighth, only three of which are in their original positions. The largest stones are in the west and south-west arcs. Excavation in 1961 revealed that many of the stones had been 'keeled' at the base of one side to aid stability and some had been deliberately 'shouldered' at the top. Finds included an undecorated cinerary urn, 30 cm high and 12.7 cm wide, which was mouth upwards in a pit and contained a deposit of cremated bone with charcoal on top. The urn contents were dated to the middle Bronze Age but the circle itself may well pre-date the burial.

16 Shianbank, New Scone   NO 156 273

This pair of circles lies 330 m E-S-E of Shianbank Cottage, east of the A94 between New Scone and Balbeggie. The northern circle has been disturbed by the erection of World War II concrete pill boxes and by forestry work, so only five stones remain in situ. It has a diameter of 9.3 m by 8.7 m and the stones average 0.9 m high. The other circle is 8 m in diameter and there are only six stones still in their original position, the largest 0.9 m high. The circles lie 13.5 m apart with the pill box between them, and originally both probably contained ten stones.

17 Tynreich, Ballinluig   NN 976 534

On the east side of the A9(T), 1 km north of Ballinluig. The circle is 6.7 m in diameter, with six stones from 0.6 m to 1.8 m in height. Excavations in 1855 uncovered four large urns, 0.6 m high and 0.3 m in diameter, full of calcined bones.

FOUR-POSTERS

1 Carse Farm, Dull   NN 802 487

This four-poster, immediately south of the B846 Aberfeldy–Keltneyburn road, lies north of a stone circle (see p. 119) and north-east of three burial cairns (see p. 112). It measures 3.7 m by 2.7 m and the tallest stone is at the south-east.

On the upper surfaces of the eastern two stones there are cupmarks – the north-east stone has seventeen cupmarks and two dumbells and the south-east stone has three cups. A decorated collared urn containing cremated bone was retrieved from a pit at the base of the inner face of the north-east cupmarked stone. The pit also contained cremated bone, black earth and charcoal.

2 Commonbank   NO 175 248

On a slight elevation, 400 m south of the unclassified Pitroddie–Bonhard road, north-west of a wood and 370 m north-west of Commonbank steading, this four-poster measures less than 3 m across and lies outwith the main concentration of four-posters. All four stones have fallen and the north-west stone has three cupmarks on its upper surface. Eight and a half metres to the east there are three recumbent boulders aligned E-N-E–W-S-E, the eastmost with three weathered cupmarks on its upper face.

3 Craighall, Rattray   NO 184 481

This four-poster lies on a mound on the edge of a terrace, immediately east of the unclassified Rattray–Drimmie road and measures about 9 m in diameter and 0.2 m in height. All four stones have fallen and the southernmost one is broken in two. Field clearance stones have been gathered around the monuments more recently.

4 Glenkilrie, Glen Shee   NO 123 625

This probable four-poster lies on top of a low knoll overlooking the west bank of Allt a' Choire Liathaich, a short detour from the Lair–Kirkmichael public footpath. Only two stones on the south-east survive, 0.6 m and 0.8 m high. The setting is central to a circular platform, 9.5 m in diameter and 0.3 m high, revetted by a boulder kerb with twenty-three stones. A depression in the mound to the north-west marks the site of an excavation.

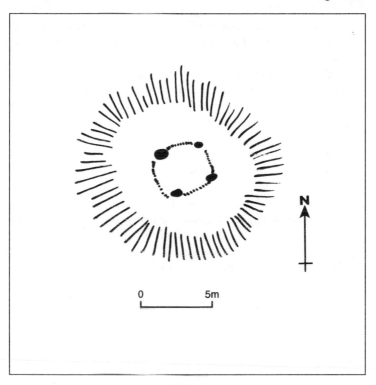

Fig. 3: Grave of Diarmid – four-poster

5   Grave of Diarmid, Glen Shee   NO 117 702

On top of a glacial moraine, 550 m E-S-E of Old Spittal farmhouse, with extensive views down Glen Shee. The stones lie
at the corners of a trapezium, the two largest 0.75 m and
0.8 m high, on the west, but as the site was excavated in
1894 these may not lie in their original positions. The slight
mound in the centre is the result of 19th-century excavations,
from which no finds were recorded.

Essential Viewing

6   Lundin, Grandtully   *NN 879 505*

*There are several sites of interest in the vicinity of Lundin farm,
south of the A827 Logierait–Aberfeldy road. The four-poster,*

4 m by 3.5 m, lies on a knoll which is at least partly artificial. Some of the stones have been keeled or undercut at one edge to aid stability.

Excavations revealed a demarcation ditch around the stones and a pit in the centre containing cremated bone and carbonised wood. The top of the mound had been deliberately hollowed-out and filled with cairn material with the four stones erected round it. A second cremation, that of a child, was discovered at the base of the north-west stone and cremated bone was found scattered over the whole central area. Sherds of an undecorated collared urn, a cord-ornamented beaker and decorated and undecorated Bronze Age domestic ware were also recovered. In addition, twenty-four quartz pebbles were found in the south-west quadrant. The finds also included a stone with two shallow hollows shaped into it, possibly part of a bow-drill, similar to that found at Carse Farm (see p. 112).

Thirteen metres to the south-east is a boulder with forty-three cupmarks on its upper surface and at NN 878 506 there is a small standing stone, 1.2 m high with a pair of standing stones nearby, 0.6 m and 1.2 m high and aligned east-west.

7 Muir of Gormack, Drimmie   NO 195 514

Along the south bank of the Lornty Burn, on a low knoll at the west end of a settlement of hut circles and field systems (see p. 139) and beyond the Buzzart Dykes (see p. 219), 2.5 km west of West Gormack. Only the west and east stones are in situ; the other two have fallen but lie close to their original positions at the corners of a trapezium. Originally, the inner face of the north-west pair opposed that of the south-east pair.

8 Parkneuk, Drimmie   NO 195 514

On gently sloping pasture ground, 250 m north of the unclassified road between Mains of Creuchies and Strone Bridge, there are three uprights and one fallen stone. The two largest stones, 1.38 m and 1.2 m high, are on the west and south.

9 Shealwalls, Hill of Alyth   NO 240 515

This four-poster lies by the unclassified Alyth–Bamff road, 750 m north-east of Newton of Bamff, amongst the rough pasture and gorse at the east end of a low ridge. From it, there are fine views to the north-east over the mouth of Glen Isla. It measures 1.3 m square and the south-west, north-west and north-east stones are 0.1 m, 0.4 m and 0.3 m in height respectively. The tallest stone was probably the fallen one on the south east which is 1 m long.

STONE PAIRS AND ALIGNMENTS

1 Balnabroich, Strathardle   NO 092 565

At the north end of small plantation on a natural mound by the entrance to Balnabroich steading, just off the A924. The northern stone of this pair is 1.45 m high with a flat top; the southern stone is irregularly shaped and leaning to the south. They are about 3 m apart, facing each other with their broad axes east-west. Nearby, in an arable field 150 m to the north, there is a 1.7 m-high standing stone.

2 Broughdearg, Glen Shee   NO 137 670

This pair lies immediately south-east of the barn at Broughdearg steading, 400 m north-east of the A93. Both stones are flat-topped, the western 1.6m high and the eastern 1.5 m high. They lie 3 m apart but do not seem to have been set in alignment as the eastern stone is 0.6 m in front of the western stone.

3 Dowally   NO 001 480

These two stones, one fallen, lie near the road, *c.* 3 m apart and aligned east-west with the smooth faces of both stones facing north. The north stone stands 2.76 m above ground level; the other is 2.33 m high.

4 East Cult, Dunkeld NO 073 422

From East Cult steading, a track leads 150 m south-west between two fields to this pair of standing stones and cupmarked boulder. The stones are 1.8 m and 2.15 m high and the cupmarked boulder may have formerly stood in alignment with them, high above the River Tay.

There are about one hundred and thirty plain cupmarks and a dumbell on the upper face of the recumbent boulder, and three cupmarks on the east face.

5 Loanhead, Guildtown* NO 148 328

At the south-east end of a plantation, 420 m north-east of Lonahead steading, off the Guildtown–Burrelton unclassified road, 1.4 km N-N-E of the Guildtown stone circle (see p. 120). The stones are 1.5 m high and 5.5 m apart with their long axes at right angles and may have been part of a larger circle. They are now part of the *South-East Perthshire Stone Circle Trail*.

6 Newtyle, Dunkeld NO 045 410

Amongst trees, just north of a sharp bend in the A984, these two stones stand in an unusual position at the foot of a steep slope and at the rear of a terrace overlooking the Tay. They are 2.7 m apart and the northern stone is 2.1 m high, the southern 1.6 m high.

7 St Madoes, Glencarse NO 197 210

Now in a flower-bed at St Madoes Primary School. Although all three stones may have been on a N-N-W–S-S-E alignment, only the two pointed boulders *c.* 1.5 m high are still upright and the third stone may always have been recumbent. The most northerly stone is cupmarked. Excavations at the site provided no dating evidence.

8 St Martins NO 159 312

One kilometre north-east of St Martins, by the farm track to Kingswell, this three-stone alignment lies in the south-east corner of a field, 920 m east of Cairnbeddie steading. Only the northern stone is upright and it measures 1.05 m in height. The central stone lies 1 m distant from it and the third, also fallen, is 2.3 m away from the second.

STANDING STONES

1 Acharn, Killin   NN 561 316

This stone, 1.2 m high and with a 1.9 m girth at its base, lies in a field below the farmhouse of Acharn, to the east of the A827, 2 km north-east of Lix Toll.

2 Belmont Castle, Meigle   NO 286 436

In the grounds of Belmont Castle, 400 m west of the B954. The stone is 0.95 m high and leans slightly to the south-west.

3 Bridge of Lyon, Fortingall   NN 731 464

Three hundred and forty metres south-east of Bridge of Lyon, the stone is 2 m high. Nearby there is a probable Neolithic long barrow (see p. 109) and a cupmarked stone in a ditch surrounding a cairn (see p. 142).

4 Craighall, Rattray   NO 185 483

To the east of the unclassified Rattray–Drimmie road, 3 km north of Rattray. This massive flat-topped stone with sloping sides is 2.5 m high and lies on the edge of a terrace, aligned north-south. It has nine cupmarks up to 80 mm by 30 mm near the base of its east face.

5 Dunkeld House   NO 014 430

Fifty metres south of the unclassified Dunkeld–Dowally road, towards the rear of a river terrace, 490 m north-east of Dunkeld House Hotel. This upright slab of schist is 1.4 m high.

Essential viewing

6   Macbeth's Stone, Belmont   NO 280 434

This massive granite stone lies at the western entrance to Belmont Castle by the gate lodge, off the unclassified Coupar Angus–Meigle road. It is 3.6 m high, tapering in thickness towards the top and both its faces are decorated with cupmarks. There are about forty cupmarks on the eastern face and twenty-four on the west face, most in a band 1.4 m above ground level.

7   Murrayshall   NO 152 263

One hundred metres west of the unclassified New Scone–Bonhard road. The stone is 1.8 m high.

8   Spittal of Glenshee   NO 109 702

On the east end of natural knoll, 17.5 m west of Spittal of Glenshee church. The slab is 1.8 m high and aligned N-N-E–S-S-W. On either edge is a semi-circular notch of unknown function, *c.* 0.8 m above ground level, probably signifying a much later re-use of the stone.

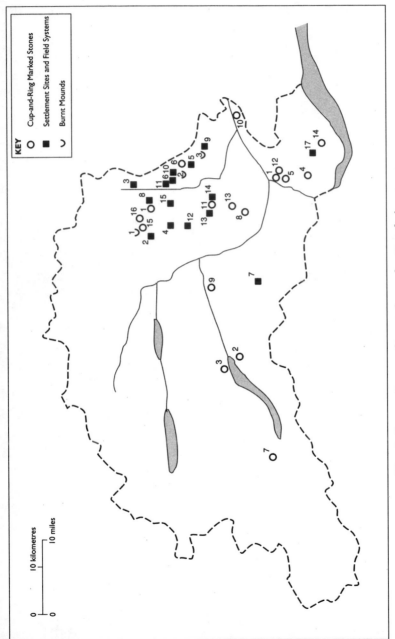

Map 4: Bronze Age – settlement sites and cup-and-ring stones

SETTLEMENT AND FIELD SYSTEMS

1 Ashintully, Kirkmichael See p. 155

2 Badyo NN 978 613

There are seven hut circles and contemporary field-systems of clearance heaps, field walls and lynchets or raised banks caused by ploughing, 750 m west of the A924. Two of the hut circles are double-walled, measuring 9 m and 15 m in internal diameter. The field system is partly overlaid by rig-and-furrow and there are foundations of later settlements in the vicinity.

Essential viewing

3 Dalnaglar, Cray NO 150 642

East of the junction of the B951 and the unclassified Dalnaglar Castle road, 600 m south-east of the castle, there are three hut circles, several sections of bank and a Pitcarmick-type building. Two of the hut circles were excavated between 1958 and 1960. The largest is 11 m in maximum diameter within a stony bank up to 2.2 m thick and 0.4 m high levelled into the slope. Few structural details emerged from the excavations but several hundred sherds of coarse pottery of the late Bronze Age were discovered, mostly from outside the hut circle. Eighty metres north-west is the other excavated hut circle and again a few fragments of similar coarse pottery were discovered. The third, unexcavated hut circle lies 65 m west of the first but is poorly preserved. One of the field banks was also excavated and was found to have a loose core of boulders. Two stone implements were found on the north side.

4 Dalrulzion, Kirkmichael See p. 155

5 Drumderg, Smyrna NO 185 534

There are three hut circles on a low rise immediately north of the unclassified Alyth–Glen Shee road, 220 m north-west of Smyrna cottage, and extensive prehistoric settlement on the south and south-east slopes of Drumderg. The double-walled hut circle on the east is particularly well-preserved with an inner face of stones set on edge. The outer wall has a diameter of 16.6 m and the inner diameter is 10.8 m. Immediately west is another double-walled example, 7 m in internal diameter, similarly faced internally with boulders and slabs set on edge. The outer wall has been heavily robbed but the empty sockets of some facing stones can still be identified. There is an entrance 1.4 m wide on the S-S-E side. A third hut circle, 9 m in diameter and single-walled, lies to the north. At the north-west it conjoins a low bank which defines the northern edge of this group of hut circles.

On either side of the road, west of the hut circles, there are about forty small clearance cairns up to 5 m in diameter and 200 m E-N-E of Smyrna cottage, at the east end of the cairns, there is a crescentic burnt mound. It is 9.7 m by 4.9 m and up to 0.5 m high with its U-shaped hollow facing the burn.

Essential viewing

6 Drumturn Burn, Corb   NO 160 579

This large group of hut circles lies around the headwaters of the Drumturn Burn and its tributaries, on the south-west flank of Beddiegrew, 1 km north-west of Corb steading off the Glen Shee–Alyth unclassified road. Most of the hut circles are at the southern end of a field system represented by segments of low walls, in three tiers, levelled into the slope. Many are extremely well-preserved, with facing-stones of both single- and double-walled huts remarkably intact. The best preserved is 9.5 m in diameter on the west of the group, with an almost complete ring of inner facing-stones. Further east is a pair of smaller hut circles, 7.3 m in diameter, and to the south-east the track continues between an unusual double-walled hut circle and a lynchet at the bottom of the field to the north-east.

In the upper tier there are four double-walled hut circles, with internal diameters of 6.6 m to 9.3 m and external diameters of 15.4 m to 16.5 m, two of them with inner facing-stones visible. On the slope there are faint traces of a platform, possibly a stance for a timber house.

The field system is composed of a number of large enclosures bounded by cleared stone banks and low lynchets and accessed by trackways.

This site is well worth visiting to see some remarkably preserved hut circles and exploration can be extended by continuing about 1 km north-west to the slopes of Knockali, east of Easter Bleaton steading (see below) where there is another large complex of hut circles, field banks, cairns and Pitcarmick-type buildings.

7   Glen Cochill   NN 905 412

These extensive settlement remains, including ten hut circles and associated field banks, clearance cairns and enclosures, lie west of the A826 Amulree–Aberfeldy road, 1.5 km south of Scotston farm. The hut circles are widely spread on terraces and small knolls and most are 7 m–8 m in diameter within 1.8 m-thick walls, with their entrances in the south-west and south-east. In the surrounding area, there are over one hundred small, clustered field-clearance cairns up to 4 m in diameter.

8   Glenkilrie, Ashintully   NO 123 623

Groups of hut circles and small cairns extend along the north-east valley of the Ennoch Burn, 300 m south of the footpath between Kirkmichael and Lair, 2 km south-west of Lair. Three hut circles and a group of small cairns lie to the north of the rocky spur overlooking Craigies farmstead (see p. 238). The eastmost is best preserved. It is double-walled with an internal diameter of 9.2 m and its outer wall lies off-centre to the inner wall with the gap between the two walls varying from 2.4 m to 4.2 m. A field-wall obscures the junction of the other two hut circles which were probably tangential. On the slope below there are cairns and banks and a large rectangular enclosure. Fifty metres N-N-W there are two stones in the middle of a circular platform revetted by a boulder platform, possibly the remains of a burial cairn.

9 Hill of Alyth   NO 228 502

The remains of seven hut circles, two ring-ditch houses and a group of small cairns lie on the west and south-west flanks of Hill of Alyth. Six hut circles and a Pitcarmick-type building (see p. 171) extend over 120 m on a low rise between a wire fence on the west and an old drove road on the east, 340 m north-east of Whiteside steading. Beside the fence are two hut circles, 12.5 m and 9.5 m in internal diameter. The larger has a deeply-splayed passage entrance like that usually associated with double-walled huts. A second pair lies 70 m to the east and north-east of the pair there is a hut circle 6.5 m in internal diameter and a double-walled hut circle 7.5 m in internal diameter and 16.3 m in overall diameter. Adjacent to the old drove road, 100 m to the east, there is a burnt mound, oval on plan, 4.5 m by 3.5 m and 0.6 m high.

About 300 m west of the group of six hut circles and north-west of a robbed burial cairn are two ring-ditch houses, 30 m apart. The larger of the two is on the edge of a terrace and is 14.5 m in overall diameter with an entrance on the south-west. The other is better preserved and lies at the foot of a slope to the north-west. It is 12.5 m in overall diameter and also has its entrance, which leads into the bottom of the ditch, on the south-west. The ditch is best defined to the south of the entrance where it is up to 3.8 m broad and 0.3 m deep.

10 Hill of Kingseat, Forest of Alyth   NO 162 556

This group of hut circles and small cairns lies immediately north of the unclassified Glen Shee–Alyth road, 350 m E-N-E of Glen Gleamnach (see p. 111). A double-walled hut circle, 10.5 m in internal diameter, lies on the edge of a terrace overlooking a row of four hut circles below. The eastmost is the best preserved, measuring 9 m by 8 m internally, with a small pen built on the west side of its interior. The next hut circle has an internal diameter of 7.5 m and is flanked by a pair with smaller diameters of 5.5 m and 5.3 m. South of the pair and clipped by a public road there is a further hut circle. There is an extensive area of field-clearance cairns over approximately twenty-five hectares from the south-east flank of Saebeg across the eastern slopes of the saddle and on to the north-east flank of Hill of Kingseat.

11 Knockali, Easter Bleaton   NO 154 588

This complex of hut circles, field-banks and small cairns lies on the western and southern flanks of Knockali. There are at least thirty hut circles, of which four are double-walled with internal diameters of 7.7 m to 9 m. The single-walled hut circles range in internal diameter from 4.5 m to 12.8 m. A row of five with prominent boulder-faced walls, one with an internal ring ditch, has been levelled into the slope at the back of a narrow terrace. On the slope above there is a stony bank, to the front there is a courtyard, and some of the nearby field banks seem to be related to the hut circles.

12 Loch Benachally, Forest of Clunie   NO 070 515

This area of settlement and field systems seems very remote now as it is only accessible by a track across rough moorland. Yet in earlier times this was a well-populated area, attractive to settlers from the Bronze Age represented by the hut circles, field systems and cairns around the loch, right up to the 18th and 19th centuries, represented by the abandoned settlement and house at Craigsheal (see p. 239).

This group of hut circles lies immediately south of the track, on a gentle, south-west facing slope on the east side of the valley, 600 m north of the artificially-dammed loch and 750 m north-east of Craigsheal. Three hut circles lie on the southern edge of a field system of small clearance cairns and stony banks. The eastmost hut circle lies on a low knoll at the rear of a broad terrace, 16.7 m in external diameter, its interior masked by an overlying Pitcarmick-type building. Two hundred and ten metres west there is a double-walled hut circle levelled into the south-west facing slope and measuring 22 m by 18.8 m externally, over an outer wall 1.4 m to 4 m thick.

13 Middleton Muir   NO 114 483

This is another large settlement complex with groups of hut circles, field systems, clearance cairns, burial cairns and a ring cairn (see p. 114). These sites have been preserved here because medieval and later ploughing has been largely confined to the southern ridge within the Buzzart Dykes deer park (see p. 219).

East of the Middleton-Laighwood march-dyke, 2.5 km north-west of Middleton and 300 m beyond the corner of the Buzzart Dykes, there is a single-walled hut-circle, a double-walled example and a ring-ditch house stance, probably not all contemporary. The single-walled hut circle, 11 m by 10 m in diameter, lies on the ridge with the double-walled hut circle 50 m to the W-N-W. The latter has an internal diameter of 11.3 m and an overall diameter of 20 m and several of its facing stones are in situ. The ring-ditch house, 9.5 m in

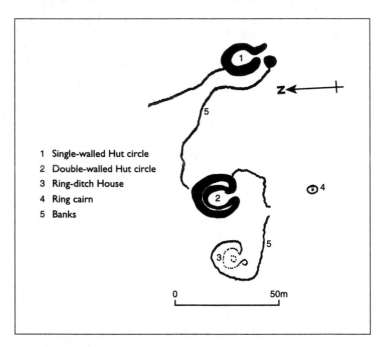

1 Single-walled Hut circle
2 Double-walled Hut circle
3 Ring-ditch House
4 Ring cairn
5 Banks

0   50m

Fig. 4: Middleton Muir – settlement, field system and ring cairn

diameter, is adjacent to the march-dyke, and the ring ditch itself is 3.8 m broad and 0.3 m deep.

A trackway passes the single-walled hut on the west and south and there is a scatter of cairns, mostly 2 m to 3 m in diameter, with two larger examples on the east measuring 5 m and 6 m in diameter to the E-S-E and south.

14 Muir of Gormack   NO 125 473 and NO 122 473

Another remarkable concentration of settlement remains lies on the south bank of the Lornty Burn, 1.7 km W-N-W of West Gormack. This particular group comprises six hut circles, field systems and small cairns, probably not all contemporary. The best preserved hut circle is 8.8 m in internal diameter and has twenty-eight inner facing stones still visible around the northern half of its wall. There are also unusual club-shaped terminals on either side of its

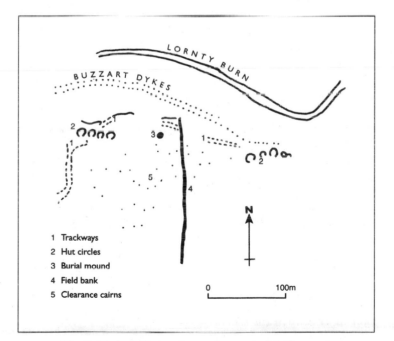

Fig. 5: Muir of Gormack – settlement and field systems

entrance on the south. The second hut circle, 9.1 m in diameter internally, has 3 m thick walls, faced inside with upright slabs and outside with low boulders and, like many double-walled hut circles, has a deeply-splayed entrance passage. The four remaining hut circles are smaller, with internal diameters of 4.5 m, 7 m, 5.6 m and 6.8 m from east to west. A long stony bank running from the top of the slope to the bottom divides the stone clearance heaps from an adjacent field system.

The second row of four hut circles 150 m to the west includes one with a medial wall-face, indicating that there were at least two separate construction phases. In its latest phase it was 8.4 m in internal diameter with a 2.8 m thick wall. There are small cairns and a burial cairn between a track and the bank along the east side of the field system.

15 Muir of Merklands, Strathardle · NO 098 576 to NO 108 568

One kilometre north-east of Stylemouth, east of the A924 Bride of Cally–Kirkmichael road. Within one square kilometre of moorland and pasture, there are ring cairns (see p. 107), a stone circle (see p. 112), burial cairns (see p. 114), Pitcarmick-type buildings (see p. 173), farmsteads and sixteen hut circles with associated field systems and clearance cairns. Most of the cairns lie east and south of Grey Cairn while the hut circles lie to the north and west.

The hut circles have internal diameters ranging from 9 m to 13 m, edged by collapsed stone walls 2 m to 3 m wide with occasional inner and outer facing-stones protruding, and some have been levelled into the slope. Most have their entrance in the southern quadrant and the entrance of one is flanked by two enormous boulders. The only artefact recovered during 19th-century excavations was a 'fragment of bronze like the pin of a brooch'.

Most of the small cairns are probably clearance cairns and on the lower slopes there are 18th- and 19th-century cultivation rigs between the cairns.

16 Tulloch Field, Enochdhu   NO 054 637

Six hut circles lie along the old river terrace 330 m N-N-W of
Tulloch Cottage and 100 m east of the A924 Rattray–Pitlochry road. Four of the hut circles lie along the top of the
terrace, the largest with an internal diameter of 10.5 m.
The other two hut circles below the terrace have been excavated. The remains of a timber house were discovered within
the 3.6 m thick walls of the southernmost. Finds included
sherds of a bucket-shaped coarse-ware vessel, 250 mm high
and 175 mm in diameter. In the second excavated hut circle
there was evidence of a double ring of post-holes, 3.5 m and
7.6 m in diameter within a low rubble wall up to 4 m thick.
A porch was defined by two post-holes on the south and
finds included many sherds of coarse pottery, fragments of
quernstones, quartz scrapers, flint flakes and a fragment of a
bronze pin.

17 Whitemyre, Glen of Rait   NO 202 284

There are two hut circles 150 m north of Whitemyre, north
of the unclassified Glen of Rait road, 7 m and 9.6 m in
internal diameter. The interior of the larger one has been
levelled into the slope.

CUP-AND-RING STONES

1 Balholmie, Cargill   NO 148 363

Originally from Newbigging, this stone is now by the lawn
at Balholmie House, west of the A93. It is a small boulder,
1.8 m long, with eight cupmarks on it. Five of the cupmarks
are surrounded by three concentric rings and one has a
radial channel extending from it.

2 Balmacnaughton   NN 773 436

On a rocky outcrop 450 m east of Balmacnaughton, high
above Loch Tay and close to a wall enclosing Kenmore Hill,
there are over one hundred and fifty cupmarks, twenty-five
ringed and three foot-shaped. Most of the grooves on the

rock – which measures 13.5 m by 4.5 m – are probably the result of weathering but some may be artificial.

3 Bridge of Lyon, Fortingall   NN 732 466

In what is probably a circular ring ditch surrounding a Bronze Age burial, 350 m south-east of Bridge of Lyon and 150 m west of the conspicuous moat site (see p. 197), this cupmarked stone may have stood upright at the centre of the burial site at one time. It is 2.4 m long and 0.9 m wide with nine cups on its western face and one cup on its northern face. Excavations during the 19th century uncovered cist flags and fragments of bone from the cairn site.

4 Brownie's Knowe, St Martin's   NO 160 309

In a clearing in a conifer plantation 370 m north-west of Rosemount there is a small stone circle with six of its original ten stones still in place. 17.7 m to the south-west of the circle there is a cupmarked boulder, 1.1 m long, 0.85 m thick and 0.5 m high. On its south-facing surface there are nine cupmarks up to 60 mm in diameter.

5 Colen   See p. 120

6 Drumderg, Forest of Alyth,   NO 185 549 and
NO 184 545

On the south-east flank of Drumderg, 1.6 km north of Smyrna cottage and to the north of the unclassified road between Glen Shee and Alyth, is a kite-shaped boulder, 1.9 m by 1.7 m, which has twenty-eight cupmarks on its south-west face. Two of the cupmarks are surrounded by triple rings and an oval cup, 100 mm by 70 mm, is surrounded by four rings. Four cups have single rings and the rest are plain cupmarks, the largest of which is 60 mm in diameter.

The second group of cupmarks is 500 m south-west on the west face of a rock outcrop, 1.3 m east-west and 0.65 m high. It comprises twenty-nine plain cupmarks up to 80 mm in diameter and eight double cupmarks up to 140 mm in length by 70 mm in width.

1. Dunsinane Hill, late Iron Age and Early Historic hill fort, from the east

2. Duncroisk, Glen Lochay, cup-and-ring stone

3. Meigle no. 2,
panel showing Daniel in the Lion's Den

4. Logierait,
Class II Pictish stone cross-face

5. Evelick Castle

6. West Toun, late medieval church

7. Castle Menzies from the east, showing stepped Z-plan

8. Weem Kirk

9. Foulis Easter, collegiate church

10. Dunkeld by John Slezer, showing the now demolished 17th-century Dunkeld House on the right, the cathedral in the centre and with the remains of the canons' manses and the tower of the now disappeared bishop's palace on the left.

11. Dunkeld Cathedral, west front

12. Scone Palace (NLS)

13. Keithbank Mill

Essential viewing

7 Duncroisk, Glen Lochay　　　　NN 532 358

One hundred metres south of the Glen Lochay public road below the first house at Duncroisk, in a field between the road and the River Lochay on a very conspicuous elongated ridge of quartzite schist. This is one of the most impressive examples of cup-and-ring decoration in Perthshire. Eight groups of markings, including over one hundred and thirty plain cupmarks, seventeen cups with single rings, and two cups with double rings, extend over about 20 m of the upper surface of the rock outcrop. The cups are up to 40 mm deep and 250 mm in diameter. There are other cupmarked rocks in the vicinity.

8 East Cult　　　　See p. 128

9 Lundin　　　　See p. 125

10 MacBeth's Stone, Belmont　　　　See p. 130

11 Muir of Gormack　　　　NO 125 472

South of the Lornty Burn and Buzzart Dykes (see pp. 139, 219), 1.6 km west of West Gormack and protruding from a south-facing slope on the fringe of a settlement and field system, there is a boulder which measures 1.6 m by 1.4 m by 0.5 m. On the upper surface there are weathered remains of three cups with single rings, one with double rings, and five plain cupmarks. The largest cup is 50 mm by 15 mm.

Essential viewing

12 Newbigging, Cargill　　　　NO 156 352

Two hundred and ten metres W-S-W of Newbigging steading and W-S-W of the unclassified Cargill–Collace road, the stone has been moved here from its original position nearby. It is roughly-pointed and recumbent, 1.8 m long, 0.95 m broad and 0.65 m thick, with about thirty-seven cupmarks on it. Three of the cups have between three and five rings surrounding them, five have single or double rings, and some are joined by radial

grooves to a vertical channel. Unusually, much of the decora-
tion is enclosed within a linear 'frame' on three sides.

13 Over Kincairney, Clunie   NO 083 440

Two hundred metres south-west of Over Kincairney farmstead and west of a possible ruined chapel (see p. 185), this
stone was ploughed up 100 m W-N-W of its current position.
It is a 1.5 m by 1.15 m slab, up to 0.4 m thick and on its upper
surface are about sixty-eight cupmarks and several lengths
of channel.

14 Rait   NO 227 268

On the west side of the carpark, marking its entrance, at
Rait steading shop development, this large boulder was
found during ploughing and moved here. There are seventy
cupmarks on its upper surface, up to 80 mm in diameter. A
rosette pattern is formed around one of the large cups by a
ring of six equally-spaced smaller cups.

15 Tulloch, Straloch   NO 053 634

West of the A924 Rattray–Pitlochry road, 280 m W-N-W
of Tulloch Cottage and on a low rise in a field with several
clearance heaps of stones. This large boulder, 2.75 m by
0.9 m and 0.6 m thick, has at least forty cupmarks on its
upper surface, up to 70 mm in diameter. Most are circular,
some are oval and one group is roughly cruciform in pattern.
There is a cairn to the north and a hut circle to the south.

BURNT MOUNDS

1 Ashintully, Kirkmichael   NO 104 622

On a slope below a number of hut circles (see p. 155),
between two boggy stream-beds 60 m north-west of the footpath between Ashintully and Lair, there is a burnt mound.
It is crescent-shaped, 7.5 m by 4.4 m and up to 0.5 m high.
The uphill side is partly buried in peat, making it difficult to
trace.

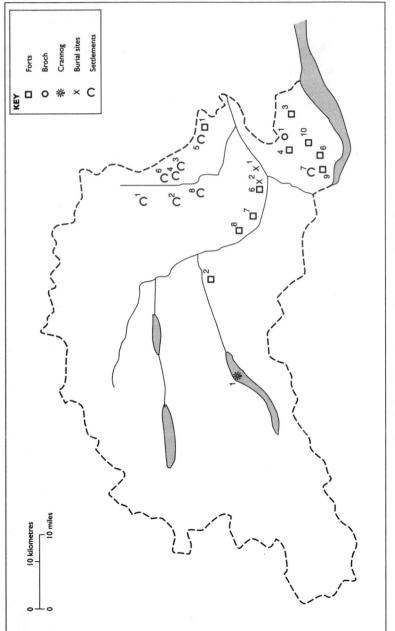

Map 5: Iron Age – forts, settlements and burial sites

IRON AGE MONUMENTS

HILL FORTS

Essential viewing

1 Barry Hill, Alyth   *NO 262 503*

This most impressively-defended fort lies 200 m east of the B954, 3.5 km north-east of Alyth. Strategically-positioned above Glen Isla and Strathmore at the east end of the long ridge which separates the two valleys, it is a prominent skyline feature when viewed from the south. It has been extended and improved during different phases of construction and the earliest fort probably lies beneath the huge inner wall. Defending this early fort were the two outer ramparts on the north and west sides of the hill and the rampart beneath the later outwork on the east.

The outwork or outer annexe, up to 15 m thick, is contemporary with the inner wall on the south and east and contains a blocked entrance on the south-east. An associated ditch, dug in segments, follows the line of an earlier ditch. The inner defences associated with this later period of construction are still massive, though they are now reduced to 10 m-thick rubble banks, and they contain the partly-vitrified evidence of a timber-laced wall. These inner defences enclose an 80 m by 25 m space.

A trackway leads from the entrance on the north-east through the outer defences to the top of the inner wall and there is a partly artificial pond on the west, between the outer ramparts. Within the fort there are the remains of more recent structures but there are no traces of contemporary domestic buildings. The hillside has been quarried for millstones in the more recent past.

2 Castle Dow, Balnaguard   NN 929 513

There is a car park off the B898 west of Balnaguard and way-marked trails lead from it up through a protected one hundred year-old juniper forest to the summit of Caisteal Dubh, 1.5 km above the road, giving commanding views over the River Tay. The fort measures 97 m by 64 m and its

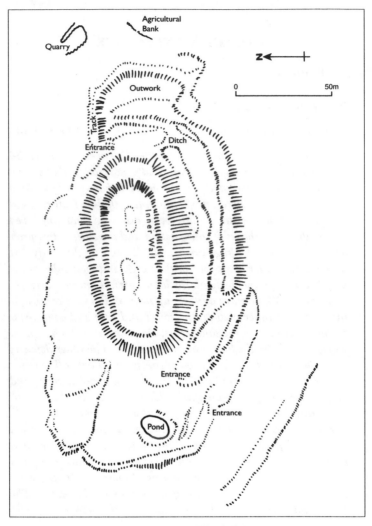

Fig. 6: Barry Hill – hill fort

boulder-faced rubble wall is 3.5 m wide, increasing to 5.8 m
at its entrance in the west. Traces of the wall-core can still
be seen along the top of the cliff in the north-east. The turf-
covered rampart is of earth and stone and there are traces of
a ditch at the east end. An annexe, 85 m by 26 m , has been

added at the south-west corner of the fort. Inside the fort, there is a modern sheep shelter but no other trace of early structures.

3 Dron, Fowlis Easter   NO 289 321

This oval fort, 100 m by 76 m, on the summit of Dron Hill, 750 m west of Dron, commands magnificent views over the eastern end of the Carse of Gowrie and the estuary of the Tay. Its remains have been heavily denuded. On the west side is a long row of large, closely-set stones representing the base of the outer wall-face but the inner face is less complete. There are traces of three outer defences on the west and the main entrance has been on the north-west.

Essential viewing

4 Dunsinane or Dunsinnan Hill, Collace
NO 214 317

A 1.5 km track leads up Dunsinane Hill from the unclassified road 300 m south-east of Collace. The fort, 54.8 m by 30.4 m, is in a spectacular position with an outlook right across lower Strathmore (though overlooked on the north-east by Black Hill). It encloses 2.16 ha and is defended by a single main rampart (up to 9m thick) and two outer ramparts. Much vitrified stone in the inner defences indicates that the walls have been timber-laced. The later entrance is probably on the north-east, reached by a trackway, but an earlier entrance on the north is accessed by a trackway which was later blocked by an outer rampart.

The interior has been much disturbed by mid 19th-century excavators, lured to the site by its association with Macbeth, but on the terrace in the southern half there are traces of crescentic scarps left by timber houses and the early excavation found a bi-lobed souterrain within the fort. A stone-walled hut circle appears to overlie the rampart on the south side, possibly as a result of upcast from the excavations. Finds, since lost, included a bronze spiral finger-ring, a quern, animal bones, midden material and the skeletal remains of two adults and one child, probably from an earlier burial site.

'*Dunsion*', *mentioned in Pictish sources, has been tentatively identified as the fort at Dunsinane, extending its occupation from the Iron Age into the early historic period.*

5 Evelick   NO 199 257

This fort is 350 m south-east of Evelick towerhouse (see p. 205), 3 km E-S-E of the fort on Law Hill, Arnbathie (see below). It is another large fort, 107 m by 78 m within ramparts, with walls up to 8 m thick and 2 m high. And again, at least two periods of construction can be identified – the two outer banks and ditches are later additions to the fort, blocking an earlier entrance on the west. The fort is protected to the east and south by steep slopes and is defended in the north and west by four ramparts, the outer two with ditches. There are three entrances, those on the south and north approached by trackways. Inside the fort there has been a large ring-ditch house, 14 m in diameter, and there are less prominent traces of stances for round timber houses. To the north there are remains of turf-covered field boundaries.

6 Inchtuthil, Caputh   NO 115 393

The fort, 750 m south-west of the Roman legionary fortress (see p. 160), can be approached from the B9099 Caputh–Murthly road, along the north bank of the River Tay. It lies on a steep-sided promontory at the south-west end of a plateau, above Inchtuthil Cottage. Excavations in 1901 revealed that the earliest structure on the site was a timber palisaded enclosure across the tail of the promontory, with ditches on the outside. After the Romans left, a new and larger native fort was built on the promontory with five ditches and ramparts. These later fort-builders made use of Gourdie stone in the inner rampart, robbed from the walls of the Roman fortress. The 1901 excavations also uncovered a paved area in the interior, possibly the floor of a circular house.

7 Kemp's Hold, Stenton   NO 067 407

A track leads from the west to this fort, 100 m above the A984 Dunkeld–Meikleour road. It is protected on the north-west and north-east by sheer slopes. Measuring 82 m by 27 m at the north-west, it narrows to only 7 m at the south-east, within an almost complete inner rampart which follows the edge of the summit. This inner rampart is remarkably complete – up to 4 m thick and with an entrance in the south-west. The outer defences are also impressive, particularly on the north-west where there are still three stout ramparts with external quarry-ditches. At the east end there is a shallow ditch with a low counterscarp or outer bank.

8 King's Seat, Dunkeld   NO 009 440

Follow the way-marked trail in the grounds of Dunkeld House Hotel, 1.5 km west of Dunkeld on the unclassified Dunkeld–Dowally road. The fort itself is not very accessible and, like many Perthshire hill forts, has been overwhelmed by *rhododendron ponticum*. Nevertheless, the trail allows an appreciation of the strategic location and natural defences of this site. It is a relatively small fort, 35 m by 22 m, within a massive wall and further defended by a series of teraces, outlying ramparts and quarry-ditches. The entrance is in the north with a trackway above to a lower entrance on the west, below which access to the fort is blocked by three terraced ramparts. The fort may have continued in use into the Pictish period when Dunkeld was an important centre.

9 Law Hill, Arnbathie   NO 170 258

Off the unclassified Bonhard–Pitroddie road, 450 m W-N-W of Arnbathie. This is another large, multi-period fort, 154 m by 90 m, with impressive defences, including the remains of a *chevaux de frise* of pointed stones to impede attackers at the northern end. This is a relatively rare defensive feature of Scottish Iron Age forts. Other examples in Scotland can be seen at Cademuir Hill and Dreva Craig in Peeblesshire, Dun Gerashader in Skye and Ness of Burgie in Shetland, but it is more common in Ireland, Wales, Spain and Portugal.

The remains of the earliest defences – three outer ramparts – are on the north approach to the hill. These were superceded by a short length of rampart at the north entrance and another rampart around the inner wall. A further rampart on the south side forms an annexe containing a stone-walled hut circle and a depression on the north-west may have been a pond or cistern. Trackways lead to the four entrances.

On the summit is a cairn, 7 m in diameter and 0.5 m high, and immediately below the defences there is an enclosure and a building. To the north of the fort there are the remains of five hut circles and there is a further hut circle below the south-eastern ramparts (see p. 156).

10 Rait   NO 230 268

Six hundred metres east of Rait, 50 m west of the unclassified Kinnaird–Glendoick road. Like Inchtuthil fort, Rait has been defended by drawing a band of massive earthworks across the neck of a steep-sided promontory. Here, a narrow, steep-sided spit of land is defended by three slightly curving mounds with external ditches and a 2 m-wide ramp entrance crossing the inner and central ramparts. The three ramparts are aligned east-west and average 50 m long with a maximum height of 2.3 m and a maximum width of 8 m. The enclosed area is relatively small at about 0.05 ha.

BROCH

Little Dunsinane Hill   NO 222 325

On a rocky knoll on the west side of the Sidlaws, 1 km north of the B953 and 1.5 km north-east of Dunsinane Hill fort (see p. 149), 150 m south-west of and below Little Dunsinane Hill. This broch is 12 m in diameter, with walls about 5 m thick. It has been heavily robbed but three courses of the outer wall survive to a height of 1.25 m on the south-west and there are a few facing-stones of the inner face in the north-east. The outer face has been set below and up to 5.5 m distant from the inner face, constructed of large basal blocks underpinned by small boulders. The entrance in the E-S-E is protected by an outer wall and just outside it there is a small annexe with a quarry pit further to the south.

CRANNOG

Essential viewing

**Oakbank Crannog, Fearnan and
The Crannog Centre, Kenmore**   *NN 723 442*

*Selected for excavation because its remains never appeared
above the surface of Loch Tay – even during extended periods
of drought – Oakbank crannog lies off-shore at Fearnan by
the A827 Kenmore–Killin road. Although the site is invisible,
paired with the nearby Crannog Centre at Kenmore where
a reconstruction based on the findings from Oakbank can be
visited, this is one of the most important archaeological projects
in Scotland. Material from the site has revolutionised ideas
concerning the culture and economy of early Iron Age Scotland,
and the outstanding preservation of organic matter in the water-
logged conditions of the submerged crannog offers insights into
daily life which no land site can equal.*

*Seventeen crannogs have been identified in Loch Tay, five
of which are islands exposed at all times of the year, including
the largest crannog in Scotland, the so-called Priory Island at
Kenmore. Of the remainder, a further five are visible at times
of exceptionally low water but seven are now submerged at all
times. Oakbank is one of that seven and has been the subject of
extensive archaeological investigation in the 1970s and 1980s.
Further excavations are planned.*

*The excavated levels of the crannog comprised a round timber
house with a laid log floor, dating from c. 400 BC–600 BC, on
an artificial platform in the loch with access via a causeway
to the shore and a landing stage. Up to 3 m-long timbers
held the crannog above water. The peaty nature of the water
and the anaerobic conditions of the sediments have preserved
organic material, including bramble, raspberry, wild cherry
and flax seeds, hazelnuts and sloe stones, and the teeth of a
cow and droppings of sheep or goats. Also preserved are jet
beads, a wooden plate and a paddle, a fishing net weight,
wooden whistle, spindle whorl and pot sherds. Wood used in the
construction of the crannog included oak, wych elm, field elm,*

rowan, alder, hazel, Scots Pine, ivy, dog rose, pear and apple. Some of the original artefacts recovered by the underwater excavations are on display at the Crannog Centre.

BURIAL SITES

1   Hallhole Square Barrow, Meikleour   NO 186 390

This site is marked on the OS map as an 'earthwork'. It lies 500 m E-S-E of Hallhole steading and comprises a low central mound, 10 m wide and 0.5 m high, standing within enclosing ditches and banks. It is surrounded by two ditches with low external banks and causeways at three corners, characteristic of square barrows. Excavation in 1903 found only small concentrations of burnt bone and charcoal within the mound. It is likely that this was just one element of a more extensive cemetery as a round barrow has been identified from cropmarks 50 m south. Excavation of a similar barrow at Boysack Mills, Angus, produced an iron pin of the early AD 1st millennium.

2   Inchtuthil Barrows, Caputh   NO 127 397

There are two visible round barrows on what may be a more extensive cemetery site to the east of the Roman fortress (see p. 160). On excavation in 1901, the largest, 28.3 m in diameter and 1.8 m high, known as 'The Women's Knowe', was found to contain a central long cist of thin stone slabs on a raised platform, lying east-west and surrounded by a ditch. Stone from the Roman fortress had been added at a later date.

The second barrow, 10 m in diameter, with a narrow ditch, is more closely associated with the Roman remains. It overlies the fortress defences and must therefore be of later date than the late AD 1st century Roman occupation. A central grave pit is covered by a circular mound of earth, 0.7m high, capped with gravel and boulders. No trace of a skeleton was found.

UNENCLOSED SETTLEMENT SITES

HUT CIRCLES AND RING-DITCH HOUSES

1 Ashintully, Kirkmichael   NO 102 622

In a glen to the north of the Ashintully estate, approached
by a track through the saddle in the hills to the south-west.
The first group of hut circles lies 800 m north of Ashintully
Castle (see p. 200) west of the Kirkmichael–Lair footpath,
on the southern spur of Cnoc an Daimh. There are five hut
circles on the terrace above the deserted settlement beyond
the improved fields to the north of the towerhouse.

Two of the five hut circles are tangential, enclosed by their
outer surrounding wall. This enclosed pair, with internal
diameters of 8.8 m and 9.4 m, lies at the edge of the terrace
and there is a possible ring ditch inside the larger of them on
the east. The other three hut circles to the north and north-
west comprise a double-walled example of 16 m overall diameter and two single-walled examples of 6 m and 12 m diameters. At the rear of the terrace to the north-west is a double-
walled hut circle and enclosure. The hut circle, 15.8 m in
internal diameter, has a well-defined ring ditch within. The
enclosure lies on a low rise to the E-N-E and measures
23.3 m by 12 m.

2 Dalrulzion, Kirkmichael   NO 123 573

Though very poorly preserved and masked by heather, this
is the type-site used to define the characteristics of double-
walled hut circles, lying north of the forest path to Loch
Mharaich, 2 km from the A93. Eight huts, two of them
double-walled, survive within a long, narrow clearing in the
plantation. The smaller of the two has an internal diameter
of 8 m and is faced with upright slabs on the north and
slabs with boulders on the south. The one metre-thick outer
wall has been reduced and an entrance can be traced on
the S-S-E. The other double-walled hut circle measures 9 m

in internal diameter and has a partially-defined inner wall of uprights slabs and an outwardly-splayed entrance on the south-east.

These and other hut circles in the area were excavated earlier this century. Finds were relatively few but included bones, pottery and saddle querns for grinding barley or oats.

7 Law Hill, Arnbathie   NO 171 262

There is a group of five hut circles 100 m east of the track across Dalreichmoor and 250 m to the north-east of the fort (see p. 151) and a sixth lies downhill from the ramparts on the south-east. Structural evidence is only visible at the latter site which has two successive external wall-faces on the south-west side. They range in size from 8.5 m to 12.8 m in internal diameter and the largest, in the saddle north of the fort, was excavated in 1950 to reveal a roughly-paved central court, a possible hearth and a later cremation deposit in a stone setting in the entrance.

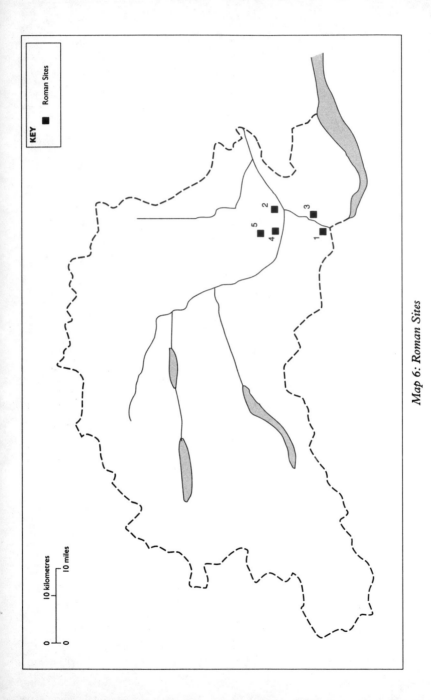

Map 6: Roman Sites

ROMAN SITES

1 Bertha, Redgorton   NN 097 268

This large Flavian-period fort, of which little trace remains,
lies at the confluence of the Rivers Tay and Almond, 3 km
north of Perth, bisected by the railway line. A faint ridge is all
that survives of the northern rampart and a short length of
the southern rampart lies in woodland by the River Almond.
In 1958 a dedication stone to *discipulina augusti*, a military
discipline cult, was recovered from the river and is now in
Perth Museum. References in early medieval chronicles to
an important Pictish and Scottish royal centre of *Rathinveramon* – 'Fort at the Mouth of the Almond' – points to a
re-use of the Roman defences.

2 Black Hill Watch Tower, Meikleour   NO 176 391

In dense undergrowth, 350 m north-east of Bridge Farm.
The watch tower was sited on a glacial knoll 18 m high and
would have been visible from neighbouring Roman forts at
Inchtuthil, Cardean and Cargill. All that now remains is the
sub-rectangular earthwork which enclosed the timber tower
and there is very little trace of the external V-shaped ditch
which was 5.2 m wide with a narrow entrance causeway on
the N-N-W. Excavations revealed the post-holes of a timber
tower 4 m square within a turf rampart, ditch and bank,
all characteristic of watch towers of the Flavian period, AD
82–7. Finds from the excavation included iron nails, Roman
glass and a piece of a bronze pin. In Strathmore, the frontier
posts, of which this watch tower was part, were all deliberately demolished and abandoned by AD 87.

3 Grassy Walls, Sherriftown   NO 105 280

On the east bank of the River Tay, 1.1 km N N E of Scone
Palace. On a Roman road, this is the largest of the known
temporary camps in south-east Perthshire, measuring 670 m
by 760 m and enclosing an area of 52 ha. It probably housed
the troops of the Emperor Septimius Severus during the

campaigns of AD 208–11. The ramparts are still partly visible in Drumshogle Wood as grassy banks, (NO 105 284) 6 m thick, with a ditch 3 m wide. The only find from the site is a AD 2nd century brass coin, now in Perth Museum.

Essential viewing

4 *Inchtuthil, Caputh*   *NO 125 397*

This fortress is situated on an extensive gravel plateau in a bend of the River Tay at Caputh. From the A984, a farm track opposite the juction with the B947 leads to a footpath which

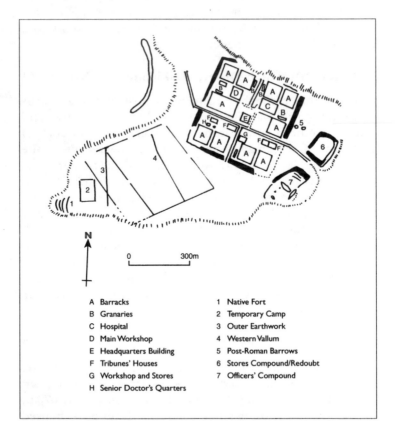

A	Barracks	1	Native Fort
B	Granaries	2	Temporary Camp
C	Hospital	3	Outer Earthwork
D	Main Workshop	4	Western Vallum
E	Headquarters Building	5	Post-Roman Barrows
F	Tribunes' Houses	6	Stores Compound/Redoubt
G	Workshop and Stores	7	Officers' Compound
H	Senior Doctor's Quarters		

Fig. 7: Inchtuthil – Roman legionary fortress

runs uphill to the fort. North of the path are the mutilated ramparts and defensive ditches of a rectangular enclosure, probably a stores compound in use during the construction of the main fortress. One hundred metres beyond is the broad east ditch of the fortress and to the west, just before a modern plantation bank, is the broad, low mound of the western rampart and its associated ditch. The southern defences, including rampart, ditch and berm or ledge between them, are quite well preserved in nearby rough ground.

Nothing remains of the internal timber-built structures but the site has been extensively excavated several times sinces 1901 and, more recently, aerial photography has contributed further to our understanding of the site. It was probably built around AD 83 to house 5500 of Agricola's troops and it encloses 21 ha within the 5 m-thick turf ramparts, the 2 m-deep ditch and the bank visible on the south and west sides. At a later date the promontory to the south of the fort, which had been occupied by temporary encampments to house the men who constructed the permanent fortification, was cut off by a new rampart and ditch known as the 'Western Vallum' of which traces can still be seen. Sandstone was quarried for the construction of a stone facing for the rampart at the Hill of Gourdie to the north-west.

The main buildings' defences enclosed sixty-four barracks and officers' quarters as well as the headquarters, hospital, store sheds, workshops and six granaries with loading bays. The long barracks were built around the perimeter in blocks of ten, one for each of the occupying legion's cohorts of six centuries. Each centurion – commander of a century – had a suite of rooms in a larger block at the rampart end of the long barrack ranges and the senior centurion of each cohort enjoyed the luxury of a large house with hypocaust underfloor heating systems. The principal streets which led to the four timber gateways and towers were lined with colonnaded rows of open-fronted timber buildings – the stores, workshops and offices.

Outside the defences to the south-west were the temporary tented accommodation blocks and the offices used by the construction workers who built the fort, and to the south-east the extramural senior officers' temporary compound with bath-house.

The fort was never completed and the buildings were delib-

erately demolished and the defences slighted c. AD 86, drains blocked up and a pit filled with nine iron tyres and 875,428 nails – presumably to prevent their re-use by hostile locals. A coin of AD 86 was found in almost mint condition, providing the presumed date of departure of the troops.

5   Steed Stalls, Gourdie   NO 115 427

Four hundred metres north-east of Craigend of Gourdie farm buildings, north of Middle Gourdie farm. On the east shoulder of the Hill of Gourdie, this small temporary camp may have been associated with the quarry for Inchtuthil. Cropmarks reveal that it measured about 145 m square and was divided in two by a ditch with a causeway at its mid-point. The northern section contains seven hollows, possibly kilns for lime production or for firing bricks.

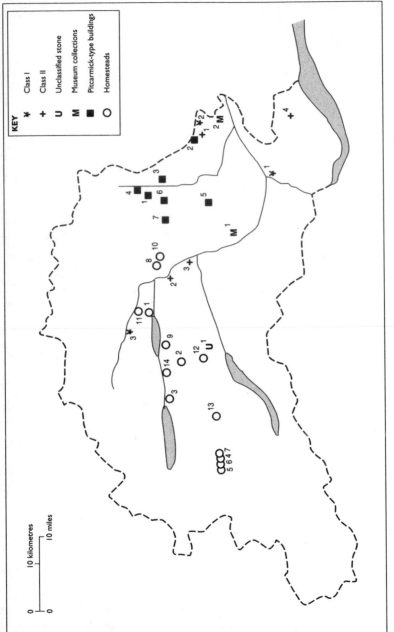

Map 7: Pictish and Early Medieval Sites – Pictish stones and settlement sites

PICTISH AND EARLY MEDIEVAL SITES

PICTISH SYMBOL STONES

CLASS I

1 **Balholmie House, Cargill**   **NO 148 362**

Now in the garden at Balholmie House, west of the A93 Perth–Blairgowrie road. The stone, a whinstone slab, 0.93 m high and 0.65 m wide, has been moved here from a wall north-west of West Whitefield Farm, Cargill. It is incised on one face with a rectangle which has a vertical line extending from its lower side on the left and a variant of the rectangle symbol on the right.

2 **Bruceton**   **NO 290 504**

In a field 400 m south of Bruceton steading on haughland of the River Isla. It is 1.4 m high and there are two incised symbols on its south face. Near the top, in the middle, there is an arch or horse-shoe and below it a beast. Bones and 'coffins' were discovered nearby last century.

3 **Struan**   **NN 809 653**

In the churchyard on the south bank of the River Garry, this is a stone of blue schistose slate, rectangular at the top but broken at the bottom. It is 1.3 m high and 0.8 m wide, incised on one face. On the front, half-way down, to the left, is a double disc and Z-rod. On the right is part of another symbol.

There is another stone in the churchyard, 8.3 m south-west of the south-west corner of the church. It is 1.1 m high and 0.6 m broad and bears two simple incised crosses on its east and west faces.

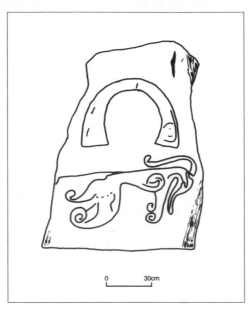

Fig. 8: Bruceton – Class I Pictish Stone

CLASS II

1 Alyth*   NO 243 487

This 1.37 m-long stone was discovered near the manse and is
now kept in the porch of Alyth High Kirk. It is a slab of grey
schist, a coarse-grained metamorphic rock which is easily
split. It bears a Latin cross on the front with an unusual
tenon or projection at the base of the shaft. The arms and
shaft are decorated with interlace and spiral bosses or knobs
fill the angles between the arms of the cross. On the reverse
there is a fragment of a double disc and Z-rod symbol.

Essential viewing

2 *Dunfallandy**   *NN 946 565*

*Signposted from the unclassified Pitlochry–Logierait road. Park
at the cattle grid and follow the path and steps up to the stone*

which is 1.5 m high, of Old Red Sandstone. On one side there is a decorated cross in relief and nine side panels. At the top left is a beast with a human head, and at top right a prostrate beast with another standing over it, interpreted as a lion breathing life into its cub, a symbol of the Resurrection. Below the right arm of the cross there is a beast with its head bent back and parallel with it on the left side there is an angel with four wings. Left of the shaft is a beast with its tongue hanging out and a stag below. On the right is a second angel. Bottom left, a monster swallows a man, possibly a representation of Jonah and the whale, and on the right there is a beast with a reptile head. At the bottom right is a beast with a curved horn biting its own tail. The panels are surrounded by an ornamental border of interlace, interrupted where the arms of the cross extend.

On the other side there is a human head in the centre between the mouths of two beasts whose attenuated bodies form a raised border terminating in fish tails at the bottom, enclosing two panels with two enthroned people facing each other across a small cross. Above the head of the left man is a beast symbol and above on the right there is a double disc. In front of them are a crescent and V-rod and in the middle is a figure on a horse with a crescent and V-rod and another beast symbol to the right. At the bottom are a hammer, an anvil and a pair of tongs.

3 Logierait   NN 967 520

In the churchyard by the A827, south of Pitlochry, beside three 18th-century mortsafes for securing coffins against body-snatchers. This is an upright cross-slab of whinstone, 1 m high by 0.6 m carved in relief on two faces but broken at the top. On the front is a cross with four small circular raised bosses in hollows between the arms and spiral terminations at the bottom of the shaft. The background of the cross is divided into four plain panels.

On the back is a single panel with the lower part of a horseman and below that a serpent round a straight rod. This is a unique instance of a serpent combined with a perfectly straight rod instead of the Z-rod with which it usually appears.

4 Rossie Priory   NO 292 308

This cross-slab is in the Kinnaird family mausoleum, formerly Rossie parish church, 150 m west of the unclassified road between the A856 and Wellbank. The stone is particularly remarkable for the detail and variety of its monsters. It stands 1.67 m high and with a cross in high relief on the front, decorated with interlace and key patterns. Its left arm is missing.

There are panels on either side of the cross-head. On the left is a beast with a human head and a curling tail; on the other side a beaked figure holds an axe with both hands as it attacks a claw-footed bird. On the left of the shaft is a beast with its tail curled over its back, a naked man being attacked by a beast and a fish-tailed monster, and a pair of confronted beasts, each swallowing a bird. On the right of the shaft there is a beast swallowing a serpent. Below is an animal with a bovine head and large eyes. And at the bottom, there is a pair of monsters with human heads complete with beards and flowing hair, fish fins, beast-headed tails, bodies intertwined, facing opposite directions, one astride the other.

On the back, unusually, there is a second cross decorated with key pattern and an ornamental border round the top and down the two sides. Down the short shaft of the cross there are three horsemen ranged vertically to form a hunting scene with two further horsemen and a pair of hunting dogs on the right. Below the left arm of the cross is an animal head and above the side-arms is an angel and a figure holding a pair of birds by their necks. On the left of the shaft and the pedestal is a crescent and V-rod, a beast and a kneeling animal, its head turned backwards to face a similar head forming the termination of its tail.

UNCLASSIFIED STONES

Dull   NN 806 492

In the upper churchyard in the village church, 300 m north of the B846 Aberfeldy–Keltneyburn road there are two recumbent cross-slabs. One, an incised circled cross, abutts a 19th-century headstone for John Menzies. A second cross-slab lies a few metres to the south, bearing a small cross in relief.

Three free-standing crosses, 1.8 m high, originate in the vicinity of the church at Dull. Two are now in Weem church (see p. 227) and one remains at Dull. These crosses reputedly marked the boundaries of a sanctuary established in the early Christian period.

MUSEUM COLLECTIONS

1   Dunkeld Cathedral*   NO 024 426

Symbol stone 1 was moved to the Cathedral from the grounds of Dunkeld House. It is a Class I symbol stone of grey sandstone with an incised figure on one face. At the top right side there is a man on horseback blowing a horn, holding a spear in his right hand.

Dunkeld 2, known as 'The Apostles' Stone', is a Class III slab which was formerly used as a gate-post at the entrance to the churchyard and is now in the chapter-house museum. It is an upright cross-slab of grey sandstone, carved in relief on four faces. On the front is a cross in one panel containing two horsemen riding one behind the other, a row of four men, three more men prostrate on the ground, one of them decapitated; a man between four beasts, possibly a representation of Daniel in the Lions' Den; and the heads of six men in a row. There are two recessed panels on each side. On the left panel is part of a beast and on the right is a beast with a long snout and tail interlaced with its legs.

On the back there are three panels. At the top are sixteen or more heads and a circular disc and two rows of six men. On the right side there is a man on horseback with a saint with a nimbus around his head and a row of three men below. On the left side all but a spiral at the top has been defaced.

Also in the chapter-house museum is a 2.1 m high tapered cross-slab of the 9th or 10th century which has been damaged by re-use as a gate-post. On one side is a cross-shaft and the other face bears a tapered shaft with a pendant motif at the top.

Essential viewing

2   *Meigle Museum**   *NO 287 446*

The twenty-six fragments of Class II and III carved stones found in and around Meigle parish church and now housed in the old schoolhouse museum illustrate its importance as an early ecclesiastical centre and school of sculpture. Some of the fragments are architectural, perhaps from an early church. Space only allows a description of selected stones from Meigle Museum but a comprehensive guidebook is available.

Meigle 1 is a cross-slab with a range of Pictish symbols on the back including a fish, beast, serpent, Z-rod, beast's head and mirror and comb. Below the beast's head is an animal with a long jaw, crouching down, and below the mirror and comb is a group of five horsemen and a hound. In front of the horsemen is a flying angel and to the right is an animal like a camel with a long neck. In the right lower corner is a beast with a coiled body. The exotic elements on this stone may have been copied from an imported manuscript or carving.

Meigle 2 is a cross-slab in high relief with unusual projections at the sides, possibly to allow it to be slotted into a wall or screen. On the front is a cross with three pairs of beasts symetrically facing each other. On the left, one man appears to haul another up the space at the side of the cross. On the right there are three beasts with convoluted bodies, one above the other.

On the back is a horseman with a pair of hounds at the top, with an angel in front. Below on the left are three horsemen riding abreast followed by another riding behind on the right. Beneath is the figure of Daniel flanked by two lions and possibly a cub. There is a centaur with an axe in each hand and a branch under its right arm; and at the bottom is a man with a club over his right shoulder and in front a dragon seizing a horned beast by the nose. Again, this stone combines native and foreign elements.

Meigle 22 may illustrate a Pictish version of the Celtic god Cernunnos in classic cross-legged pose. A similar figure appears in the Book of Kells. This may be an architectural piece as it is very well preserved, suggesting it was incorporated inside a building.

Meigle 25 is a hog-back monument, so-called because of its shape. The ridge is characteristically decorated with roof-tile motifs and interlace design. At its head, the ridge terminates in outward-facing beasts' heads with pointed ears and the tip of a raised snout protrudes.

Meigle 26 is a highly decorated 9th-century recumbent grave-slab designed to lie horizontally over a grave with a socket on the top, possibly for an upright cross. The vertical end panel shows a beast pursuing a naked and apprehensive man looking over his shoulder and the sides and top have animal, abstract and human motifs, including a swastika of four crouched human bodies, each clasping the foot of its neighbour.

SETTLEMENT SITES

PITCARMICK-TYPE BUILDINGS

1 Ashintully, Kirkmichael   NO 108 625

Close to the edge of a terrace, by the Kirkmichael to Lair footpath. This Pitcarmick-type building is 25 m by 8.1 m at its widest point over a bank which is 2 m thick and 0.2 m high, narrowing at both ends. The eastern half has been scooped out to a depth of 0.4 m. Immediately to the south is a D-shaped enclosure, 6 m by 3.5 m within a bank.

2 Hill of Alyth   NO 228 502

On a terrace on the south-west flank of Hill of Alyth, 500 m south of the unclassified Alyth–Newton of Bamff road, 300 m north-east of Whiteside steading and immediately south of seven hut circles and two ring-ditch houses (see p. 136). It is 26 m long by 7.8 m at the west end and 6.4 m at the east end over walls which are 2.8 m thick and 0.2 m high.

3 Knockali, Glen Shee   NO 153 581, NO 152 586
                                              and NO 155 587

The remains of at least five Pitcarmick-type buildings can be found on the heather moor at the head of the valley of the Drumturn Burn – four on the lower slopes of Knockali to the east of Easter Bleaton farm. The southernmost of those on the west of the valley is 17 m long with a maximum width of 8.4 m, narrowing to the south-west. There has possibly been a partition 3.2 m from the south-west end.

The Pitcarmick-type building at NO 152 586 lies within an enclosure in a saddle on the south-east flank of Knockali. It measures 18.3 m by 7.6 m, narrowing at the east end. The wall, 1.5 m thick, is a low earth bank with an outer face of boulders and slabs set on edge. There are traces of an inner face on the north. The surrounding enclosure may be contemporary or may date to the earlier field system.

One hundred and forty metres east is another Pitcarmick-type building, 19 m long and narrowing in width at the east, with 2 m-thick walls. The entrance on the south incorporates a small porch and the interior has been partly excavated into the slope. There is an annexe on the south-west.

At NO 155 587, at the foot of a south-facing slope is the fourth Pitcarmick-type building, 21 m long by 5.58 m broad and excavated into the slope, with an entrance midway along the south side. It has been extended on the east by one or two annexes.

4   Lair, Glen Shee   NO 139 638

Two hundred and fifty metres west of the A93, 480 m north-west of Lair farmhouse and 32 m east of Lair ring cairn (see p. 105), there is a building which measures 22.5 m east-west by 7.7 m wide at the west end and 5 m wide at the east end, over 1–2 m thick walls which are now 0.4 m high. There are two opposed entrances at the mid-point and the eastern half is sunken. At the south-west corner is a small D-shaped enclosure. Immediately to the north of it is a second similar building, 19 m east-west by 6 m wide, its south wall underlying the north wall of the first building. The entire length of its interior is sunken and there is a drainage gully on the north side. A third Pitcarmick-type building, 18.8 m by 6.8 m, lies end-on to the first and 200 m north-west on a terrace there is a round-ended building, 17 m long, 5.5 m wide at the S-S-E with a sunken interior and 7 m wide at the N-N-W.

5   Muir of Gormack, Kinloch   NO 132 469

One hundred metres east of the ruined 19th-century farm-stead of Marleehill and the unclassified Kinloch–Middleton road, within an area of rig-and-furrow, on a south-facing slope. It measures 15.5 m by 6.1 m at its widest point over a low turf-covered bank and is widest at its eastern, rounded end. The western half has been scooped out. There is an entrance midway along the south side. Fifty metres south-east there is a poorly-preserved building, 15.8 m by 6.1 m.

6   Muir of Merklands, Strathardle   NO 099 575

There are at least six Pitcarmick-type buildings amongst the cairns and hut circles to the north-east of Stylemouth (see p. 140). The principal building, which has been levelled into the slope, is crossed by a track, 40 m east of a stone dyke. It is 30 m long and 8.5 m wide though the south-east end narrows to 4.5 m wide and has been hollowed out internally. There are also traces of an annexe with a separate entrance.

At NO 100 575 there is a second Pitcarmick-type building with low banks, 15 m long and 6 m broad with an entrance midway along the south-west side. The south-east end is hollowed out and an annexe is sited immediately to the south.

At NO 106 569 there are four Pitcarmick-type buildings round a natural basin. Two of them are on low ridges to the north-west of the burn, of which the westernmost is bow-sided, narrowing at the south-east end. It measures 16.3 m by a maximum of 8 m over 2 m thick earthen walls which are 0.3 m high. The eastern building narrows a little at the east end and measures 15.6 m by a maximum 7.4 m overall. The earth bank wall has an external stone kerb and there has been an entrance on the south-west, possibly with a porch. An enclosure with stone-cored walls has been attached at the north-west end and there is a low bank from the east corner.

The third Pitcarmick-type building is on a low ridge 200 m to the E-S-E, 19 m by a maximum 8.5 m, narrowing to the south-east. It has a small annexe on the south of the entrance and an enclosure in the north-west.

The fourth Pitcarmick-type building lies in deep heather, 200 m N-N-W. It measures 23.5 m by 10 m maximum over 1.6 m thick walls, 0.6 m high. The interior has been deeply scooped into the slope. There is an annexe north-west of the entrance and an enclosure on the south-east.

7 Pitcarmick   NO 051 567

This is the type-site for Pitcarmick-type buildings, typically in an area of dense Bronze and Iron Age settlement and amongst deep heather which can make it difficult to locate all the hut-circles, cairns, shielings and the eight Pitcarmick buildings on the slopes and terraces to the north and north-east of Pitcarmick Loch. Follow the path from Pitcarmick steading out to the north-west end of Pitcarmick Loch then walk northwards.

On the southern edge of a terrace overlooking the west end of Pitcarmick Loch, 325 m north of the Loch is a Pitcarmick building which is 30 m long and up to 7.8 m wide at its western end and 6 m wide at its eastern end. The outer face is composed of slabs set on edge backed by an earthen bank 1.3 m thick. One hundred and ten metres to the south-east is a second Pitcarmick building with its east end hollowed out and 180 m south-east of it, there is a third, 23.5 m long, narrowest at the east end which is also hollowed out. On the north side of the building there is a drainage gully.

HOMESTEADS

Essential viewing

1 Allean Forest, Queen's View, Loch Tummel*
NN 863 602

A waymarked track leads up to the homestead from the Forestry car park at Allean Forest on the north side of the B8019. It is near-circular, 24 m by 22.7 m with a stout outer wall, 3 m to 4 m thick, which is preserved to its original height for most of its circumference. It is more defensible than most similar structures, located on a terrace high above Loch Tummel, but it is open to the east, south and west with no natural defences. Pollen analysis indicates that when the homestead was first built it was surrounded by light woodland and pasture.

Excavations at the site revealed twenty-three post-holes which measured 0.3 m in diameter and 0.2 m in depth and several still contained packing stones to hold timbers in place. So at least part of the interior must have been roofed over. Two of the timbers were in the entrance on the west, marking where a porch had stood. The entrance passage is 4.01 m long, 1.5 m wide at the inner end and 1.75 m wide at the outer end, with a buttress protruding beyond. The entrance passage has been paved and upright slabs were positioned 2.5 m from its outer end to support a wooden door. There was no firm identification of an occupation layer. Rather, the ground seemed to have been trampled, suggesting that at least part of the structure was used to shelter animals.

Very few finds were made during excavation. These included pieces of two rotary querns, a stone lamp, a small yellow bead, possibly Anglian of c. AD 700–900, and 25 kg of slag.

Two depressions were identified in the interior, from which much of the slag came. This has been identified as the residue of smithying rather than smelting and represents a secondary phase of use, possibly in the 17th or 18th century by the people from the nearby settlement to the west (see p. 237). During this second main period of use, another entrance was made in the east, wide enough for carts to be brought in and out. At the same time, a corn-drying kiln was built on the outer wall at the south-east.

2 Braes of Foss   NN 753 560 and NN 755 563

The first homestead lies on a flat-topped grassy knoll in a non-defesive position overlooking good arable land, east of Braes of Foss and north of the Kinloch Rannoch-Coshieville road. Although it has been largely removed by ploughing, a few outer-facing stones of its 3 m thick walls can still be seen protruding through the green mound. It has an internal diameter of 22 m by 19 m. Inside the homestead there are the turf-covered remains of a later rectangular building.

The second homestead, on a low knoll by Kynachan Burn, has an internal diameter of 21 m by 17 m and the usual

3 m-thick wall. There are traces of later settlement around and possibly within the homestead.

3 Bunrannoch, Kinloch Rannoch   NN 666 580 and
NN 665 579

The smaller of the two homesteads by Bunrannoch House, ·1 km south-east of Kinloch Rannoch, is found on the north side of the road on hummocky ground, amidst clearance cairns and later buildings. It has an internal diameter of 11 m and its wall is 3 m thick. A gap in the west probably represents the entrance. A rectilinear enclosure south-west of the homestead may well be contemporary with it.

The second homestead, on the south side of the road, is 20 m in diameter with a 3.5 m-thick wall. An earthfast stone in the south-east may have been a door jamb.

4 Caisteal a' Chambaican, Cashlie, Glen Lyon
NN 483 417

Between the unclassified Glen Lyon road and the river, 200 m west of the access road to Dalchiorlich. This oval homestead, 27 m by 20 m, is situated on a low-lying natural shelf which has been artificially levelled. Its wall is 3–4 m thick, of huge boulders up to two courses high. There is an indistinct entrance in the east.

5 Caisteal an Deirg, Cashlie, Glen Lyon   NN 475 416

This is the westernmost of the group of four homesteads at the west end of Glen Lyon, 1 km west of the access road to Dalchiorlich on the north bank of the River Lyon. Most of its east side has been destroyed but originally it was 14 m in internal diameter with 3.6 m-thick walls. Inside are the footings of two rectangular buildings.

6 Caisteal an Duibhe, Cashlie, Glen Lyon NN 479 417

This homestead lies immediately north of the unclassified Glen Lyon road, 500 m west of the Dalchiorlich access road. It has an internal diameter of 13.5 m and a wall 3.5 m thick which incorporates a massive boulder, 7 m by 3.5 m by 3.5 m. There is a 1.4 m-wide entrance passage on the west with a door check on its north side.

7 Caisteal MhicRheil, Cashlie, Glen Lyon NN 491 418

This homestead lies opposite Cashlie Farm, between the Glen Lyon road and the river. It is oval in shape with an internal diameter of 13.8 m and 2.8 m-thick walls. There are traces of inner and outer wall faces but no sign of an entrance. Later buildings are situated in the south-west of the interior.

8 Drumchorrie, Pitlochry NN 932 595

The interior of this homestead now forms the site of a tee on Pitlochry Golf Course. It measures 27 m in internal diameter, with a 4 m-thick wall which has been partly robbed and is adjoined by a later settlement. Though the wall is mutilated, a few inner and outer facing stones are still evident.

9 Drumnakyle, Foss NN 786 574

Fifty metres along the Drumnakyle access road from the B846, immediately east of the track. This oval homestead, 21.5 m by 24 m, lies on a low knoll. It has been heavily robbed and is best preserved on the north-east where some outer facing stones survive. There has been a possible entrance on the E-N-E and the top of an upright stone protruding on the north side of it, 1.8 m in from the outer face, may represent the door-jamb.

10 Edradour, Pitlochry NN 952 577

A footpath from the southern outskirts of Pitlochry leads up through woodland to this homestead below Black Spout waterfall. Only the southern half survives as a stone wall 2.7 m thick with an outer face four courses high in the south-west. Originally, it must have had an external diameter of about 27 m.

11 Glen Fincastle, Balavoulin NN 873 616

This homestead, 50 m north-west of Balavoulin, above the unclassified Glen Fincastle road, measures 15 m in diameter internally, with a 3 m-thick wall. Some of the outer facing stones survive on the south-west. A bank of turf-covered rubble on the north represents modern clearance and a late wall overlies the homestead on the south-west.

12 Litigan, Keltneyburn NN 766 497

On the west side of the Keltney Burn, 250m south-east of Litigan. This homestead had an interior of 15.5 m in diameter and walls 3 m thick. Excavations revealed two concentric rings of post-holes 3 m and 4.5 m from the centre where there was a 1 m square hearth slab. The inner and outer face of the wall is built of large boulders and blocks of stone with smaller stones between. Fragments of rotary querns and stone discs were found with pieces of slag and charcoal, dating the site to *c.* AD 840 to 1020.

13 Roro, Glen Lyon NN 627 468

At the base of a hill slope adjacent to cultivated haughland on the south side of the River Lyon, by the farm track 500 m beyond Balnahanaid, accessed from Camusvrachan. This is a well-preserved homestead with an external diameter of 23 m by 22 m and a wall 4.2 m thick. The outer face of the wall is continuous in the south-west arc but the inner face is largely obscured by tumble and later building. The 1.7 m-wide entrance has been in the north-east. The homestead has been robbed to build the ruined school building within its walls.

14 Tullochroisk, Kinloch Rannoch NN 711 578

On a low wooded knoll, overlooking good agricultural land immediately west of the farm track leading to Tullochroisk, 200 m from the unclassified Braes of Foss–Kinloch Rannoch road. This homestead measures 24.5 m by 25 m and its outer wall-face is visible for much of its circumference with occasional inner facing stones protruding through the turf. The mutilated entrance is in the east and a possible contemporary turf-covered bank curves from the north and east for 10 m.

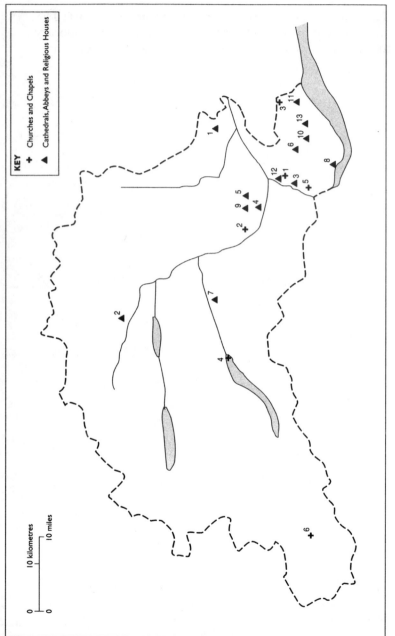

Map 8: Middle Ages – religious sites

KEY

+ Churches and Chapels

▲ Cathedrals, Abbeys and Religious Houses

MEDIEVAL SITES

CHURCHES AND CHAPELS

1   Alyth Old Parish Church and Burial Ground
NO 245 488

On a terrace close to the centre of the burgh 120 m E-N-E of
the present parish church. The surviving portion of the late
medieval north wall and aisle arcade, 25.4 m long, suggests
that originally Alyth church comprised a square-ended choir,
nave, aisle of three bays carried on octagonal piers, and a
north aisle chapel or sacristy. The fragment of north wall
incorporates a plinth, round-headed doorway and window-
opening, and to the east end, aumbries or recesses and a
sacrament house.

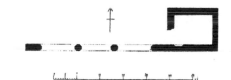

Fig. 9: St Moluc's Church, Alyth – plan

Fig. 10: St Moluc's Church, Alyth – arcade

The three-arched arcade probably survived destruction in 1839 when the new church was built because it was deemed to be 'Saxon' on account of its round arches. Another arcade was demolished at that time, suggesting it was built in a different style, considered not worth sparing. In the wall of the burial ground, by the north gate, there is a skewputt or gable coping-stone, bearing a coat-of-arms, and a lintel with the date 1629.

A record of 1352 refers to a church dedicated to St Moluag and the original village fair was called St Moluag's. The church was erected a prebend, and granted as the stipend or fee of the canons of Dunkeld Cathedral by Bishop Thomas Lauder in the mid 15th century.

2 Blair Church*   NN 866 665

Signposted in the grounds of Blair Castle, 300 m north-west of the Castle (see p. 229), north of the Blair Atholl service road. St Bride's Church and the nearby village of Old Blair was the main settlement area until the road was re-routed to the south during the 19th century. The church is on record in the late 13th-century rolls of the papal tax-gatherer, Boiamund di Vicia.

Few datable features survive in the roofless ruin, a plain rectangular structure with a later burial aisle added on the south side, but it is probable that the main fabric of the building is medieval. Within the church there is a 1579 gravestone in the north wall and the the burial place of Viscount 'Bonnie Dundee' Claverhouse who died at the Battle of Killiecrankie in 1689. In the graveyard there are several 17th and 18th-century graveslabs.

3 Cambusmichael Church and Burial Ground
NO 115 326

The church of St Michael lies within the burial ground, overlooking the Tay on a bluff, 0.5 km north-west of Cambusmichael and the unclassified Old Scone–Cambusmichael road. In the 12th century the chapel here was part of a monastic estate belonging to Scone Abbey but the ruin

Fig. 11: Cambusmichael Church

we see now dates largely to the 15th century when it was the parish church.

It is a plain rectangle on plan, 15.5 m by 6.4 m, its gables still standing to their full height. Medieval features include a round-arched door on the south side towards the west end; an aumbry in the north wall; a pre-Reformation belfry on the west gable; and a medieval grave-cover incorporated in the embrasure of the lintelled doorway. Central to the south wall there is a small round-headed window with two larger window openings to either side. The medieval church was later remodelled but it was already ruinous by 1711. An enclosure of 1.5 ha round the church has been identified from cropmarks, probably dating to the period when the site was an administrative centre belonging to the Augustinian abbey at Scone.

4 Caputh Parish Church and Burial-Ground
NO 083 400

The medieval parish church stood in the burial ground on Mute Hill, indicated by a depression, 22 m by 7.8 m. At the west end is a 17th-century burial vault, the west end of which incorporates a mock-Romanesque chancel arch. In the burial ground there are two 17th-century gravestones. The medieval church was built when the parish of Caputh was erected from Little Dunkeld by Bishop George Brown of Dunkeld (1484–1505/6) and was replaced by the present church in 1798.

5 Clunie Parish Church and Burial-Ground
NO 109 440

West of the motte (see p. 197), the medieval parish church stood where the Kinloch of Gairdie burial enclosure now is. The only survival from the earlier building is a recon-structed, composite arched doorway of the late 12th century which has been re-used in the small, detached building to the south-west of the present church. Stones from the earlier church are also incorporated in the wall of the burial ground, including two with masons' marks at the eastern end of the north wall. In the church there are a number of pewter vessels, communion tokens and a small oak chest. The medi-eval church was on record by 1236.

6 Collace, Kirkton of Collace   NO 197 320

By the unclassified Kinrossie–Pitcur road, 0.75 km south-west of Collace. The medieval parish church stood to the south of the present church where the Nairne of Dunsinnan aisle now lies. Built into the middle of its south wall is a very fine, partially-restored, 13th-century doorway with dog-tooth markings from the early church. There is a fragment of a medieval disc-headed cross in the burial ground. The church was on record by 1242 when it was dedicated to St Euchan by the Bishop of St Andrews.

7 Grandtully*   See p. 223

8 Kinfauns Church, Glen Carse   NO 166 222

The present ruin, 250 m north of the A85(T), measures 21.6 m by 7.9 m, and dates from the 15th century when it attained parochial status. An earlier chapel is on record in 1226 when it was declared a chapel of Scone Abbey. The church has been re-modelled several times since the 15th century but retains several medieval features, including the south doorway and the east window in the south wall. The arched recess in the north wall is probably a 16th-century Easter sepulchre where the reserved Sacrament and Crucifix were housed from Good Friday to Easter.

The 'Gray Aisle' on the south side, founded by John and Janet Chisholm in 1598, is roofed with a late example of groined vaulting (two vaults intersecting at right angles), and displays the Lindsay coat of arms in the central panel and the Charteris arms on the east side.

In the burial ground there are several medieval coped grave-covers. One, at the western end of the south wall, is carved with a floriate-headed cross and a pair of shears; a second has been incorporated in the lintelled embrasure of the north doorway; and a third has been cut to serve as the lintel of a square-headed window at the eastern end of the south wall.

9 Over Kincairney, Clunie   NO 083 440

This chapel lies west of the farmtrack and 180 m S-S-W of Over Kincairney steading, amongst trees and bounded by a low, stony bank. It is 11.8 m by 5.3 m and there is probably an entrance at the west end of its south-western wall.

10 Rait Parish Church and Burial Ground

NO 227 268

Rait church, to the east of the village, a plain rectangular medieval church, is now an ivy-clad ruin, 20.1 m by 6.1 m. Though the east gable is still entire, the other walls stand to a height of only 2.5 m. There is a doorway in the south wall near the south-western corner and two windows in the east side, one at ground-floor level, the other possibly lighting a loft. In the 12th century it was a chapel of the priory of Scone and in the 15th century it became the parish church.

11 Rossie Church and Burial Ground   NO 291 308

In woodland in the private policies of Rossie Priory, 300 m east of the 19th-century mansion. Permission to visit this site should be obtained from the estate office. This bicameral medieval church, 20.5 m by 6.9 m, may well be on an earlier Pictish site – a splendid Class II cross-slab is preserved within the church. Mention in records of 'The Abbacy of Rossie' does not mean that an early monastery existed at this site, for reference to abbacies or *abthainn* lands most often simply records the former ownership of the property by a monastic community elsewhere. It retains a substantial medieval core, including the fabric of the northern and eastern walls and the north doorway which is probably a restored original. In the floor of the chancel, which is now the Kinnaird family mausoleum, there is a slab of Tournai marble depicting a knight and lady of *c.* 1260.

The church was gifted by David I to Matthew, Archdeacon of St Andrews who in turn conveyed it to the canons of St Andrews, a deed confirmed by Malcolm IV. In 1670 it was abandoned when the parish was conjoined with Inchture but it was restored in the 19th century and adapted as a mausoleum.

12 Stobhall, Cargill See p. 217

13 Westown Church and Burial Ground   NO 249 274

On the west side of the unclassified Kinnaird–Westown road, 300 m north of Westown. This late-medieval bicameral or two-compartment church, 15 m by 6.85 m, stands on a ridge of high ground in the Carse of Gowrie. It was dismantled in *c.* 1800 when the chancel was removed but the nave and the blocked-up chancel arch have survived and the west gable, capped by a small belfry, is almost intact. Its early features include slit windows, a round-headed doorway with roll mouldings and lancet windows with cusped head and moulded surrounds. In the south wall, the doorway and two square-headed windows all have glazing grooves. A stoup or vessel for holy water has been removed from by the south door and joist sockets in the middle of this wall may indicate the former position of the post-Reformation pulpit.

The church is on record in 1331 and it is referred to in a charter as the Church of the Blessed Virgin of Inchmartin.

CATHEDRALS, ABBEYS AND RELIGIOUS HOUSES

1 Campsie Linn, Guildtown   NO 124 339

On a rocky promontory on the east bank of the River Tay, 250 m north of Campsie, to the west of the A93 at Campsie Linn, are the wall footings of five ruined buildings round a yard on the site of the residence of the abbots of Coupar Angus. The chapel is 12.5 m by 7 m and was dedicated to St Adamnan.

William I granted the chase of Campsie to the abbey in 1173–78 to provide it with meat, fish, timber and pasture and according to a lease of 1474, 'Robert Pullour shall inherit the mansion of the abbot until further provision, and shall also have the acre of St Adamnan'. Although the lands had been leased out to secular tenants by the 15th century, the abbot and monks of Coupar Angus retained the buildings as a rest-house. A record of 1551 lists the abbot's residence at Campsie as a hall, chapel, chamber, kitchen, bakehouse and brewhouse. Furnishings in the rest-house included four feather beds and four other beds for servants.

Essential viewing

2 *Dunkeld Cathedral*   *NO 023 426*

Although Dunkeld Cathedral is largely medieval, it lies on the site of a much earlier monastic community, the only trace of which can be seen in some of the early sculpture preserved in the chapterhouse. The church is dedicated to St Columba, some of whose relics were brought here for safe-keeping by Kenneth McAlpin from Iona when that island was under threat of attack from Norse invaders. In what was probably a shrewd political move, Kenneth McAlpin then made it the ecclesiastical centre of his united Picto-Scottish Kingdom and it remained so until primacy was removed to St Andrews c. AD 943. The medieval history and development of the cathdral were chronicled by Abbot Alexander Myln of Cambuskenneth in the early 16th century.

Alexander I may have revived the ecclesiastical power of

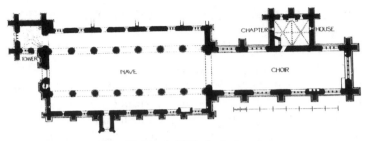

Fig. 12: Dunkeld Cathedral – plan

Dunkeld soon after his accession to the throne in 1107 but most of the fabric of the surviving buildings dates to 1260–1501. The aisleless choir, now used as the parish church, is the oldest part of the present cathedral. It was re-built by Bishop William Sinclair in the early 14th century, completed in 1350 and re-modelled in the early 19th century. An original fragment can be seen in the damaged first pointed arcade in the north wall near the west end, below window sill level. In the north wall, near the pulpit, is an opening: probably a 'lepers' squint', an aperture through which these social outcasts were able to watch the celebration of the mass. It could alternatively have been a window through which pilgrims could see the shrine of St Columba, which was located behind the high altar in the choir. Bishop Sinclair's headless effigy is at the east end of the choir, behind the screen of the communion table and near the effigy in full armour and chain-mail, believed to be that of Alexander Stewart, the Wolf of Badenoch, son of King Robert II.

To the west of the choir is the nave, begun in 1406 by Bishop Robert de Cardeny whose canopied tomb of 1436 is in the Chapel of St Ninian at the east end of the south aisle. De Cardeny, who had been kidnapped from his palace on the south side of the cathedral, had completely rebuilt his residence for greater security. In place of the undefended hall inherited from his predecessors, he constructed a stone towerhouse and adjacent hall-block, which survived until the early 18th century. His work on the cathedral was finished by Bishop Lauder in 1464 during which time the windows were decorated with glass, the roof was completed and the cathedral was dedicated. The plan of the new seven-bay nave with an aisle down each flank was partly conditioned by the way the east walls of the aisles had been built during the mid and late 13th century when the choir was first built.

The cathedral is small by European standards and certain economies can be detected – for example, the corbels and vault springings in the nave suggest that whereas stone vaulting was planned in the south aisle, only timber vaulting was intended for the north aisle. Nevertheless, the internal elevation indicates that Bishop de Cardeny had ambitions for his cathedral. Three distinct storeys have been arranged with a strongly horizontal emphasis, the round arches of the triforium stage echoing the earlier Romanesque style. This revival of the Romanesque in Scotland evidently took place in the late medieval period for it is also prevalent in major 15th-century work at Aberdeen, Stirling and Iona. Alongside such 'old-fashioned' borrowings from an earlier period, there are more modern developments too – the arcade bases are typically late Gothic with their deep profile and the marked separation of the circular base from the polygonal sub-base.

Bishop Lauder added the porch on the south side of the nave and work started on the square chapter-house on the north side of the choir on 13th April 1457. It probably also served as a sacristy, with the treasury in the upper storey. It is now a mausoleum for the Dukes of Atholl and a small museum, housing several fine Renaissance and Pictish monuments. The lower storey is vaulted and the windows have been fitted with shutters, some of which are still in place. A small stoup is cut at the base of the doorway leading to the choir. Bishop Lauder also installed the painting of the twenty-four miracles of St Columba at the high altar, the bishop's throne and the stalls in the choir.

Lauder's most important contribution to Dunkeld Cathedral was the four-storeyed campanile (bell-tower) at the north-west corner of the nave, started in 1469 and completed by his successor, James Livingston. In the ground floor chamber of the tower the most complete scheme of medieval painting to survive in Scotland can be seen on the walls and ceiling vault, giving some indication of the blaze of colour which once adorned the interiors of Scotland's medieval churches. This room was used as an ecclesiastical court room and the paintings present appropriate biblical scenes, including the judgment of Solomon, possibly work of a Flemish artist.

Lauder also altered the west front of the cathedral by building a narrow platform out over the the west door, carried on arches. Above the platform was inserted a six-light window, of which only the stubs of tracery survive.

Bishop George Brown (1483–1515) remodelled the window in the west bay of the south aisle where he established a chapel dedicated to the Virgin. Several furnishings were imported from the Low Countries, but were destroyed in the Reformation.

Following the Reformation, the See was declared void in 1571 and all images, altars and monuments of idolatry were removed and burnt, and the roof was removed. In 1689 there was further plunder when Dunkeld was ransacked by the Covenanting forces who probably burnt down the bishop's palace, the canons' houses and the hospital of St George. It is recorded of the Cameronian regiment that, 'For rendering the place more secure they brought out the seats of the church, which made pretty good defences'.

Essential viewing

3 Fowlis Easter Collegiate Church   NO 322 334

This collegiate church, dedicated to St Marnoch and on record in 1180, lies in the village, east of the unclassified Star Inn–Fowlis road, 10 km west of Dundee. It was built in 1453 for Andrew, Lord Gray as an endowed non-monastic community of secular clergy and retains part of the original timber rood screen, an elaborate sacrament house and painted decoration. It is oblong on plan and may have replaced an earlier mid 12th-century parish church. In its 15th century form it was an unbuttressed timber-roofed rectangle of 27 m by 8.5 m and despite restoration work carried out in 1889, the basic structure of the building is largely medieval. The principal lay entrance was through the south doorway which is surmounted by an ogee or double-curved hood-mould. There is a smaller entrance on the north and the priest's doorway is on the south side of the chancel. Most of the windows are on the south and west and two of them are traceried.

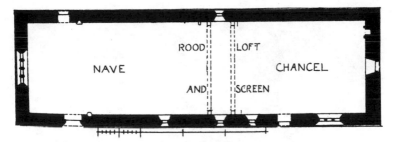

Fig. 13: Fowlis Easter Church – plan

Internally, Fowlis Easter has surprisingly lavish furnishings and fitments for a rural collegiate church. The choir and nave were separated by a timber chancel screen and a loft which was carried on corbels in side walls. Low-level windows to the north and south lit nave altars in front of the screen, with a single upper window on the south side lighting the loft. The timber doors of the screen itself have since been re-set in a modern screen towards the west end of the church.

Part of the Crucifixion painting above the screen has survived as one of the finest pieces of medieval panel painting in Scotland. The painting's edge line indicates the profile of the original ceiling, rediscovered after 1746. Other paintings to have survived include an elongated panel illustrating Christ with apostles and saints, possibly from the front of the loft, and a panel showing Christ as Salvator Mundi, perhaps from an altarpiece.

The Salvator Mundi theme is continued into the sacrament house where Christ is shown flanked by angels holding the cross and flagellation post, over an ogee-headed locker. Above is a carved scene illustrating the Annunciation. The font, though badly damaged, is amongst the finest of its type in Scotland, illustrating scenes of the Passion and Resurrection.

4 Priory Island, Kenmore   NN 766 454

At the north-east end of Loch Tay, near Kenmore Bridge, this is one of the largest crannogs in Loch Tay at 30 m in diameter. Sybilla, Alexander I's wife died and was buried here in 1122, following which the king granted a charter to

Fig. 14: Fowlis Easter Church – sacrament house

the monks of Scone to build a priory on the island, but there is no evidence that this plan was ever put into effect. It later became a nunnery and in the early 16th century the Campbells of Glenorchy converted it to a fortified house, the ruins of which can still be traced.

5 Scone Abbey*   NO 115 265

There are no structural remains of the abbey which probably stood south of Moot Hill and west of the present graveyard in the grounds of Scone Palace (see p 000). Surviving architectural fragments scattered throughout the palace grounds include a fine Romanesque capital, fragments of tracery and the inscribed grave-slab of Abbot Mar.

There may have been an early Christian community established here by Culdees but the first certain foundation was *c.* 1120 when Alexander I founded an Augustinian priory, probably colonised from Nostell, Yorkshire. The priory was elevated to an abbey in 1164 after the previous church was destroyed by fire and at that time the 'Stone of Destiny' was listed amongst its possessions. The Stone was removed by Edward I in 1296 and only returned to Scotland in 1996 but Scone remained a place of coronation even in its absence. In 1318 a Parliament at Scone first recognised the claims of the Stewart succession and in 1371 Robert II was crowned there. The last Scone coronation was that of Charles II in 1651.

In 1559 Scone abbey was ransacked by the Reformers following John Knox's inflammatory sermon at St John's Kirk in Perth and in 1581 it was erected to a temporal lordship when the lands passed to the Earl of Gowrie.

6 Strathfillan Priory, Crianlarich   NN 358 284

The priory lies on the West Highland Way footpath, 50 m west of Kirkton and 4 km north-west of Crianlarich. It is ruinous, its walls standing to a maximum of 3 m high, and the north-west corner has been completely destroyed. To the south-east of the church there are faint traces of other structures represented by stony banks. The priory of Augustinian canons was founded by Robert I in 1317/18 when the church of St Fillan in Glendochart was bestowed on Inchaffray Abbey. Priors are recorded from 1414 until the dissolution of the priory in 1607.

St Fillan became an unofficial patron saint of Scottish kings in need of unifying their country. Not only did Robert I found Strathfillan Priory but he is also reputed to have carried the relic of St Fillan's arm into battle at Bannockburn. There are six relics associated with St Fillan, including a crozier or bishop's staff and a handbell. Similar Celtic bells can be seen in Fortingall and Innerwick churches. Each of St Fillan's relics was in the guardianship of local families who were *dewars* or custodians of the relics by hereditary right. St Fillan was also associated with local healing rituals – healing stones can still be seen in Killin, and the Holy Pool, 5 km from Crianlarich, was the site of bizarre attempts to cure mental illness. Veneration for springs, wells and pools, many of which were – into this century – associated in Perthshire with healing, may be a vestige of an older Celtic religion.

7   Coupar Angus Abbey   NO 223 396

Little remains of the great Cistercian abbey of St Mary the Virgin, founded in 1164 by King Malcolm IV and, by the late Middle Ages, the richest monastery of that order in Scotland. The only remnant is a stumpy pinnacle of masonry in a fenced enclosure beside the main Dundee–Coupar Angus road, comprising a portion of a gate-pend with one jamb of a large window which lit a first floor chamber. Around the 19th-century church, which is believed to largely occupy the site of its medieval predecessor, architectural fragments have been grouped as well as early grave stones recovered during grave-digging operations in the cemetery which overlies the site of the cloister.

Plans for the foundation of an abbey here may have been set in motion by David I, but it was not until 1159 that his successor, Malcolm IV, granted the royal lands of Coupar to the Cistercians. The founding colony arrived to commence building work in 1161 and formal foundation followed three years later. Building operations on the church continued intermittently for nearly 80 years and, although the choir had been completed and was in use for services by 1186, the completed building was dedicated only in 1233. The community appears to have suffered badly in its early years, the worst experience coming in 1186 when Malcolm, Earl of Atholl, cornered a band of outlaws within the monastic precinct. The leader of the captured rebels and his nephew were beheaded in front of the high altar in the church, while the remaining fifty-eight men were burned to death in the abbot's hall, where they had taken refuge.

The later Middle Ages brought wealth and power based on the production of wool from the flocks grazed on the abbey's extensive upland pastures in Strathardle, Glenshee and Glenisla. Its abbots received mitred status in 1464, which gave them the powers of a bishop over their community. At the end of the 15th century, Abbot John Shanwell, whose tomb slab survives, attempted to reverse the decline in religious life amongst the Cistercian order in Scotland, but after his death the abbey became the focus of attention for a succession of wealth-seeking time-servers. The last abbot died in 1563, after whom a succession of commendators was appointed by the Crown until it was erected in 1606 into a temporal lordship for James Elphinstone. Elphinstone appears to have converted the cloister into a private house, which survived until 1645 when it was ransacked by a detatchment from the Royalist army. By 1682 the once extensive buildings were described as 'nothing but rubbish'.

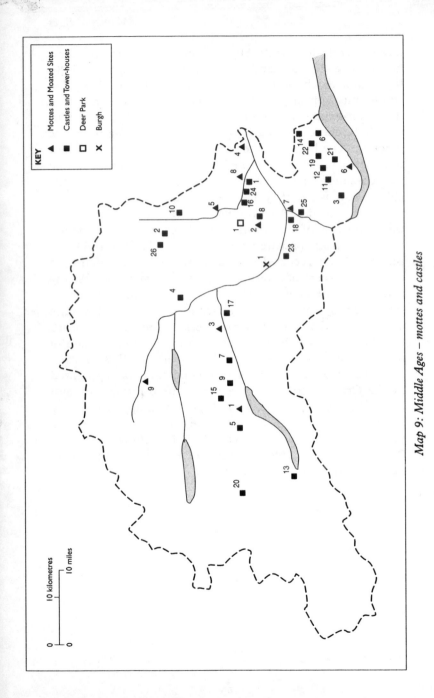

Map 9: Middle Ages – mottes and castles

MOTTES AND MOATED SITES

1 Bridge of Lyon, Fortingall   NN 734 466

On a flat river terrace in a field 200 m south-east of the junction of the Bridge of Lyon and the Glen Lyon unclassified roads. The central area of this medieval homestead moat site, 70 m by 63.5 m, sits 1.5 m above the area around it, with an entrance causeway on the east flank, surrounded by a bank and a broad wet ditch, 15 m wide. There is no trace of the timber buildings which would have stood on the raised inner area. A medieval copper vessel with beak, handle and three feet and a small jar have been recovered from the site.

2 Clunie   NO 111 440

This motte lies on the west bank of the Loch of Clunie on the summit of Clunie Hill, 75 m east of Clunie Church (see p. 184). The 13th-century royal castle on this site probably replaced and incorporated the earlier motte. On the south end of the summit traces of a large building and a curtain wall are still visible. The castle was accessed from a terraced track on the south and the sides of the hill are also terraced.

Clunie is recorded in the Pictish period and later as a royal seat, possibly as a hunting lodge for the Forest of Clunie from *c.* 1141, and in 1296 it was occupied by Edward I. Stone was robbed from the castle to build the towerhouse on the island in Loch of Clunie (see p. 204) and in 1513 four men were employed for a year to clear the remaining rubble.

3 Edradynate Castle, Weem   NN 880 521

The motte, 1 km north of the unclassified Pitnacree–Weem road, is 5 m high with a level summit, 22 m by 6 m. At its base is a ditch and an outer rampart. There are traces of two buildings on the summit.

4 Hallyards, Meigle   NO 279 464

On low-lying arable land, 300 m south of Hallyards Farm and west of the unclassified Bridge of Creuchies–Ruthven road. Unfortunately, this rectangular site, 85 m by 80 m, on a slight eminence and within an 8 m wide ditch, has been severely wasted by ploughing. The interior is featureless and no entrance can be identified. The teinds of Hallyards were recorded in 1506 and in 1727 the house of Hallyards was described as protected from the floodwaters of the River Isla, 'by ditches encompassing it'.

5 Lady Lindsay's Castle, Glenericht   NO 177 488

On a sheer-sided promontory on the west bank of the Ericht Gorge, 400 m east of the A93 and immediately south of Craig Liach. A 4 m-broad ditch and low internal bank with causeway cut across the neck of the promontory to protect this medieval earthwork, 22 m by 18 m. On the south-east are the remains of a rectangular building, 7.1 m by 5.1 m with an entrance in its west wall. There may have been a second building to the west.

'Lady Lindsay' was Janet Gordon of Huntly, wife of Alexander Lindsay, who died in 1489, though there is no documentary evidence to confirm the association.

6 Law Knowe, Errol   NO 231 224

This motte, 750 m north-west of the B958 Errol–St Madoes road, at the west end of a broad ridge in the Carse of Gowrie, has a roughly oval summit, 13 m by 11 m. There is no evidence of a bailey. In the late 19th century a burial vault was built into it and a stone cross was added to the summit.

This was probably the *caput* or seat of the Hays of Errol who received lands from William I in 1178–82. The 'Mote' of Errol is on record in 1507.

7 Meikleour   NO 153 387

Thirty metres west of Meikleour House, on the edge of a river cliff on the east of the River Tay. This motte is 5 m high on the S-S-E, with a circular summit 22 m in diameter. A slight depression on the summit is the site of a doocot.

At the beginning of the 13th century, Meikleour was held

by the earls of Strathearn. In 1318 it was granted by Robert II to Malcolm de Innerpeffray and in 1363 David II confirmed its sale to John Mercer.

8 Rattray   NO 210 454

Two and a half kilometres east of Rattray, 300 m south of the A926 Rattray–Alyth road. Unfortunately, the motte and two baileys were mutilated by quarrying in the 1970s. Only parts of the upper bailey with its 2.5 m-thick enclosing bank, and the outer bailey, 28 m by 11 m with its bank and 7.6 m-wide ditch, now survive. The Rattray family owned the site from the reign of Malcolm Canmore (1057–93) until the early 16th century.

9 Tom an Tigh Mhoir, Struan   NN 807 653

On the south bank of the River Garry, 150m west of Old Struan church. This large grassy mound, nineteen square metres, has an irregular flat top and a ditch on the south and west. The foundations of a rectilinear enclosure may be modern.

CASTLES

1 Ardblair, Blairgowrie   NO 163 445

This privately-owned castle, 50 m south of the A93 and clearly visible from the road, is one of few to retain its courtyard intact. It is a three-storey-and-attic L-plan tower-house built in the late 16th century, at which time it may have been defended by a loch, since drained. A wing projects from the main block to form a re-entrant angle, on both sides defended by gunloops. A pediment above the fine-arched gateway is dated 1688 and the entrance in the inner re-entrant angle has an ornate but uninscribed panel above. A wide staircase leads to the first floor in the wing which is panelled in 18th-century style.

The lands – a fifth of the parish of Blairgowrie – were granted by David II to Thomas Blair in 1399 and passed to the Oliphants of Gask through marriage in 1792. The Castle houses material relating to Lady Caroline Nairne (*nee* Oliphant, 1766–1845) who wrote a number of popular songs, including 'Charlie is My Darling' and 'Caller Herrin'.

2 Ashintully, Kirkmichael   NO 101 612

This privately-occupied, small, stepped L-plan tower-house of the late 16th century is 2.5 km from the Kirkmichael Hotel where the public footpath to Lair in Glen Shee begins. It comprises a main block of three main storeys. Extruded on the south-west is a four-storey accommodation and stair-wing. It has an unusual single open parapet or bartizan which crowns the wallhead above the doorway on the south side. The entrance in the south-east re-entrant angle is surmounted by an elaborate heraldic panel with the initials of Andrew Spalding, and the date 1583, inscribed, 'THE LORD DEFEND THIS HOUS'. Additional defences include wide-splayed gunloops at basement level on the south, west and east and a circular shot-hole on the north front at second-floor level. The tower-house was much restored, altered and extended in the 18th and 19th centuries and although the ruinous Whitefield Castle nearby (see p. 219), was built for the Spaldings on exactly the same plan, it is now difficult to make comparisons between the restored Ashintully and the ruinous Whitefield.

In 1587, local lairds besieged Ashintully and took Andrew Spalding prisoner. John, Earl of Atholl, put up bail for the agressors who were his kinsmen so when they did not appear in court they were outlawed and John was accordingly fined. In 1677 Ashintully was erected to a free barony with rights to hold two fairs each year and a weekly market.

3 Balthayock, Kinfauns   NO 174 229

At the west end of Glen Carse, 100 m east of the unclassified Oliverburn–Kinfauns road, by Balthayock House. This fine example of a late 14th or early 15th-century keep has been the seat of the Blair family since the reign of William I (1165–1214). Rectangular in plan, 15.9 m by 11.7 m, it has three storeys with walls 3.6 m thick, and an open parapet carried on continuous corbelling. There are machicolated projections at second-floor level on the south front, over-hanging a precipitous ravine. A 19th-century forestair leads up to the first-floor main entrance, replacing an earlier remov-able timber stair and an heraldic panel bears the date 1578 and the initials AB and GM. Tusking at the east angle indi-cates the former presence of a barmkin or outer wall.

The tower was remodelled *c*. 1870 with the addition of the crenellated parapet, the forestair, and the caphouse crowning the stair to the parapet: and the floor levels have also been altered.

4 Caisteal Dubh, Moulin   NN 947 589

In a field, 300m south-east of Moulin church, 90 m west of the footpath between Moulin and Edradour. A fragment of this 13th-century stronghold, 30 m by 26 m, with 2 m-thick walls up to 9 m high, survives on a platform. It has been a large quadrangular enclosure surrounded by high, solid walls, strengthened with round towers at each angle. The foundations of the south-west tower and an internal wall can still be traced. Though there is no evidence of a moat, there may have been a loch here in the medieval period.

When the estate was forfeited by the Earl of Atholl, Bruce gave it to his brother-in-law, Sir Neil Campbell of Lochawe. His second son, Sir John Campbell, had no heirs, so the estate passed back to the Crown. It was conferred on William Douglas, Lord of Liddesdale, who resigned it in 1341 in favour of Robert, Great Steward of Scotland.

5 Carnbane, Invervar   NN 677 479

In woodland to the north of the unclassified Glen Lyon road, 1.25 km south-east of Invervar. This 16th-century tower-house sits on the spur of an escarpment which is ditched to the north, possibly on the site of an earlier motte. There are horizontal gunloops on three sides. On the east there is a vaulted storage cellar and on the south an unvaulted kitchen. A stair-tower has been added at the south-west, blocking entry to a small court to the south because of its location on the spur. There are wall foundations around the perimeter of the court .

6 Castle Huntly, Longforgan   NO 301 291

This 15th-century L-plan tower-house lies 1.25 km south-west of Longforgan, west of the unclassified road between Longforgan and Powgavie and is now a Young Offenders' institution. It stands on a volcanic knoll above the Carse of Gowrie and is built of sandstone quarried from Kingoodie. Erected for the 1st Lord Gray of Fowlis Easter in 1452, it originally comprised three main storeys. There are three vaulted cellars, part-cut into the rock, one of them probably a prison pit accessible only from a trap-door in the guardroom above, and in the floor of another was sunk a well, now filled in. There was no permanent internal stair to the main levels – a passage in the guardroom vault was accessed by a removable ladder.

The property belonged to the Grays until 1614 when it was sold to Patrick Lyon, Lord Glamis and it was sold again in 1777 to George Patterson. A high barrel vault in the hall was removed in the 17th century when an extra floor was inserted and in the 18th century the top storey was altered again with the addition of sham angle turrets, battlements, and a windowed caphouse. At the same time, a Georgian two-storey building with two wings and an entrance hall with oval, glazed cupola was added to the east.

There is a mid 17th-century ice house built of hand-made bricks in the face of the slope 100 m north-east of the castle. Entry is by a 3 m-long passage.

Essential viewing

7 *Castle Menzies, Weem**   *NN 837 496*

This excellent example of a Z-plan tower-house, signposted 150 m north of the B846, is now open to the public as the Clan Menzies museum. Its main block comprises three storeys and an attic and the square towers at opposing corners each house

Fig. 15: Castle Menzies – view from south-east

*five storeys. On the vaulted ground floor of the main block are
the kitchen, larder, stores and guard rooms. The hall and withdrawing rooms are on the first floor and on the second floor are
the private apartments, strong room and guest rooms.*

*Comrie Castle (see p. 205) was the first seat of the Menzies
clan, and when it was burnt down, Sir Robert Menzies built
a new mansion known as 'The Place of Weem'. This, in turn,
was burnt down by Neil Stewart of Garth and a new castle was
built here at Castle Menzies by Robert's great-grandson, James.
It is in a strategic position, commanding Strath Tay and the
road to Rannoch, and there are a large number of gunloops at
every aspect of the tower-house – little wonder given the record
of the previous two Menzies strongholds.*

*In 1577 the upper storey and roof were altered and dormers
with elaborate pediments were added. One dormer pediment
bears the initials IMB, the date 1577 and the motto 'IN OWR
TYME' and a lintel is inscribed 'PRYSIT BE GOD FOR
EVER'. The original entrance at the south-west tower, guarded
by gunloops, is surmounted by an heraldic panel with the arms
and initials of James Menzies and his wife, Barbara Stewart,
daughter of the Earl of Atholl, commemorating their marriage*

and the concession by *James* to his wife of the life-rent of Weem
in 1571.

In 1646 the castle was occupied by General Monck's forces
and in 1715 the *Jacobites* took and occupied the castle. In 1746
the family were ejected and the Duke of Cumberland's forces
moved in, four days after Charles Edward Stuart had spent
two nights there.

In the early 18th century, the angle of the north tower and
the main block were enclosed by a new set of apartments with a
connecting stair. The present entrance and the west wing were
added in 1840 and extensive interior redecoration was undertaken. In 1918 it ceased to be the seat of Clan Menzies and
during the 1939–45 War it became a Polish Army medical
stores depot. Finally, it was acquired and restored by the Clan
Menzies Society in 1957 and the 18th-century north wing
which was beyond repair was demolished.

8 Clunie   NO 113 440

On an island in Loch of Clunie, between Dunkeld and Blairgowrie. This ruined L-plan tower-house was built for the
bishops of Dunkeld. In the mid 15th-century, the island and
old castle on the west shore of the loch became the refuge of
robbers. They were evicted and by 1506 construction of the
tower-house had begun. A survey of the submerged portion
of the island suggests it is probably artificial. The edge of the
island is enclosed by the remains of a low rubble wall and
there is a small quay on the south.

There are three storeys and an attic in the main block of
the tower-house and five storeys in the wing. The stair tower
is round and at the top there is a watch tower with twin
windows, possibly not original. The entrance is protected by
high level machicolation and arrow slits and opens to a newel
or spiral stair. A straight mural stair, now blocked, gave independent access to the first-floor hall and chapel in the wing.
The kitchen with large fireplace is in the basement of the
main block. Several alterations were made between the late
16th and 19th centuries. The tower was still roofed in the
earlier part of this century.

At the Reformation, Bishop Crichton sold the Clunie lands to his relative, Robert Crichton, on the condition that they would revert to the Church if the Reformation collapsed.

9 Comrie   NN 787 486

This ruined Menzies stronghold can be seen from the road-side in a private garden, 50 m east of the unclassified Keltneyburn–Fearnan road. It was burnt down in 1487 and rebuilt *c.* 1600 as the home of a cadet branch of the family. It is a small L-plan keep, 7.9 m by 5.8 m, of three storeys and an attic, with a vaulted basement. The doorway in the re-entrant angle is roll-moulded and above it the base of the corbelled stair-turret survives.

10 Corb, Forest of Alyth   NO 164 568

All that remains of this castle which lies by Corb farmstead, 1.5 km north of the unclassified Alyth–Glen Shee road, is a low grassy mound, 18 m by 12 m. Nearby, there are more than five buildings reduced to turf-covered footings, measuring from 10 m by 5 m to 27 m by 6 m. It is said to have been the hunting seat of the Scottish kings and of the earls of Crawford. From the 17th to the mid 18th-century, it was the property of the Rattray family but by 1783 it had become ruinous.

11 Evelick, Kilspindie   NO 204 259

This ruined late 16th-century, stepped L-plan tower-house lies immediately south of the unclassified Kilspindie–Dalre-ichmoor road. It comprises a three-storey-and-attic main block and a wing which has its main entrance and stair in the semicircular tower in the south-east re-entrant angle. Above the main entrance is an empty panel space. The doorway in the north re-entrant is probably later though it has also been protected by gunloops. The vaulted basement and the floors above have collapsed and the attic storey has also gone except for the gunloops below its dormer windows. Additional accommodation was provided in a 17th-century

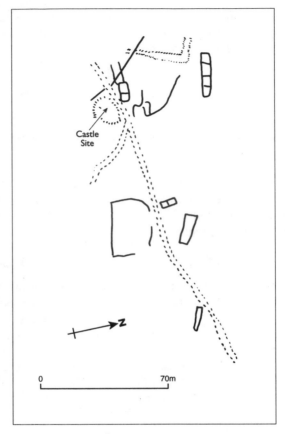

Fig. 16: Corb Castle

two-storey range indicated by openings and tuskings in the east gable. The Lindsay family owned Evelick from at least 1497 until 1799 when the last Evelick Lindsay died in a drowning accident.

12 Fingask   NO 228 274

This late 16th-century L-plan tower-house of three storeys and an attic, 500 m north-west of the unclassified road between Baledgarno and Glendoick, has been much altered.

A wing was added at the west in 1674 and further additions were made in the 18th and 19th centuries. It has also lost its square stair-tower from the re-entrant angle and no towers or turrets remain though there are a number of original gun-loops and shot-holes and iron yetts over the windows. The vaulted kitchen in the basement of the wing has a gunloop at the back of the arched fireplace. On the first floor is a fine hall with withdrawing room in the wing with garderobes and mural closets while the floor above contains accommodation.

The earliest known owners were a branch of the Bruces of Clackmannan who sold the estate to the Threiplands, a Peebleshire family. It was forfeited following the first Jacobite uprising but Lady Threipland bought it back from the notorious York Building Company. However, dragoons once again occupied the towerhouse during the second Jacobite uprising and it was not restored until 1816, after which it was again alienated from the family. There is notable topiary work in the garden and 19th-century figure groups which include Charles Edward Stuart and Flora MacDonald.

13 Finlarig, Killin   NN 575 338

On a knoll by the entrance to Finlarig Mains, 500 m along Pier Road in Killin, beyond the cemetery. This has been a Z-plan tower-house but the tower on the north-east angle has been demolished and the rest of the building is in a dangerous condition. It is built on a mound, probably on the site of earlier castles, and is dated to 1609 by a panel over the entrance which bears the royal arms and the intials of James VI. On the vaulted ground floor there is a kitchen with stone drains, two cellars and a good square staircase in the wing. The hall is, as usual, on the first floor with private rooms in the wing. A small modern, brick-built chapel replaces the early 16th-century burial place of the Breadalbane family on the mound, but this itself is now derelict and choked with rubble. To the north of the tower-house there is a stone tank with overflow drain, probably for storing water but known as the Execution Pit. Nearby are the Gallows Tree and Judgment Hill, a small artificial mound.

Fig. 17: Finlarig Castle – view from south-east

14 Fowlis Easter   NO 322 334

Now a farmhouse and formerly the village alehouse, this was a much larger establishment comprising a quadrangle with high outer walls, corner towers and a portcullis, the seat of the Lords Gray. The remaining part is the Lady's Tower or Bower, dated to the early 17th century but incorporating earlier phases in the lower masonry: for example the wide-splayed gunloop at the front of the massive chimney stack. It is a simple oblong with a more recent wing added to the north, with a circular stair-tower and projecting chimney stack on the south front. The chimney is outstanding, housing the flue for the huge kitchen fireplace, offset at each floor level as it rises. The main block is three storeys and an attic high, and the stair-tower is one storey higher. The pediment of an original dormer window, dated 1640, has been incorporated in an adjoining property. The main doorway in the foot of the stair-tower gives access to a newel stair and the upper floors.

Fowlis Easter was granted by David I to Wiliam de Maule

for gallantry at the Battle of Sauchie. In 1138 it passed to his son-in-law, William de Mortimer, and in 1377 to Sir Andrew Gray, first Lord Gray of Fowlis. Sir Andrew also built Castle Huntly and owned Broughty Castle.

15 Garth, Keltneyburn   NN 764 504

The square tower, 1.5 km north-west of Keltneyburn, privately owned and occupied since its restoration in 1950, sits in a well-defended position on a promontory between two deep stream gullies. Around the promontory there are faint traces of a curtain wall which is also indicated by tusking or protruding stonework in the outer wall of the 12.7 m by 9.0 m keep. Within the castle there is a basement with two vaulted pits, lit only by arrow slits. The first floor, formerly vaulted, contained the hall with a huge fireplace and windows with stone seats. The vaulted storey above provided dormitory accommodation for men-at-arms.

The castle was built on land acquired by Alexander Stewart, the Wolf of Badenoch, under whom construction may have begun. In the early 15th century, his descendants, the Stewarts of Atholl, occupied, rebuilt and restored it. In 1502 Nigel Stewart of Garth raided Weem Castle, burned it and took Robert Menzies prisoner, incarcerating him in the vaulted dungeon at Garth and threatening to starve him to death unless he gave up his rights. Stewart also reputedly arranged the murder of his own wife and was imprisoned in the tower for nine years until his death in 1554.

16 Glasclune, Blairgowrie   NO 154 470

One kilometre east of the unclassified Kinloch–Middleton road, and 140 m E-S-E of Glasclune steading this ruinous tower-house of *c.* 1600 is composed of two detached elements which were possibly joined at an earlier period. On the south is the surviving part of the L plan block with a stair-turret in the north-west re-entrant angle. A portion of the accommodation wing with stair-turret survives on the north and on the north-east is a three-storeyed circular tower, most of which has collapsed since it was sketched over a century ago.

There is a walled courtyard to the west. Glasclune belonged to the Blairs in the 17th century.

17 Grandtully Castle   NN 891 515

This privately-occupied Z-plan tower-house, 100 m south of the A827, can be viewed from above from St Mary's Church (see p. 223). It incorporates an earlier free-standing keep, built into an L-plan tower-house in 1525, and now comprises an oblong main block with square towers at opposite angles, each one storey higher than the main block. Unusually, a circular stair-tower has been added in the south-west re-entrant, heightened to form a watch-chamber with an ogee roof, dormer windows and angle turrets in 1626 when the entire upper floor and roof-line were re-modelled for Sir William Stewart and his wife, Agnes Moncrieff. A guardroom protects the entrance in the south-west tower, with a prison pit below. Abutting the north-east wing is a small chapel, the loft of which can be entered from the first floor of the house.

The ground floor is vaulted with two parallel cellars in the main block and a kitchen in the north-east tower, with garderobes off the passage. The wood-panelled hall on the first floor and the laird's private chamber in the north-east tower are accessed by a passage in the thickness of the east wall with garderobes off it. A dormer window on the circular stair-tower is dated 1626 with the Stewart arms. Grandtully has been the headquarters of various military commanders including Montrose, General MacKay, Argyll and Charles Edward Stuart and belonged to the Stewarts from the 14th century.

18 Kinclaven Castle   NO 158 377

On the west bank of the River Tay in woodland, 150 m south of the unclassified Meikleour–Murthly road. This is a square courtyard enclosure, formerly with square towers at each corner. Nothing remains of the interior lean-to buildings which would have been built against the curtain wall.

Kinclaven Castle was built between 1210 and 1236

Fig. 18: Grandtully Castle

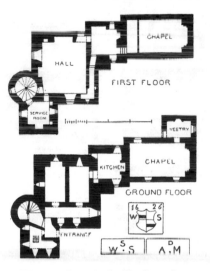

Fig. 19: Grandtully Castle – plan

following the destruction in a flood of the royal castle at Perth and was a favoured residence of Alexander II. Its plan is very similar to that adopted at that king's other major building projects – Tarbert in Argyllshire and Kincardine in the Mearns. A large quadrangle with the main apartments (hall, chamber, kitchens etc.) ranged round the inner face of the courtyard. Although it is still recorded as a royal castle in 1264, during the reign of Alexander III – it was probably by then mostly occupied as a garrison castle rather than a royal residence. Either way, it has had a chequered history, having been destroyed by Wallace in the mid 13th-century, held by Edward III in 1335, and recaptured by the Scots in 1336.

19 Kinnaird Tower   NO 241 289

On a terrace, reached by a flight of steps, this 15th-century oblong keep with small projecting tower or buttress at the south-west angle is 400 m north-west of Kinnaird church. Still occupied as a private house, it is 11.8 m by 8.4 m and

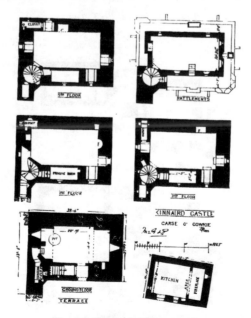

Fig. 20: Kinnaird Tower – plan

Fig. 21: Kinnaird Tower

18.3 m high, with four storeys and a gabled garret above the parapet. There has been a courtyard or outer bailey on the west and there are the remains of an enclosing wall at the north-west corner.

The entrance to the tower at basement level is through an arched doorway protected by an iron yett or gate. A straight flight of stairs then joins a wheel stair to the upper floors. A second entrance at first-floor level in the buttress tower is now reached by a stone forestair. This entrance is fitted with double doors, the outer one folding over like a drawbridge, and the sockets and iron ring for raising and lowering the chain are still in place. Originally, it would have accessed the parapet walk round the top of the walling of the courtyard, 4.5 m above ground. The parapet has machicolated projections.

The ground floor has only been vaulted at either end, the central section supporting a timber ceiling on corbels. There is a dungeon-pit cut out from the rock, 5.5 m deep and 1.4 m in diameter and in the south-west wing there is another small pit in the thickness of the buttress base.

A stair rises to the first floor in the thickness of the wall, leading to the hall with two stone window seats, mural chamber and garderobe with drain. A turnpike stair in the wall of the south-west corner leads to the upper floors, each room with round chambers and garderobes. There are garderobes in the walls of the upper floors and the soil at the north end is thrown clear of the walls by projecting sloping stones.

To the east of the tower is a free-standing two-storey 17th-century building. The later kitchen within this building has an enormous fireplace and hatch at the gable next to the tower. A dormer window on the second floor bears the initials PT and MO and is dated 1610. In the reign of William I (1165–1214), the castle belonged to the Kinnaird family but the estate was bought by Sir Patrick Threipland of Fingask in 1674. It was roofless in the mid 19th-century until restored in 1880.

20 Meggernie, Glen Lyon   NN 554 460

This 16th-century privately-occupied castle 300 m south of the Glen Lyon road probably incorporates an earlier building. It is a square tower of five storeys with square corbelled corner-turrets to which a more recent mansion has been added. The door in the south front leads to a vaulted basement and there are shot-holes beneath many of the window sills. Meggernie was a stronghold of the Menzies family of Culdares.

21 Megginch, Errol   NO 242 246

This privately-occupied Z-plan tower-house 750 m east of
the A85(T) was sited on marshland originally. Although it
was re-modelled in the 19th century, the north front is largely
unaltered. It comprised a simple oblong main block of three
storeys and an attic with a circular stair-tower on the south,
corbelled out to a square at the top to form a watch-chamber.
Two conical-roofed corner-turrets at the north-west and
north-east ends of the main block are connected by the
parapet, interrupted by the stair-tower. There are several
wide-splayed gunloops at ground level. The main block has
a kitchen and two vaulted cellars on the ground floor, with a
hall and a chamber on the floor above.

Over one window is inscribed 'PETRUS HAY AEDIFI-
CIUM EXTRUXIT AN 1575'. Originally the towerhouse
belonged to the Hays, later to the Drummond family. The
various window levels give some indication of the amount of
alteration undertaken since the 16th century.

22 Moncur, Inchture   NO 283 295

The ruins of this late 16th or early 17th-century Z-plan
tower-house, 200 m north of the A85(T), lie in the policies of Rossie Priory. Permission to visit the ruins should
be sought from the estate office. It comprises a three-
storey main block with two towers. The north-east tower
is square; that on the south-west is circular. The entrance
was in the re-entrant angle of the square tower. The main
building houses the kitchen, with springing for a large fireplace, oven and slop-sink, and a service-corridor connects
the kitchen with two store-rooms. The ground floor has
been vaulted but only the portion over the wine cellar
survives and from one of the cellars, a service-stair leads
to hall level and the upper floor. The first-floor hall has a
wide fireplace, mural press and garderobe. On the second
floor there have been two chambers. Accommodation was
in the two towers.

During the 15th century, the tower-house belonged to a
branch of the Kinnaird family and in the 16th century it

became the family seat. It was abandoned after a fire in the early 18th century.

23 Murthly Castle   NO 072 399

The castle lies 2.5 km along a track, accessed from the B9099, on the south bank of the River Tay. In the 16th and 17th centuries, this was a small free-standing square tower with later extensions to form three sides of a square. The early tower was four storeys and an attic high with angle-turrets decorated with quatrefoil gunloops. Near roof level on the east front there is an heraldic panel bearing the Stewart arms and dated 1617. The upper storeys were altered in the late 16th century when angle turrets were added along with the first extensions, including a gabled tower to the south-east, linked by a later building. In the mid 18th-century a two-storey pedimented entrance hall with Venetian doorway approached by an external staircase was added. A walled garden was laid out in 1669 in Dutch fashion with terraces, pools and clipped hedges.

In the medieval period Murthly Castle may have been a hunting seat of the Scottish kings. In 1615 it came into the possession of the Stewarts, Barons of Grandtully, and in the early 19th century, the sixth baronet began building a new mansion, still unfinished, near the castle.

24 Newton Castle   NO 171 452

This is a privately-occupied, late 16th-century Z-plan tower-house with square and round towers and a watch-chamber. The main block is three storeys and an attic high with a stair-wing on the south-east and a round tower corbelled square to form a watch-chamber on the north-west. Only the west wing of the main block is vaulted. The original door in the square stair-tower is protected by a gunloop and in the lowest corbel of a tiny stair turret above second floor level on the east front, a human face has been carved.

Newton Castle belonged to a branch of the Stobhall Drummond family. There are some fine 18th-century interiors.

25 Stobhall, Cargill NO 132 343

The medieval chapel on this site, 250 m east of the A93 and 3 km south-west of Cargill on the east bank of the River Tay, influenced the design of the tower when it was converted to a ground floor hall. There are four unconnected buildings at different angles and levels, all within an irregular retaining courtyard wall – the dower house with kitchen and parlour by the pend; the laundry block on the west wall; the chapel and accommodation block in the centre of the courtyard; and the kitchen block in the east wall.

The entrance is through the pend by a long two-storey block with dormer windows and crow-stepped gables: this was the dower house with large kitchen and living room

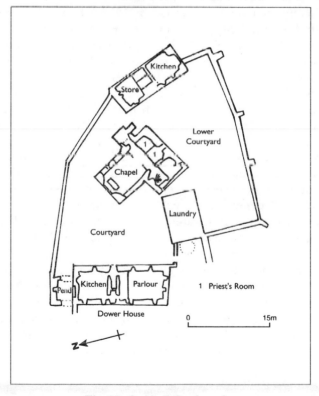

Fig. 22: Stobhall Castle – plan

and accommodation above. The early 17th-century arms of John Drummond, second Earl of Perth, and his wife Lady Jane Kerr, are carved above the entrance. This dower house which, more recently, was the home of Ruskin, Effie Gray and John Everett Millais, includes a turretted priest's house: for the Drummond family remained Catholic beyond the Reformation and continued to hold Roman Catholic services. The priest's house rises to three storeys and an attic with two conical towers on the south-west angle.

The late 16th-century L-plan chapel and three-storey-and-attic dwelling block has a two-storey angle turret at the south-west corner. It was erected by David, 2nd Lord Drummond whose arms and initials are on the outside, dated 1578. The rectangular, medieval private chapel, 13.4 m by 6.8 m, was converted for secular use in 1578 when it became a ground-floor hall attached to the tower-house until its restoration in 1840. Despite these alterations, it retains a number of medieval features, including a zoomorphic skewputt at the south-east angle; a deeply-splayed trefoil-headed window in the north wall; an aumbry door; a stoup or vessel for holy water; an altar slab; and an arch-pointed doorway re-set at the entrance of the basement created beneath the west end of the chapel. The ceiling was decorated in 1642 and has been heavily re-painted since then. It is divided into five compartments, each containing two kings on horseback (with the exception of *rex mauritanae* who appears on an elephant) and ornamental panels, with the Drummond arms and motto. One compartment illustrates a row of caltraps or spiked balls, thrown to the ground to deter cavalry attacks, with the highly-appropriate Drummond motto, 'Gang Warily'.

Next to the chapel is the late 16th-century laundry range, two storeys high, with brewhouse and bake-house. To the east is a later domestic range, since remodelled as a library.

This was the main seat of the Drummond family, granted to them by Robert I after Bannockburn. It became the dower house when Drummond Castle was built in 1487.

26 Whitefield   NO 089 617

This ruinous stepped L-plan tower-house is 2 km north-east of the A924, up a private track from Dalnagairn. It was built for the Spaldings in the 16th century, altered in the late 18th century, abandoned by the early 19th century, and partly demolished to build the neighbouring steading. A panel above the entrance is dated 1577.

The ground floor is divided into two barrel-vaulted compartments. To the east is the kitchen which has an arched fireplace, stone basin and drain. A recess behind the door would have held a block of wood placed to prevent the back bars of the entrance door from being forced from the outside. On the south is a service-corridor and in the west wall there is a mural service-stair to the hall. A scale-and-platt stair leads to the first floor hall with a turnpike stair to the upper levels.

To the south are the wasted remains of a barmkin or wall connecting on the north-west with a ditch. The bank may be an original causeway.

Ashintully Castle, 1.2 km E-S-E, renovated and occupied, is very similar in its plan and features (see p. 200).

DEER PARK

Buzzart Dykes, Middleton Muir   NO 127 473 and
                                            NO 134 479

The south side of the deer park enclosure lies 1.25 km W-N-W of West Gormack, parallel with the south bank of the Lornty Burn. The north side is 1 km W-N-W of Middleton steading. A bank up to 1.4 m high and ditch up to 1.2 m deep encloses around 86 ha of deer park on Middleton Muir. The enclosure has been obliterated on the east by cultivation but is quite well preserved on the west where it is up to 10.1 m wide. There is no evidence of the original entrance.

BURGH

Essential viewing

Dunkeld   NO 026 426

The River Tay is said to have been bridged at Dunkeld by 1461 and a hospital is recorded there in 1506. It was erected as a burgh of barony in 1511/12, by which it was granted increased privileges, including the right to hold an annual fair and a weekly market. Much of the town was destroyed by fire after the battle of Killiecrankie in 1689 when the Cameronians, government troops, drove out the Jacobites by setting fire to the town, and only one 17th-century house, the Dean's House, now survives. The sites of other buildings can be identified from the blocked windows and doors in the precinct wall of the cathedral. The houses of the secular canons on the north and west were levelled by the Atholls for the policies of Dunkeld House. Lining the sides of Cathedral Street and The Cross are the 'Little Houses', built to replace the medieval houses burned in 1689.

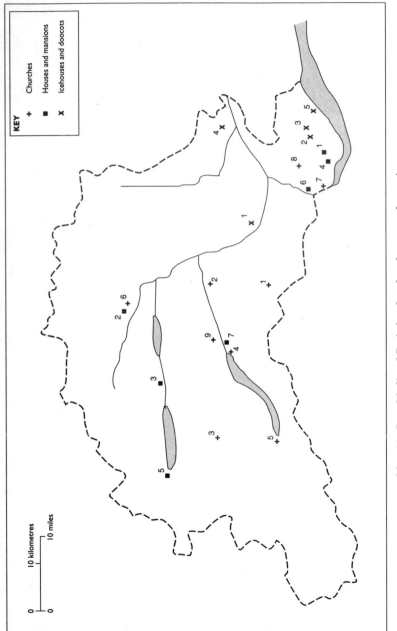

Map 10: Post-Medieval Period – churches, houses and mansions

KEY

Churches   +

Houses and mansions   ■

Icehouses and doocots   ×

POST-MEDIEVAL SITES

CHURCHES

1 Amulree   NN 899 366

Amulree church, west of the A822, was built between 1743 and 1752 and remodelled in 1881–2 by John Douglas of Edinburgh who was also responsible for the church at Killin (1743) and who Palladian-ised Blair Castle (1736) and designed Taymouth Castle (1746).

The church has a vaulted ceiling, carved oak pulpit with matching carved 'table' and spacious windows. The bell was cast in 1519 in Mechlin, Belgium, by William van den Ghein who also made the bell for Henry VIII's warship, the *Mary Rose*.

Essential viewing

*2 Grandtully**   *NN 886 506*

St Mary's Church is signposted from the A827 Logierait–Aberfeldy road and a footpath leads to it from the car park. It is a simple pre-Reformation church on plan, first recorded in 1533 when Alexander Stewart of Grandtully gave lands to the priory of St Andrews as an endowment for a priest to serve here. The pre-1533 building was shorter than the later one and the two principal building phases can be traced on the outside of the south wall, seen from the burial ground. All the original windows on the south have been blocked up. Within the church, there are two aumbries or cupboard recesses in the east and north walls, the latter a sacrament house for storing the Host after Mass.

Alexander's great-grandson, Sir William Stewart, enlarged and repaired the church in 1636, adding a remarkable Renaissance-style painted timber vault over the eastern third of the interior. There are twenty-nine panels in the painted ceiling, interspersed with fruit, flowers, cherubim and birds. They depict the arms of local landowners, including the Lairds of Grandtully and the Earls of Atholl, as well as biblical illus-

223

trations with scriptural texts. The central panel promotes the virtues of a Christian death, showing the figure of Death about to claim the occupant of a fine canopied bed.

The door and two flanking windows towards the west end are not framed by dressed stone and are probably part of the 1636 additions. There is a lintel over the window in the gable end inscribed with the initials of Sir William Stewart and his wife.

3 Innerwick, Glen Lyon   NN 587 475

On the south side of the unclassified Glen Lyon road. An Act of Parliament of 1824 allowed for the building of forty-two new Parliamentary churches in the Highlands and Islands. Thomas Telford was to supply standard plans and specifications for these churches, of which this is an example. A Celtic bell from an earlier church at nearby Bridge of Balgie is now kept in the porch of Innerwick Church.

4 Kenmore   NN 772 454

William Baker, an architect from the Midlands, designed Kenmore church in 1760 in a style of architecture ahead of its time. Gothic Revival did not become popular until the early 19th century and Kenmore church seems to have had no local impact on the design of churches. The present church, at the west end of the village by Loch Tay, incorporates an earlier church built in 1669 and was remodelled around 1869 when the tower was added. The bells, cast in 1759, were made by Thomas Janaway of London.

5 Killin   NN 573 334

Immediately east of the A827, this Renaissance-inspired church of 1744 was built by Thomas Clerk, a Dunkeld mason, to plans by John Douglas. It is octagonal in plan with a pyramidal roof, a slated cupola, belfry on the north gable, aisles projecting to the east, west and north, and a centrally-placed pulpit. The aisles had lofts and to the south is a low projecting session house. It was altered in 1831 when the east and west aisles were widened on the north side, the octagonal gallery inserted and the windows altered. Further alterations were made in 1903.

6 Kilmaveonaig Chapel, Blair Atholl   NN 879 657

St Adamnan's Episcopal Church, 300 m north of the Blair Atholl service road, was rebuilt in 1794 to replace the church of 1591. The 16th-century church itself replaced a parish church which is recorded here in 1275. It is one of very few old parish churches which is still in the possession of the Scottish Episcopal Church. For some years after 1688 the four parish churches of Blair Atholl, Struan, Lude and Kilmaveonaiag continued in use, with Episcopal services held at the latter two until they were combined *c.* 1700.

Kilmaveonaig church was restored in 1866–71 and enlarged in 1899. Its old bell is dated 1629 and was brought here from Little Dunkeld.

7 Kinnoull   NO 123 233

On the east bank of the River Tay, on the outskirts of Perth, an older church on this site was rebuilt in 1779 and the present church dates from 1826. In the north aisle of Kinnoull church is the fine Jacobean tomb of Lord Chancellor Hay, first Earl of Kinnoull, who died in 1634. The monument depicts him standing in his Lord Chancellor's gowns, surrounded by ornate *momento mori* symbols.

8 St Martins   NO 155 304

South of the farm track to Rosemount, this 1842 church displays several features of the Perpendicular Gothic style. It is T-plan with porches and stairs in the re-entrant angle and with gable belfries. It was designed by Andrew Heiton Senior of Perth and its original fittings include an imposing pulpit with crocketed sounding board, precentor's desk and double stairs. There is a 17th-century mural memorial by the steps leading to the boiler house, and a detached session house.

A church was recorded here in the 12th century, known

Fig. 23: Monument in Kinnoull Church

then as Megginch church but later dedicated to St Martin of Tours. During the medieval period, it belonged to the abbey of Holyrood.

It is the third church design on this site since the Reformation, replacing others of 1622 and 1733.

Essential viewing

9 Weem*   *NN 843 498*

The old church, dedicated to St Cuthbert, is at the west end of Weem, on the north side of the B846 Aberfeldy–Killin road. Collect the key from the custodian as directed on the kirk door. It now houses a small collection of local carved stones, including two early medieval free-standing crosses from Dull (see p. 168), as well as the mausoleum of the Menzies family. A church at Weem is first recorded in a charter of 1235 but the present building is mostly the result of remodelling of the medieval church by Alexander Menzies in 1609 to conform to Reformed practices, and later modifications in the 18th century. The initials of Sir Alexander Menzies and his first wife, Margaret Campbell, appear with their coats-of-arms above the outer door lintels.

There are some surviving features of the late medieval church, which would have been a simple rectangular structure, probably with a thatched roof. The chancel at the east end would have been divided by a simple wooden screen from the nave and the altar would have stood against the east wall with a wall recess or aumbry on either side.

After the Reformation, the altar and chancel screen were removed and the pulpit became the central focus. The transept was converted into the laird's loft with a small retiring room at the rear with a fireplace in the north wall. At the same time, the windows were enlarged and a belfry added over the west gable. During the 18th century, the kirk was heightened by 0.6 m and later, a gallery added at the west end. The 18th-century iron jougs or neck collar survive and are on display in the church.

The Menzies Memorial is a very fine Scottish Rennaisance carved stone cenotaph of 1616, erected by Sir Alexander Menzies to celebrate his maternal ancestors and two wives. The two kneeling figures are Sir Alexander on the left and his first

Fig. 24: Monument in Weem Church

wife, Margaret Campbell, on the right. The two large figures are representations of Faith (right) and Charity (left).

Around the walls of the church there are several funeral escutcheons belonging to the Menzies family. These banners were displayed outside the homes of the deceased during the period of mourning and were in use in the 17th–19th centuries.

HOUSES AND MANSIONS

1   Balthayock House, Glen Carse   NO 175 230

East of the unclassified Oliverburn to Kinfauns road, this house was built in 1870 by James MacLaren, incorporating French and Scottish elements. Its unusual features include a granite-columned loggia and a front door which slides on rollers. The interior was sumptuously decorated with columns, stained glass and carved balusters.

Essential viewing

2   Blair Castle*   NN 865 661

Signposted to the north of Blair Atholl village. Blair Castle has had a chequered history. Most of what is seen today dates to the 1870s but there have been at least three earlier periods of major construction on the site. In 1269 a complaint was made by David, Earl of Atholl to Alexander III that John Comyn of Badenoch had begun to build a tower at Blair. The foundations of that tower probably lie under what is now known as Comyn's Tower at the extreme right. In 1530, the Hall range was built by the 3rd Stewart Earl and in the 18th century its two upper storeys, turrets and parapets were removed during its trans-formation to 'Atholl House', an early Georgian mansion, by James Winter in 1747–58. The interior is decorated in superb Rococo style by the plasterer Thomas Clayton and the English carpenter Abraham Swan, engaged during Winter's remodel-ling.

In the 1870s, David and John Bryce of Edinburgh were commissioned by the 7th Duke of Atholl to remodel the house. They obliterated all of its Georgian features with their

Scots Baronial design, adding crowsteps, turrets and bartisans, features of which John Comyn and the 3rd Stewart Earl would probably have approved.

In 1633 Blair Castle was stormed by Cromwell's commander and was held by his troops until the Restoration and in 1689 it was garrisoned by Claverhouse before the battle of Killiecrankie. Like many Atholl families, the Murrays were divided over the Jacobite Rebellions. The Duke of Atholl and his second son were loyal to the government in 1715 but the elder son, William, Marquis of Tullibardine and his younger brothers, Charles and George, were Jacobites. In 1745 Charles Edward Stuart stayed at Blair Castle but the house was then occupied by Hanoverian troops and attacked by the Jacobites. Queen Victoria visited in 1844 and presented the Duke with Colours for his men, the Atholl Highlanders, the only remaining private army in Europe.

3 Dunalastair   NN 710 588

South of the B846, Kinloch Rannoch–Tummel Bridge road, this house was built in the 1850s around the core of an older building for General Sir John MacDonald by the Perth firm of Andrew Heiton and Son. In lively Scots Baronial style, with a symmetry reminiscent of French chateaux, it is crowned with a huge pepper-pot tower and features a very fine ornate doorpiece with carved mouldings and coat-of-arms. The main internal feature was a grand double staircase, now collapsed. The earlier house, known as Mount Alexander, was built around 1796 by Alexander Robertson.

4 Kinfauns Castle   NO 150 226

Lying 250 m north of the A85(T), the situation of Kinfauns Castle largely dictated the plan of the building with its two main fronts facing south and east tied together by a square keep behind which offices cluster round small open courts. Designed by Sir Robert Smirke, 1820–26, architect of the British Museum, in the castellated Gothic style for Francis, 14th Lord Gray, the effect includes two ruined watch-tower follies on the crags above. The castle stands on a raised terrace, with a frontage of 48.8 m and an imposing central flag tower, 25.6 m high. Alterations were made by Sir Robert Lorimer in the 1920s.

The estate was held by the sons of Robert II in the 14th century and in the 15th century it passed to the Charteris family. The fine home farm and dairy were designed by Robert Lorimer in the 1920s.

5 Rannoch Lodge, Bridge of Gaur   NN 507 574

At the head of Loch Rannoch, this was one of the early 'gentry mansions', constructed in the remoter parts of upper Perthshire after the 1745 uprising. It was built for Sir Robert Menzies in the mid 18th-century as a two-storey, three-bay mansion, and altered for him between 1798 and 1803 to serve as a shooting lodge when two asymmetrical wings with splayed ends were added. It was damaged in 1985 by a bad fire.

Essential viewing

6 *Scone Palace, Old Scone**   *NO 113 265*

Signposted from the A93 Perth–Blairgowrie road, 0.75 km west of Old Scone. This is an early example of an asymetrically-planned Neo-Gothic Georgian mansion. It was designed by the English architect, William Atkinson, who also designed Abbotsford, and it was completed in 1813 for the 3rd Earl of Mansfield. It incorporates fragments of an earlier, 17th-century house built for David Murray, Lord Scone, who was granted the estate in 1604 by James VI for support during the Gowrie plot. Charles II resided here for his coronation ceremony in 1651.

The palace encloses three inner courtyards and its roofline is battlemented, with square and polygonal towers along the four facades. The interior has some extremely fine plasterwork in the style of Robert Adam and as the 2nd earl was ambassador to the court of Louis XVI, there are also excellent collections of French furniture and porcellain.

The pinetum was begun in 1848 by the 3rd earl and features Douglas firs grown from seed sent here by the former sub-

gardener, David Douglas. In order to establish the pinetum as well as the lawns and terraces, the old village of Scone was completely removed to a new site. The village cross, gateway, moot hill and a bit of the parish church are all that remain, scattered about the policies.

7 Taymouth Castle, Kenmore   NO 784 466

The castle lies 1.5 km north-east of Kenmore and its grounds now incorporate the remnants of a 20th-century military camp and a golf course. The 16th-century tower-house, Balloch Castle, former seat of the Campbells of Breadalbane, was remodelled in 1733 by William Adam who added to the main block two low-flanking classical wings, only the altered west wing of which remains. The square central block, designed by Archibald and James Elliot, architects of Edinburgh's Register House, dates to 1806–10. In 1838, Adam's west wing was enlarged and remodelled by James Gillespie Graham who also added a high Gothic room to his remodelled chapel. It is thought that Gillespie Graham was assisted by Pugin in the design of this room which, with its profuse use of intricate carving of wood work, highlighted by gilding, is extremely rich. When Victoria and Albert visited in 1842 this room was the state dining room. There are very fine neo-Gothic interiors with plasterwork by Bernasconi and ceiling decoration by Frederick Crace.

ICEHOUSES AND DOOCOTS

1 Dunkeld House Icehouse, Stanley Hill*
NO 029 427

Park in the public car park at the north end of Dunkeld from which the icehouse is sign-posted a short distance along a woodland path. Ice houses were widespread on country estates in the 17th and 18th centuries to ensure supplies of fresh meat in winter. Usually, they were sited on well-drained slopes, with most of the building below ground and blocks of ice deposited above – up to three years' supply at once. The entrance was secured by insulated doors edged with leather.

This icehouse probably dates to the 18th century and supplied fresh meat to the Dukes of Atholl at Dunkeld House, built in 1627 and demolished in 1825. At 6.25 m deep, it held about 20–30 tonnes of ice.

2 Kilspindie Doocot   NO 219 258

This late 17th-century rubble-built lectern dovecot, 7.9 m by 5.1 m, is in a field to the north of the unclassified Kilspindie-Evelick road and to the north-west of where the tower-house is thought to have stood, close to the 19th-century farmhouse. There are three gables with landing ledges in the roof, stone boxes, and a stepped rat ledge. The doocot incorporates a fragment of medieval tracery above the rat-ledge in the south wall.

3 Kinnaird Castle Doocot   NO 242 288

This rubble-built rectangular doocot with sloping lectern roof and plain gables possibly dates from the 17th century, though the skews and back wall cope are 18th century. A sculptured stone tomb slab featuring incised concentric circles interlaced with straight lines, and a pair of shears, has been re-used in the inner lintel of the door.

4 Polcalk Doocot, Alyth   NO 233 464

Three hundred metres south of the A926 Rattray–Kirriemuir road, at the west end of a range of outbuildings on Polcalk Farm. This 17th-century rectangular lectern doocot has a string course and a lean-to slated roof and is divided into two compartments with three hundred and eighty stone nesting boxes. The walls have been harled and whitewashed and at a later date crowned with a battlemented parapet.

5 Waterybutts Doocot, Grange   NO 277 259

This fine two-compartment lectern doocot, 8.7 m by 4.6 m, lies 0.5 km north of the unclassified Errol–Inchture road,

90 m E-N-E of Waterybutts farmhouse. At the skews there is a stone dated 1733. Though now roofless, it is stepped and finialled and retains its original iron-framed doors and iron yetts. There are paired bird entry ports in the side walls and originally in the roof also. The rat-course has been stepped but on the south wall it has been cut back.

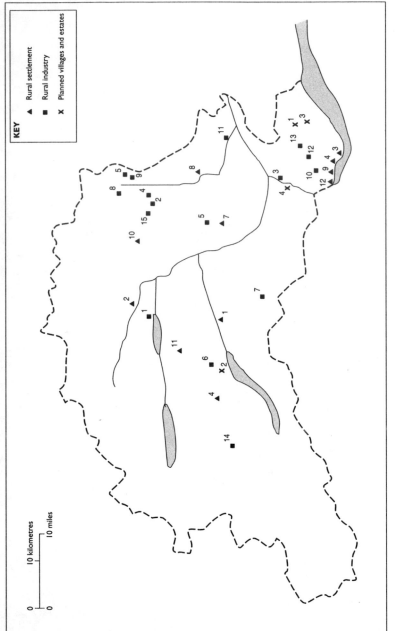

Map 11: Post-Medieval Period – rural settlement and industry

RURAL SETTLEMENT

Essential viewing

1 Allean Forest Settlement, Loch Tummel*
NN 859 603

Park at the Allean Forest car park on the north side of the B8019, 500 m west of the Queen's View Visitors' Information Centre, and follow the way-marked track up to this settlement. Excavations in the 1970s revealed that it was probably established some time prior to the mid 18th-century and abandoned in the 19th century. There are three buildings, each with their own small yard and, on the north-east, a corn-drying kiln.

House I has been reconstructed using the cruck holes on the north and south to carry a birchwood roof. During the early period of occupation it was a dwelling house with a central hearth but, at a later stage, it seems to have been adapted as a work room for wool processing. A pile of heather roots found on cobbles in the eastern half may have been intended as a source of dark brown dye, and a pit showing evidence of burning was the likely site of the cauldron used for concocting such dyes. Two uprights with an elaborate drainage system below were possibly used for hanging up newly-dyed fleeces to drip, while at the north end there were postholes for a carding loom.

House II had no hearth and was probably never in domestic use, for its two opposed doors suggest it was a winnowing barn, which would have required a good through draught.

In House III only the two gable ends survive. The drystone fireplace at the west end indicates that this was a dwelling house in the final phase of occupation at least.

The corn kiln lies across the track to the north-east, its chamber part-cut out of living rock. Originally, its lintelled flue would have been short but it has been lengthened at a later date for the burning of limestone. The inhabitants of this settlement may have been involved in smithy work at the re-used homestead site to the east (see pp. 174–5).

2 Ashintully Settlement, Kirkmichael   NO 102 621

Follow the old head-dyke to the southern spur of Cnoc an Daimh, 200 m west of the Kirkmichael–Lair public footpath to this *fermtoun* above the improved fields. There are two separate groups of buildings, 50 m apart. In the western group there are four units, each with a yard, and a kiln-and-chamber to the east. Further to the east is the second group of buildings with a kiln. Although the area is within the barony of Ashintully, erected in 1615, it cannot be identified with any lands recorded prior to the early 18th century when it is documented as *Brae of Ashintully.*

3 Cargill Cruck-Framed Cottage   NO 150 369

The remains of this 18th-century cruck-framed cottage lie in a field W-N-W of Cargill Parish Church, 400 m north-west of the A93 Perth–Blairgowrie road. It is gable-ended, 12.9 m by 5.6 m, divided into four bays by crucks. The walls are built of clay-bonded rubble masonry and there is a mason's mark on the jamb at the S-S-W end of the W-N-W wall. Original features include a fireplace, slab-lined aumbries, the window and a blocked press. It was re-roofed and slated in the 19th century and other modifications have been made this century, including the demolition of the N-N-E gable for use of the building as a garage. It is illustrated *c.* 1760 on 'A plan of the Mains of Cargill'.

4 Craigies Settlement and Corn-Drying Kiln
NO 119 624

The settlement of Craigies is scattered along the lower slopes of Lamh Dearg to the north of the Ennoch Burn, accessed by the Kirkmichael–Lair public footpath. It comprises about twenty buildings, corn-drying kilns and small enclosures separated from the hill land by the head-dyke. The buildings vary in size from 5 m by 3 m to 37 m by 4 m and some are very well preserved. There would appear to have been two main phases of depopulation, the first in the early 19th century and then again in the early 20th century.

To the south-east of the main building at Craigies, is an extremely well-preserved kiln-barn, 12.6 m by 4.7 m and up to 1.5 m high. The bowl is 2.1 m in diameter and 1.1 m deep and the lintelled flue can still be identified.

Downslope from the farmstead to the north-west is a group of lynchets – banks resulting from ploughing – up to 2 m high and 4 m broad, bounded by a head-dyke.

5 Craigsheal Laird's House and Fermtoun

NO 063 511

To the north of the track, at the break of the slope below Craigsheal, 530 m north-west of Loch Benachally, 7 km north of Butterstone amidst an area of Bronze Age settlement (see p. 137). These are the ruins of a *tacksman's* or

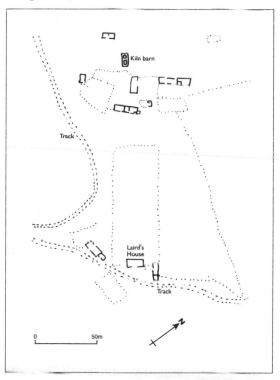

Fig. 25: Craigsheal – fermtoun and laird's house

laird's house and a small *fermtoun* of the late 17th or early 18th century. The rectangular gable-ended house, formerly two-storeyed, measures 14 m by 7 m over clay-bonded walls. The entrance is in the south-east wall, flanked by two splayed window-openings and in the north-east gable there is a lintelled fireplace. In the north corner there is a flue, probably for an oven, and in the upper storey there can be seen a fireplace and a mural press.

The laird's house is flanked by two buildings and 100 m uphill there is a kiln-barn and a three-compartment building. Two hundred metres W-N-W of the *fermtoun* on a terrace there is a single shieling hut. To the north of the laird's house and fermtoun, the hills form an amphitheatre where, on the north and east, there are at least twelve shielings, some overlying hut circles.

Craigsheal was amongst the lands inherited by Thomas Tynie of Drumkilbo in 1635. The laird's house was ruinous by the late 18th century though the *fermtoun* may have been occupied into the 19th century.

6 Drumcharry Shielings, Fortingall   NN 748 487

North of the unclassified Keltneyburn–Fortingall road, 1.25 km north-west of Drumcharry, there are nine shielings astride a hollow way from Drumcharry farm. They are turf-covered foundations of earth and stone, 6 m long and 2 m–3 m wide. Several have dividing walls and two have bowed long walls, one with a rounded end. One building has been excavated into the hillside, 9.7 m by 4.8 m with a 1.2 m-wide entrance. Halfway between the shielings and Drumcharry and close to the west side of the hollow way there is a flax retting pond with a building below.

7 Glen Cochill Shielings   NN 902 408

Five hundred metres west of the A826, below Meall Dearg and within an old field wall are ten oval and circular turf and stone shielings, 1.8 m–4 m in diameter and 0.3 m–0.7 m high. On the west side of Glen Cochill and 500 m south-west of White Cairn there are about twenty shieling huts, small cairns, rigs and banks. The shieling huts are in two groups on the east and north sides of an enclosure defined by a stony bank, 1.5 m thick and 0.5 m high. Several huts have outshots, and mounds outside two of them may have been middens. In the western half of the enclosure there are traces of rigs with furrows 4 m apart.

Essential viewing

8 Glen Shee Settlements   NO 107 704 – NO 112 705

The 2.4 km between the church at Spittal of Glen Shee and Dalmunzie to the north-west, west of the A93, is an excellent example of a pre-Improvement landscape. Most of the settlements which include fermtouns, farmsteads, buildings, mills and shielings, are to be found across the breach of the hill slope, along the turf-and-stone head-dyke. Below is a short description of some of the major settlement sites on the north side of the Shee Water, accessed from a track between Spittal Church and the bridge. Unfortunately, there is no convenient crossing point on the river to allow a circular walk which takes in the sites on the other side of the river, listed at the end of this account.

Essential viewing

8.1   NO 107 704

At the foot of the plantation, 200 m N-N-W of Spittal Church, just below the head-dyke is the fermtoun of 'Spittale of Glensche', recorded in 1542 and in 1615 as 'Chapel-crofts'. Most of the sixteen buildings are set around yards and the largest is of three compartments, 22.4 m by 5.4 m, probably of more than one period of construction. On the slopes below there are the remains of rig-and-furrow cultivation and a series of lynchets, much destroyed by ploughing. Below the track, on the haughland or meadow land by the river, there are clearer traces of cultivation. This settlement site was still in occupation in 1808.

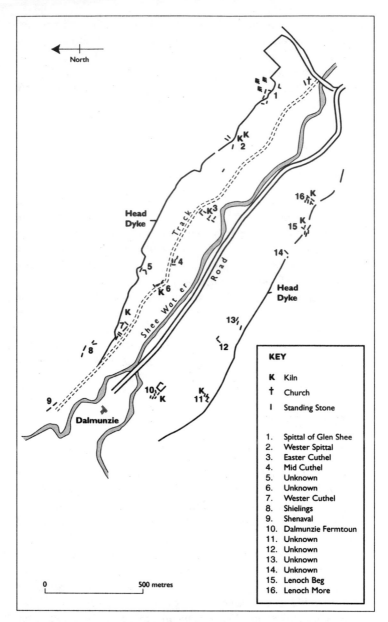

KEY

K	Kiln
†	Church
I	Standing Stone

1. Spittal of Glen Shee
2. Wester Spittal
3. Easter Cuthel
4. Mid Cuthel
5. Unknown
6. Unknown
7. Wester Cuthel
8. Shielings
9. Shenaval
10. Dalmunzie Fermtoun
11. Unknown
12. Unknown
13. Unknown
14. Unknown
15. Lenoch Beg
16. Lenoch More

Fig. 26: Glen Shee – settlements

Essential viewing

8.2   NO 105 705

Further along the hillside, on the neck of a spur above a small plantation, is the ruined farmstead of Wester Spittal which had been long abandoned by the early 19th century. The main building is of two compartments and measures 23 m by 4.2 m. In the lea of a hollow on the S-S-E side there are two corn-drying kilns, one with a chamber, and uphill from the head-dyke, terraced into the hillside, there are two buildings at opposite ends of a yard.

Essential viewing

8.3   NO 102 702

The farmstead of Cuhacherach, later Easter Cuthel, lies on either side of a modern field-wall, 320 m W-N-W of Wester Spittal. There are six buildings and a kiln around three yards.

Essential viewing

8.4   NO 099 709

Near where the track fords an unmarked burn and 270 m north-west of Easter Cuthel is the farmstead of Mid Cuthel, consisting of four buildings. North of the building is a probable mill, 9.3 m by 5.2 m, set end-on to the burn. To increase the flow of water to the mill, a tributary has been diverted upstream, and the burn has been canalised and partly dammed. West of the mill is a kiln.

Essential viewing

8.5   NO 099 710

At the rear of a hollow by a burn and interrupting the head-dyke is a small farmstead with buildings on two sides of a yard. On the north side, there is a two-compartment building with rounded angles, 14.3 m by 4.2 m. The east wall incorporates a byre-drain and a drainage bank extends along the rear wall.

Essential viewing

8.6 **NO 098 709**

Seventy metres W-N-W of Mid Cuthel (see 8.4) is a farmstead of six buildings, a yard and an enclosure which has been culti-vated. To the south and east there are some excellent examples of lynchets up to 2 m high downslope, partially overlain by rig-and-furrow.

Essential viewing

8.7 **NO 097 711**

The remains of Wester Cuthel are located 120 m north-west of 8.6 (see above), clustered in two groups of buildings. In the E-S-E cluster there are two buildings at right angles to each other, with a kiln and an enclosure. The north-west building with its opposing entrances was possibly a threshing barn. Its neighbouring building on the east has two compartments, each with a central byre drain, and a drainage bank extends the length of the rear wall. To the front there is a stone-revetted terrace on the S-S-E of which are two rick-bases. Upslope are the remains of a kiln. The second cluster is on a terrace to the north-west and also features buildings with byre drains and external drainage banks. Below the farmstead are traces of rig-and-furrow and a kiln, while on higher ground to the N-N-W lies a possible shieling hut, 8.2 m by 4.2 m.

Essential viewing

8.8 **NO 095 713**

At the foot of scree on the south-west flank of Ben Gulabin, to the north-west of 8.7 (see above), are the remains of four shieling huts and enclosures, measuring from 5.1 m by 3 m to 9 m by 4.4 m. The best preserved and largest has round-angled corners.

Essential viewing

8.9   **NO 091 715**

One hundred metres north-west of 8.8 (see above) is the farm-stead of Sheanval, by the ruins of a 19th-century cottage. There are two buildings, a small yard, and traces of rig-and-furrow to the south-west.

There are similar settlement remains on the other bank of Shee Water:

NO 092 710	Dalmunzie fermtoun – eleven buildings, two enclosures and a kiln
NO 092 707	farmstead of seven buildings and kiln
NO 095 706	two buildings in an enclosure, a possible flax mill and retting pools
NO 096 705	three buildings
NO 100 703	two buildings, a yard and an enclosure
NO 101 702	farmstead of 'Lenoch-beg' – six buildings, a kiln and chamber, and an enclosure
NO 103 701	'Lenoch-more' – nine buildings, a kiln, rig-and-furrow, and lynchets
NO 112 705	Mill of Spittal – traces of a mill, lade, weir and pond.

The lands of 'Spittale of Glensche' were on record in 1542 and of Cuthil and Dalmunzie in 1510 and 1543. Spittal fermtoun may be of this date or earlier. Dalmunzie and Cuthel were mapped *c.* 1600 with 'scheeles' or shielings at the head of Gleann Taitneach and Glen Lochsie. By the time of Roy's Military Survey of 1747–55, Spittal fermtoun had been abandoned and the population had moved near the mill at the Military Road. There were then three farmsteads on the north side – Shanwell, Chial and Cuhacherach – and three on the south side – Dalmunzie, Lennoch-beg and Lenoch-more. By the late 18th century the population had expanded and there were seven farmsteads on the north, Cuthell having divided into Wester and Easter. Dalmunzie was probably the seat of the McIntosh laird and a lintel over the door of the cottage at Leanoch Mhor bearing the inscription, 'THE LORD DEFEND THIS HOUS', with the initials PMT and IR and dated 1658, probably came from the earlier laird's house. Most of the Glenshee settlements had been abandoned by 1808, by which time the population centre had shifted to the site north-east of the chapel at Spittal, beside the Military Road and close to the Mill of Spittal.

9 Invereddrie Fermtoun   NO 136 689 – NO 135 678

There are very extensive and well-preserved settlement remains to the north and south-west of Invereddrie farmhouse, 1 km east of the A93. It includes at least sixty-four buildings with enclosures, yards and pens, three kilns, two mills and a head-dyke. The land and mill of 'Innereddre' are recorded in 1510 and 1629 and a map of 1783 shows a fermtoun of three building clusters and mills. There is a particularly well-preserved early improvement farmstead in the lea of a knoll, 600 m N-N-E of Invereddrie steading. The largest building has a drainage gully to the rear and a stone-revetted terrace in front, separating the building from the midden which is evidenced by a scoop on the south-west. There are extensive traces of rig-and-furrow to the west.

10 Law Hill Settlement, Arnbathie   NO 171 258

On a narrow terrace, below the eastern defences of the fort (see p. 151), south of hut circles (see p. 156) and 50 m east of the unclassified road between Glendoick and Bonhard. This rectangular structure, 10.3 m by 5.4 m, has been reduced to low footings, 0.3 m high, though several outer and inner facing-stones can still be identified. A low field bank abuts the north-east corner of the building and there is a small enclosure on the north-west side.

11 Old Mains of Rattray Laird's House   NO 206 452

By the farm-track, 550 m W-N-W of Mains of Rattray stands

the roofless ruin of a late 17th-century laird's house which was re-modelled in 1770 and 1800. It is two storeys and an attic high with clay-bonded walls and originally it had a symmetrical five-bay frontage. A weathered lintel over the entrance is inscribed with the name and arms of David Crichton and dated 1694. Details include moulded skews carved with human heads and an original fireplace on the ground floor. Glazing grooves in the window jambs witness the use of leaded lights over timber shutters and there is evidence of barred ground floor window openings. The roll-moulded surrounds of the attic windows may have been re-used from an earlier building.

In 1720 a single-storey extension was built on to the west gable of the original house, incorporating a large kitchen fireplace. This annexe may have been a brewery, a common feature on farms into the mid 19th-century.

12 Over Fingask Settlement, Rait   NO 226 288

Seven hundred metres north of Over Fingask up a track beyond Fingask Castle (see p. 206), off the unclassified Rait-Baledgarno road, on the east side of an extensive field system, there are the wall-footings of five buildings and two rectangular enclosures, 10.4 m by 5 m. The largest building, 13.9 m by 6.4 m, is L-plan in shape, with a principal range of two compartments.

13 Pitmiddle   NO 244 296

In the Braes of Carse, 600 m west of the unclassified Abernyte–Kinnaird road, lies a jumble of low walls and mounds, some of the first post-Agricultural Revolution improved buildings. The site has long been deserted and overgrown, with walls averaging 0.6 m wide and to a height of up to 4 m. The earliest reference to Pitmiddle is in a charter of 1172/74, in which William the Lion granted Kinnaird to Ralph Rufus, except *Petmeodhal*. The tenants paid *cain* or tribute to their lord into the 17th century in the form of *cain fowl*.

Pitmiddle was a typical toun with single-storey thatched houses, shared with animals at one end. Its lands were divided into sunny and shady portions and in the 17th century its main crops were bere, oats and flax.

Improvements in the Carse of Gowrie began *c.* 1735 and drainage commenced *c.* 1760, allowing a new turnpike road to be built between Perth and Dundee. Pitmiddle never had a piped water supply and was finally abandoned in 1938 when its population emigrated to Canada and to towns and cities with better amenities.

14 Riadhailt Shielings   NN 582 416

There are around one hundred shieling huts and pens along both sides of the upper Allt Bail a Mhuilinn on the southern side of the unclassified Bridge of Balgie–Lawers road, leading to Coire Riadhailt. There is a further concentration of settlements on the river banks of the Allt Breisleich, 2 km north-west, to the west of Allt Bail a Mhuilinn. Most are of typical stone-walled construction, banked up externally.

15 Whitefield Settlement   NO 085 616

There are a number of farmsteads around the tower-houses of Ashintully and Whitefield (see pp. 200, 219). This group lies 400 m W-S-W of Whitefield Castle, on the north side of the track and on the lower slopes of Whitefield hill. There are five buildings and four pens at the foot of a knoll and another of each to the north. They range from a single compartment, 11.5 m by 5.1 m, to a four-compartment building, 25.5 m by 4 m. About 100 m to the north, across a burn, there is a kiln and three retting pools. This is probably the settlement marked as *Edenarnochkie* on a map of 1783 and recorded within the barony of Downie in 1510 and 1629.

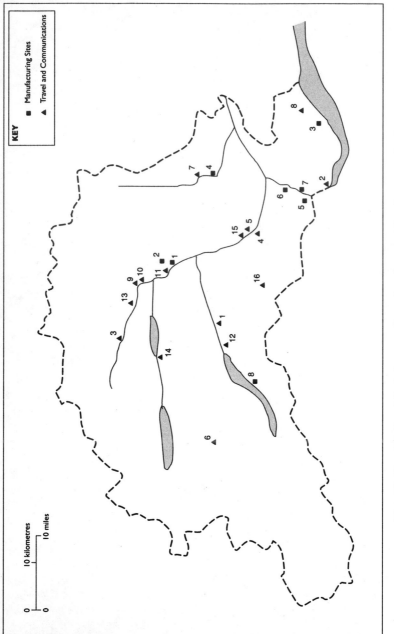

Map 12: Post-Medieval Period – manufacturing sites, travel and communications

KEY

■ Manufacturing Sites

▲ Travel and Communications

RURAL INDUSTRY

1 Aberfeldy Watermill * NN 855 491

Signposted south of the A827 in the centre of the town, this is a two-storey rubble building on an L-plan with brick and wood additions and a pyramidal roofed kiln with unusual ventilator, built in 1825. The mill lade runs 150 m from the Birks of Aberfeldy underneath the town to the Mill. It has a 6.1 m diameter, eight-spoke overshot water wheel of wood and iron which powers two pairs of 1.4 m diameter French burr stones, each weighing 1.5 tons, plus ancillary milling equipment. The mill was restored to full working order in 1987.

Essential viewing

2 Blair Atholl Watermill* NN 872 652

Signposted from the Blair Atholl service road in the centre of the village. There has been a water mill on this site since the early 17th century though the current mill building dates from c. 1830–33. A gabled kiln projects from a bay, with a small roof-ridge ventilator. The eight-spoke paddlewheel, 4.27 m in diameter, has wooden spokes and paddles and iron rings and axle. The oldest part is the main three-storey block to which the kiln and two-storeyed granary have been added. The mill stopped working in 1929 but has been refitted and re-opened since.

3 Cairnie Fishery, St Madoes NO 196 192

The oldest of the 19th-century buildings on the north bank of the River Tay are two one-storey-and-basement rubble-built stores. From the rear, there is a 0.6 m guage railway, partly laid with bridge rails, which runs to the beach on the Tay for loading salmon. Into the 20th century, a small cobble boat ran between the Pier and Ferryfield on the opposite bank. The bothies or lodges for the fishermen comprised a single room with seven wooden bunks, with no light or ventilation.

4 Inchyra Village and Pier   NO 183 203

The village and small rubble pier date to *c.* 1800 when Inchyra was a busy commercial centre. There are two rows of two-roomed rubble cottages and a two-storey 'pier-house' with oriel windows on the upper floor.

Essential viewing

5 *Invereddrie Still, Green Glen*   NO 143 707

Park at Glenshee Lodge and follow the footpath and landrover tracks east of Invereddrie for 3 km, out towards the shieling area. Shortly after the track meets the Allt an Daimh, look out for a large pyramid-shaped boulder to the west of the track, south-east of Carn an Daimh. Behind the pyramidal boulder, hidden from view, there are the remains of a probable still and a ruined building. The still, divided into three bays by crucks, has been built into the north-west side of a knoll and was mostly below ground level. Water was chanelled into the building through a lintelled opening from the nearby burn by a lade. Diametrically opposite is a plinth and outflow channel, the latter obscured by the rebuilt side wall.

The two principal requirements of an illicit still, seclusion and water, are well met at this site. Within the building would have stood the copper pot-still, lyne arm and coiled pipe or worm for the distillation processes, all easily joined and dismantled at a moment's notice.

On a spur 90 m west of the still on the scree above, lies a ruinous two-compartment building while W-N-W of the still lies a group of thirteen huts and pens around an enclosure. There are several other clusters of shielings on both banks of the Allt an Daimh, in the vicinity of the still.

6 Invervar Lintmill, Glen Lyon★   NN 665 483

Signposted opposite the telephone box in the village, to the north of the unclassified Glen Lyon road. This small, late 18th-century lint mill, probably designed and built by Ewan Cameron of Lawers, is circular and two-storeys high with a conical roof. The site of the narrow waterwheel can be identified on the west and the lade is still clearly defined. The mill was entered at ground floor level on the south and at first floor level on the north and was positioned to achieve the maximum fall of water. The upper floor was probably used for storage as there is a trap door through which the flax could be fed down to the machinery below.

The flax was pulled before it ripened then soaked in retting pools to open the fibres. Prior to mechanisation, after it was dried it was beaten with a mallet to release the flax fibres. Then it was 'scutched' or whipped to separate the fibres from the woody 'boom', before it was spun.

With mechanisation in the 18th century, the flax was bruised by rollers and then revolving blades separated the boom from the fibres. This small mill at Invervar probably only housed bruising rollers.

7   Leduckie Horse Gin, Butterstone   NO 068 466

Three-quarters of a kilometre north of the A923 Dunkeld-Blairgowrie road. This 19th-century horse gin has an open horse wheel with its wooden arms removed, mounted on a circular mound edged with a drystone rubble wall. The spur wheel of the threshing mill drive survives.

8. Old Milton of Drimmie, Glenericht   NO 160 512

This well-preserved building lies at the foot of a slope, 110 m south-east of Old Milton of Drimmie, off the unclassified Strone Bridge–Drimmie road. It measures 12.7 m by 6.5 m and on the north is a debris-filled kiln which would have been accessed from a forestair to the kiln floor. Traces remain of the scarcement for the stone floor and the wheel-pit's position can still be identified. The lade can be clearly traced to the W-N-W. Tracks lead down from Old Milton of Drimmie to the mill which was already without its roof in 1808.

9   Seggieden Commercial Icehouse, Kinfauns
NO 163 216

This commercial icehouse, south of the A85(T), was built in the 18th century. It is one of the smallest commercial icehouses recorded, though the salmon fishery there was one of the largest on the Tay. During the 18th century, fish sales to Billingsgate Market in London increased with the development of ice-packing to keep the fish fresh.

Icehouses were designed to allow the ready quarrying of ice. In winter, they were filled with broken ice, then sealed and insulated, and during the fishing season the ice was used to fill the fish-boxes.

10 Straloch Lime Kiln, Strathardle   NO 044 641

North of the A924 Pitlochry–Rattray road. This is an 18th or 19th-century dry-stone rubble kiln of circular plan.

11 Tomphubil Lime Kiln, Foss*   NN 778 545

East of the B846, this large single-draw kiln built in 1865 is rectangular in plan with a segmental draw arch. During the 18th and 19th centuries, limestone was quarried and taken to small kilns along the Tay Valley and peat and coal were imported by railway and steamboat. Tomphubil lime kiln went out of production in the early 20th century.

12 Walnut Grove, Perth   NO 137 218

On the north bank of the River Tay, south of the railway line, 2.5 km south-east of Perth. This collection of buildings of the late 19th and early 20th centuries is typical of the North Tay salmon fisheries. It included a single-storey range of stores, a mess room and other offices with an awning on the riverside. It was linked to a cart track by a 0.6 m gauge hand-worked railway.

PLANNED VILLAGES AND ESTATES

1 Baledgarno, Inchture   NO 276 302

Baledgarno, east of the B953 Inchture–Abernyte road, was established *c.* 1791 for Lord Kinnaird's Rossie Estate workers. It comprises a long street of single-storey estate workers' cottages. To the north of Rossie Priory Gates there are two-room cottages, each with a decorative porch added in the

1880s; to the south, there are one-room cottages. There is an early 19th-century school in the field to the south and the Factor's House and Baledgarno steading lie on the hillside to the east.

Successive Lords Kinnaird attempted to improve workers' conditions and in the 1830s the village reading room and school were built.

Essential viewing

2 Balnald Cottages, Fortingall   NN 739 470

Sir Donald Currie of Glen Lyon House, ship owner, commissioned James Marjoribanks McLaren, pioneer of the Arts and Crafts movement in Tayside, to design the reed thatched cottages and estate buildings in the village. The tradition of reed-thatching had been long abandoned before this time in the area but reeds harvested from the Tay Estuary were brought to provide the distinctive roof finish. The cottages, built between 1886 and 1890 for agricultural and estate workers on the Glenlyon Estate, are based on pre-Agricultural Improvement, Lowland vernacular buildings from Kinross-shire. Glenlyon Farmhouse, steading, laundry, kennels and Fortingall Hotel are all based on neo-vernacular forms associated with Scottish tower-houses. MacLaren also designed Fortingall Parish Church and when he died, aged 47, his practice was inherited by the partnership of William Dunn and Robert Watson. They rebuilt Glenlyon House and designed Fortingall Hotel with its harling, gables, crow-steps and dormers and two huge dressed piers on either side of the entrance. Between these piers is a stone lintel bearing the title of the hotel in lettering which nods at the style of Charles Rennie MacIntosh.

3 Inchture   NO 280 287

Inchture, south of the A85(T) Dundee–Perth road, is a good example of a 19th-century estate village built in two stages in the 1830s and 1860s for Rossie Priory estate workers. During the 1830s, pattern-book type single-storey ranges of three or four dwellings were constructed while in the 1860s, the new houses were mainly one and a half storeys high with upper floor dormer windows. All the Tudor-style cottages incorporate slightly different details.

At the western end of the village, separate from the other 19th-century buildings, is the Inchture horse-tram terminus, a long single-storey range with a large doorway at the west end of the south facade. The Inchture horse tramway linked the village to Inchture railway station, 2 km to the south.

4   Stanley – see below

MANUFACTURING SITES

1   Blair Athol Distillery, Pitlochry*   NN 946 577

On the north side of the A9(T), on the south side of Pitlochry. Founded in 1798 and rebuilt in the late 19th century, this is one of Scotland's oldest distilleries. It comprises a group of one, two and three-storey rubble buildings.

2   Edradour Distillery, Moulin*   NN 959 579

Signposted from the A924 on the unclassified road between the Moulin and Donavourd, 5km from Pitlochry. Alternatively, a footpath leads up through Black Spout Wood on the south side of Pitlochry. The buildings and plant of the smallest distillery in Scotland are almost intact and include a minute malt barn and kiln, two-storey production building, six-bay store and the offices for the manager and excise officer. The distillery was built in 1837 and the two-roller malt mill or bruiser is one of the smallest and earliest of its type. Between the filling store and the warehouse range is the original whisky store where, before the Maturation Act of 1915, whisky was sold direct from the cask.

In 1644 the Scottish Parliament introduced a malt tax of 2/8d on a pint of 'strong liquor' and after the Union a Board of Excise was established to enforce the tax. By 1820 there had been 14,000 successful raids on illicit stills in one year, making legal distilling more attractive. In 1823 an Excise Act reduced the minimum legal still size from five hundred to forty gallons and within two years a group of local farmers had set up Edradour distillery as a co-operative though it has changed hands several times since.

3 Inchcoonans Brick and Tile Works, Errol
NO 238 233

Two kilometres north-west of Errol, by the unclassified Errol-Inchcoonans road. This is one of the last surviving 19th-century brickworks in Scotland. It was established to produce bricks and field drainage tiles which were required to implement the agricultural improvements of that time. There is a notable group of circular and rectangular kilns with four square-section chimney stacks, drying sheds and other buildings. A 'jubilee' tip railway wagon is preserved outside the office. The clay-pit was on the east side of the road but has been back-filled.

4 Keithbank Jute and Flax Mill, Blairgowrie*
NO 175 465

Signposted west of the A93, 1.5 km north of Rattray, Keith-bank Mill can also be reached by a scenic woodland and riverside walk along the River Ericht from Blairgowrie. This is one of a group of flax and jute mills established on each side of the River Ericht, originally all driven by water wheels and exploiting an excellent water supply. Keithbank was built in 1864-5. It comprises a seven-bay, two-storey-and-attic main block with ancillary buildings and was driven by a wood and iron breast wheel, 4.27 m wide by 5.49 m in diameter, engineered by J. Kerr of Dundee in 1865. A horizontal single-cylinder drop-valve engine by Carmichael and Co. of Dundee was kept as a stand-by. The disused breast-wheel and horizontal single-expansion condensing engine with 5 m flywheel are still in working order.

A school log-book of 1903 from nearby Rattray records that mill children spent 'one day in the mill from 6 a.m. to 6 p.m. and the next day in the mill from 6 a.m. to 8.30 a.m., at school from 9.30 a.m. to 4.15 p.m. and then in the mill from 4.30 p.m. to 6 p.m'.

Other mills on the Rivers Lornty and Ericht

NO 172 467	Bramblebank Mill
NO 173 465	Brooklinn Mill
NO 192 448	Erichtside Works, Ashgrove Mill
NO 177 463	Oakbank Mill
NO 173 465	Westfield Mill

5 Luncarty Bleachworks   NO 099 299

On the west bank of the River Tay, 1 km north-east of Luncarty, off the B9099. Founded in 1732 by William Sandeman, this had become one of the largest bleachworks in Britain by the late 19th century when it spanned 52 ha. There is now a large group of single-storey rubble-built workshops.

Perthshire was famed for its bleachfields, centred on the city of Perth and spread along the Rivers Tay and Almond, and established in the 18th century with government subsidies to serve the growing linen trade, initially using basic croft bleaching processes. The cloth or yarn was exposed to sunlight for lengthy periods and moistened using soft water. The cloth was dried in workshops and treated by beetling to close up the texture of the fabric.

Essential viewing

6 Stanley Cotton Mill*   NO 114 328

On the north bank of the River Tay, 3 km east of the A9 Perth–Inverness trunk road. The mill was founded in 1785 by George Dempster and Sir Richard Arkwright with the backing of a group of Perth merchants. It is built around a courtyard with a free-standing chimney. The oldest part is the Bell Mill, completed in 1790, comprising five storeys and a basement with bellcote on the north gable. The twenty-bay East Mill was constructed c. 1840 and these two mills were linked by the Mid Mill of c. 1850. The ancillary buildings include a Gothic three-by-three cottage, a circular gatehouse with ogee or double-curved roof and circular chimneys of c. 1876, an octagonal wooden summerhouse and a circular turbine house, now gutted.

The lade system includes a rock-cut tunnel. The mills were origi-nally powered by seven water wheels which produced 400 horse-power. The bricks for the mill were made on-site from local clay.

By 1795, 100 families provided 350 workers for the mill, many of them from the Highlands and 300 of them women and children under the age of sixteen. At its peak, there were 2000 people in the village. In the 1840s adults worked in the mill from 5.30 a.m. until 7.30 p.m., with an hour for dinner while children worked from 9.45 a.m. until 3.00 p.m. then went to school. Tuberculosis, pneumonia and bronchitis were common ailments for factory workers. Later, the shortage of cotton and increasing competition meant there was less work but after the 1939–45 War, there was a shortage of labour, and young women were brought over from Germany and Italy. The factory closed in 1989 and it is now under the guardianship of Historic Scotland.

In the village above the mill, two-storey terraced houses on a rectangular plan were built during the late 18th and early 19th centuries to house the mill workers. By 1828 the village also had a church, shops, school and tenement block. There are two main streets – Percy Street/Store Street and Duchess Street/King Street; and three cross streets – The Square, Char-lotte Street and Mill Street. The best examples of mill workers' cottages are on the north sides of Percy and Store Streets and the brick range on the south side of Store Street but most have been remodelled.

7 Stormontfield Bleachworks   NO 105 297

On the east bank of the River Tay, opposite Luncarty (see above). This bleachworks was built *c.* 1820 but the main building has since been destroyed by fire. A two-storey brick block incorporating a dwelling house survives, plus some one-storey buildings. There are also one-storey brick storehouses, a range of one-storey-and-attic cottages, and a single-storey nine-bay beetling mill with low-breast paddlewheel, 4.24 m wide by 4.11 m in diameter. The lade, which is 4.8 km long and 5.49 m wide, was cut in 1847.

8   Wester Tullich Copper Mine, Kenmore   NN 691 378

The copper mine and associated chemical works were operated here by the Marquis of Breadalbane between 1833 and
1862. The mine's single-storey rubble buildings are now roofless and the chemical works are overgrown.

TRAVEL AND COMMUNICATIONS

Essential viewing

1   *Aberfeldy Bridge*   *NN 851 492*

*The bridge crosses the River Tay on the north-west side of
Aberfeldy on the B846 Weem–Kenmore road. This is a Wade
Bridge, built in 1733 to a design by William Adam. At the time
of its construction it was the only bridge across the Tay as both
Dunkeld and Perth bridges had been destroyed. It was one of
forty stone bridges constructed between 1726 and 1735 as part
of General Wade's 402 km of road construction in the Highlands, 'for securing a safe and easy communication between the
high lands and the tradeing towns of the low country' as the
inscription on the parapet reads.*

*It is a five-span bridge, 112 m long and 4.5 m wide, hump-
backed, with a wide central arch with raised parapet and
four obelisks. The chlorite schist for its construction was quarried between Aberfeldy and Kenmore and it took two years to
prepare the stones which were all dressed, marked and numbered
at the quarry.*

2   Barnton Toll, Perth   NO 128 220

Immediately south of the A85, 0.5 km south of Barnhill. This
is a very fine toll house with classical facade, tariff board and
the remains of the toll bar. Although the toll house can be
seen from the busy A85, there is no convenient parking area
in the vicinity.

3 Drochaid na h-Uinneige, Eye of the Window, Old Clunes   NN 791 668

Park at Bruar and walk west along the B847 and underneath the railway bridge on to Wade's military road. Follow the abandoned road into woodland where the bridge crosses the Allt a' Chrobaidh. The military road can be traced for a further 2 km until it is joined by the A9(T). The bridge was built in 1728 and comprises a semi-circular arch of roughly covered rubble, only one abutment of which is set firmly on the rock shelves of the river bank.

4 Dunkeld and Birnam Station   NO 031 416

Immediately west of the A9(T) at Birnam. This was one of the 'cheap railways' of the 1850s, originally built for the Perth and Dunkeld Railway and it has some very fine features, including large stone building-ends with decorated bargeboards and the massive lean-to awning with rare surviving pendant gas casement lamps.

Designed in 1856 by Andrew Heiton Junior, as a two-platform through-station, its principal building is on the up-platform, a fine single-storey structure with two ornamental gables and a projecting porch at the rear. On the platform side is a bracketed awning with steeply-pitched roof. There is a small wooden shelter on the up-platform. Other features include a rubble goods shed, wooden coal office, and lattice-girder footbridge.

In 1854 the Perth and Dunkeld Railway Company secured the necessary legislation to allow the building of a railway line starting at the Scottish Midland Junction at Stanley and terminating at Birnam. The line was taken over by the Inverness and Perth Junction Railway Company and in 1863 operation of the service between Birnam and Pitlochry commenced.

Essential viewing

5 Dunkeld Bridge and Tollhouse   *NO 027 425*

In 1803 Thomas Telford was appointed Surveyor and Engineer to the Commission for Highland Roads and Bridges and in

261

1805 designed this bridge which was completed four years later. It is 8 m wide and 208 m long with seven spans. Dunkeld's prison was built into the north abutment of the bridge. The tollhouse at the south end has a semi-hexagonal projecting bay, Tudor-style chimneys and windows with diamond-shaped panes.

When Dunkeld and Birnam Station was built in 1856, the people of Dunkeld were outraged that they had to pay just to reach the railway station across the Tay. In 1868 toll riots erupted and a detachment of Royal Highlanders was sent in to deal with them. The toll gate was finally removed in 1879.

6   Glen Lyon to Loch Rannoch Old Road
NN 588 476 – NN 618 574

Park in the public car park at Innerwick. The footpath begins opposite Innerwick church (see p. 224). This 3.6 m wide old road can be traced for about 12 km from Innerwick, across Lairig Ghallabhaich at NN 591 514 and down by Allt na Bogair through Rannoch Forest to Carie on the southern shore of Loch Rannoch. It is well-engineered, stone bottomed and kerbed. At NN 587 499 unmortared blocks carry the road across a steep and narrow ravine.

7   Haughs of Drimmie Suspension Bridge, Glenericht Lodge
NO 170 502

East of the A93 Rattray–Bridge of Cally road, in the grounds of Glenericht House. This wrought-iron framed double cantilever suspension bridge crosses the River Ericht 4.8 m north of Blairgowrie. It was built *c.* 1830 to designs by John Justice of Dundee, using a complex 'basket' or multi-stayed suspension across the 32 m span. Each pair of pylons is held in position by three anchor-stays and suspended from them are seven wrought-iron rod stays with intermediate stabilisers secured to pylons. Its iron-framed timber deck, 3.2 m wide, is supported by diagonal rods. The adjoining lodge dates to the late 18th century. There is another Justice bridge dating to 1824 at Kirkton of Glenisla, Angus.

8 **Inchture Horse Tramway Terminus** See pp. 225–6

9 **Killiecrankie Toll** **NN 918 623**

On the east side of the A9(T), 250 m south of the visitors' centre. The earliest comprehensive road system was established in the early 19th century with the completion of the turnpike system, stimulated by the need to get increasing produce to markets. These roads were constructed and financed by trust companies, with toll houses like this one every 9.6 km (6 miles) which were leased to toll-keepers. All traffic except the Public Stage Coaches and the Royal Mail coaches had to pay a toll until the system was abolished in 1878.

10 **Killiecrankie Viaduct** **NN 917 625**

To the west of the A9(T), south of Killiecrankie, follow the foot-path downhill from the Killiecrankie Visitors' Centre. This is a Joseph Mitchell viaduct, built in 1863 for the Inverness and Perth Junction Railway. It is 155.5 m long, 16.5 m high, of ten spans. There are castellated towers at both ends and in the centre a denticulate string course. Beyond the viaduct arches, the masonry is continued with a turreted retaining wall and a deep barrell-vaulted underbridge crossing a burn.

11 **Pitlochry Station** **NN 938 581**

This station was opened in 1863 by the Inverness and Perth Junction Railway and rebuilt *c.* 1890. It is a two-platform through-station with its main building on the up-platform. Its single-storey H-plan structure has wings at both ends, crow-stepped gables and Tudor-style chimneys. On the down-platform is an elaborate wooden shelter. Other features include a wooden goods shed, lattice-girder footbridge and typical Highland Railway signal box.

12 **Taymouth Castle Chinese Bridge, Kenmore**
NN 782 467

The Chinese Bridge is 1.6 km downstream from Kenmore Bridge, by Taymouth Castle. It was built in the mid 18th century by the 3rd Earl of Breadalbane for light carriages and pedestrians. Its three equal spans are supported at each bank by stone abutments and in the river by two stone piers. With its Tudor arches and Gothic cast-iron railings, the Chinese Bridge is rather a misnomer. The more functional Newhall Bridge (NN 790 469) is 1.2 km downstream.

13 Tilt Viaduct, Blair Atholl   NN 873 652

Park in Blair Atholl and walk along the banks of the River Tilt. The viaduct was constructed by Fairburn and Sons of Manchester in 1863 for engineer Joseph Mitchell's Inverness and Perth Junction Railway line. The viaduct is 78 m long with a single diamond lattice truss span of 46 m on stone abutments on platforms of 15 cm timber secured to piles driven into the river bed. The girders are wrought-iron. The Duke of Atholl would only allow the railway through his land if he could be convinced that it would not be detrimental to the estate. The highly-castellated portals resulted.

14 Tummel Bridge   NN 762 592

This bridge on the B846 was built for Wade by John Stewart of Canagan. It was built with approaches wide enough, 'to render it easily passable for wheel carriage and cannon'. The main 16.8 m arch is set high with a humped roadway over it. The parapet is 1.2 m wide reducing to 0.76 m at the ends. The road itself is 3.3 m wide. On the north side there is a segmental flood arch at a twenty degree angle to the main arch. The nearby farmhouse may be a Kingshouse, where the soldiers who built the roads and bridges were billeted.

15 Wades Road, Dunkeld   NO 005 430

A short 3 km stretch of Wade's Road can be traced along the east bank of the River Tay in the grounds of Dunkeld House Hotel, formerly the home of the Dukes of Atholl. On the uphill side, the remnants of a stone retaining wall can be seen. The old road north from Edinburgh via Perth ended at

Inver, about 0.8 km upstream from Dunkeld Bridge where there was a ferry for pedestrians and wheeled traffic.

16 Wades Road, Glen Cochill

NN 902 369 to
NN 888 444

The Crieff–Dalnacardoch military road, built in the 1730s, survives as a well-made track flanked by earth-and-stone banks. It leaves the modern road at Amulree and runs over the shoulder of the hill into Glen Fender and on into Glen Cochill. There is a well-made bridge at NN 910 378 but no indication of how Glenfender Burn was crossed.

SELECT BIBLIOGRAPHY AND FURTHER READING

Coutts, H., *Ancient Monuments of Tayside* (Dundee Museums, 1970).

Fawcett, R., *Scottish Medieval Churches* (HMSO, 1985).

Fawcett, R., *Scotland's Cathedrals* (London, 1997).

Foster. S., *Picts, Gaels and Scots* (London, 1996).

Hume, J.R., *The Industrial Archaeology of Scotland* (Batsford, 1977).

Oram, R.D., *Scottish Prehistory* (Edinburgh, 1997).

Ritchie, A., *Picts* (HMSO, 1989).

Ritchie, G. and Ritchie, A., *Scotland: Archaeology and Early History* (Edinburgh, 1991).

RCAHMS*, *North-East Perth: an Archaeological Landscape* (HMSO, 1990).

RCAHMS*, *South-East Perth: an Archaeological Landscape* (HMSO, 1994).

Salmond, J.B., *Wade in Scotland* (Edinburgh, 1938).

Tabraham, C., *Scottish Castles and Fortifications* (HMSO, 1986).

Tabraham, C., *Scotland's Castles* (London, 1997).

Tranter, N., *The Fortified House in Scotland* (Edinburgh, 1963).

Walker, B. and Ritchie, G., *Exploring Scotland's Heritage: Fife and Tayside* (HMSO, 1987).

Wickham-Jones, C.R., *Scotland's First Settlers* (London, 1994).

Yeoman, P., *Medieval Scotland: an Archaeological Perspective* (London, 1995).

---

*Royal Commission on the Ancient and Historical Monuments of Scotland